"*Building a Successful Software Business* is a marvelous guide through the complexities of marketing high-tech products. Its range of topics, and Radin's insights, make the book valuable to the novice marketeer as well as the seasoned veteran. It is the Swiss Army Knife of high-tech marketing."

*—Jerry Keane, Vice President of Sales Marketing, Universal Analytics*

"This is the best book I've ever seen for running a software business. It's also the only business book I've seen that understands software development issues."

*—Gregg Reed, President, Reed Systems Inc.*

"*Building a Successful Software Business* is about making your dreams come true."

*—Philippe Kahn, Founder, Borland International (from the Foreword)*

"Developers sometimes fail to realize that a good marketing strategy is paramount to success. In *Building a Successful Software Business*, David Radin lays out the marketing, sales and other business issues that we must address and tells us how we should address them to boost our profits and enhance our chances of success."

*—Paul Clark, President, Clark Software*

"The critical component for success in high technology markets is not a superior product but the ability to quickly and efficiently bring those products to market. Dave has provided software entrepreneurs a map to success through the sales and marketing maze."

*—Bob Davidson, Ira Rogers and Company, Austin, Texas*

"Dave Radin's *Building a Successful Software Business* is an insightful book, full of ideas that can make the difference between a profitable company and an also-ran. Dave's involvement with companies at all stages makes him uniquely qualified to merge the insights of other capable managers in the industry with his own insights, analysis, and advice. Written from a real-world perspective, his book is a must for software executives."

*—James D. Norrod, President and CEO, Telebit Corporation*

D1401623

# Building a Successful
# SOFTWARE BUSINESS

# Building a Successful

# SOFTWARE BUSINESS

*David Radin*

*O'Reilly & Associates, Inc.*
103 Morris Street, Suite A
Sebastopol, CA 95472

**Building a Successful Software Business**
by David Radin

**Editor:** Mike Loukides

**Printing History:**

April 1994: First Edition.

This book is printed on acid-free paper with 85% recycled content, 15% post-consumer waste. O'Reilly & Associates is committed to using paper with the highest recycled content available consistent with high quality.

ISBN: 1-56592-064-3

# ⚘ Table of Contents ⚘

# 1
## Marketing Strategies & Tactics

# 2
## Customer Fulfillment, Training, & Support

# 3
## Finances and the Young or Growing Company

# 4

# Special Information for Startup and Fledgling Companies

# Appendix
# Business Resource Guide

# List of Figures

# ☙ List of Tables ☙

# ⁓Foreword⁓

As a student of computer scientist Niklaus Wirth, I was well prepared for one critical aspect of business success: the creation of superior products. When I started Borland International in 1983, I brought such a product, Turbo Pascal, to market. But it turned out that creating a product wasn't the whole story: I found myself facing issues for which my academic training hadn't prepared me. The business decisions were daunting, reminding me of Carl Jung's description of a dream as "the theater where the dreamer is at once scene, actor, prompter, stage manager, author, audience, and critic." Although I have learned how to play many roles since, at that time I had to rely upon my own competitive fires to compensate for my inexperience.

David Radin's *Building a Successful Software Business* presents not only that which I learned the hard way, but also the strong sense of commitment that separates the great businessperson from the merely ambitious. If your goal is to attract venture capital and to cash out, good luck and look elsewhere. But if you want to position yourself as a player in determining the course of global technology, the advice in this book will greatly increase your chances of success.

As the author states, "It takes a full complement of ingredients that, when combined under the right conditions, permit entrepreneurs to capitalize on their creations." I liken what he's saying to competitive sailing.

Ocean conditions often aren't "right," but they are equalizing. One boat may be faster in high winds and another in choppy seas. I faced both conditions in the 1988 Pacific Cup race from California to Hawaii, which meant that my boat had the advantage at times, and at other times my competitors' did. With the goal crossing the finish line first, victory came down to having the better prepared crew, superior tactics, better knowledge of the opposing captains' strengths and weaknesses, the intuition to anticipate and the knowledge to react to wind changes, and the will not to flinch in close quarters. The "fastest boat" doesn't necessarily win: the team that's best suited to meet all the challenges that it faces will succeed.

You will read this book and realize how much there is to learn, and will begin to understand the chronology of the steps needed to launch your company successfully. *Building a Successful Software Business* is about making your dreams come true. The open market is equally rewarding and unforgiving: there's nothing more satisfying than success, but the best ideas don't necessarily succeed. While there is no substitute for experience, we shouldn't let our lack of knowledge prevent us from trying. For, in the words of Arthur William Edgar O'Shaughnessy,

> We are the music-makers
> And we are the dreamer of dreams,
> Wandering by lone sea breakers
> And sitting by desolate streams;
> World-losers and world-forsakers,
> On whom the pale moon gleams:
> Yet we are the movers and shakers
> Of the world forever, it seems.
> —*Ode, stanza 1*

Philippe Kahn
Scotts Valley, CA

# ❧Preface❧

Just like the rest of the computer industry, the software business is characterized by rapid innovation. As quickly as one technology catches on, the next one comes along to make it obsolete. The latest technologies come as new applications, new algorithms, and new methodologies—sometimes major innovations, other times, simple enhancements. In this rapidly advancing environment, only three things are certain:

- Things will change.
- They'll change fast.
- New people and new companies will be instigating many of the changes—not only the current and traditional industry leaders like Microsoft, IBM, Adobe Novell, and Borland.

Like their predecessors, the new entrepreneurs will find the opportunities in the market, and then seize them by developing products that meet the needs of the market. Perhaps you are one of these entrepreneurs.

You don't need a large staff or lots of money to start a software business. For every large software company like Microsoft, there are thousands of small companies that produce and market their products with only a handful of people. Even Bill Gates started with only one associate.

To extract maximum profit from your software company, you need to take care of four critical areas of business: product development, marketing/sales, finance, and operations. This book covers the three areas that developers often overlook, don't understand, or don't bother with: marketing/sales, finance, and operations. I have also included a special section about organization issues, written specifically for new companies and entrepreneurs.

# *Audience*

This book is intended for anybody who wants to make money in the software industry. It certainly has information that would be of interest to the technical entrepreneur, but it can be used effectively by most computer industry professionals too, as well as end users and non-technical entrepreneurs who have identified a need in a market or have a software product (or idea) that can also apply to other people's problems.

- If you are thinking about going out on your own with a new software product, you'll find out what's in store for you and how to make money in a fiercely competitive environment.

- If you have recently started your own business (or if you are about to), you can use the special information for startup and fledgling companies to decrease your personnel burden and increase your profit.

- If you are an office worker (or an end user of any type) who has put together software to solve your own problem, your solution may be marketable. Use this book to identify what you need to meet your challenges.

- If you are a developer in a software company, you can get a better feel for the challenges facing your marketing staff and other managers, allowing you to increase the value of your company.

- If you are new to the software industry, you'll learn about the industry from a business perspective, making you more valuable to your current employer and in the job market.

- If you are thinking about investing in a software company, you can use the book to understand more about the challenges facing your new company.

In addition, anybody in the industry can use the resource guide at the end of the book to locate important sources of information, customers, and industry partners. The information in this book applies to all parts of the computer industry including DOS, Windows, Mac, UNIX, mini-, super-, mainframe, and new environments.

Sure, I hope everybody gets a great idea from each page. But let's face it, even if you get only one good idea from reading this book, you'll have made a small investment that returns many times its selling price.

# *Approaching This Book*

Even though this book is aimed at both technical and non-technical readers, it has been written on a non-technical level because the issues I discuss are better addressed separately from the technical issues that are involved in software development. So, whether you are a technical person or not, you should be able to benefit from each chapter.

Nevertheless, you may have specific goals in reading the book:

- If you are new to the industry or if you are a non-business oriented technical person, start with Chapter 1 and read the whole book.

- If you want to improve your understanding of the marketing and sales aspects of the industry, read Chapters 2 through 11.

- If you need to understand how to better manage your finances, read Chapters 14 through 17.

- Anybody who has just started a company, or expects to start one, should read Chapters 12 through 14 and 18 through 22, in addition to any other chapters of interest. Chapters 18 through 22 are specifically oriented toward startups.

- To recharge your battery or get back to basics, read Chapters 1, 2, and 3. They are filled with a lot of common sense issues that we all forget easily.

- Refer to the resource guide to find resellers, trade associations, industry periodicals, computer company partners, books, databases, and many other resources.

## *Conventions and Definitions*

This book is meant to be a practical guide, not a theoretical textbook. I have stayed away from pure theory, with only a few instances in which I had to quantify the points I was making.

This book uses many examples from the entire world of business, although most come from the computer industry with the bulk of those from software companies. I have used a combination of real world examples from Marketing Masters' clients, small companies, individuals who have volunteered information, and large well-known companies. They come from all segments of the industry: DOS, UNIX, MAC, mini-, mainframe, and supercomputer. Some are specific to the segment, others are relevant to all segments. I have also included simplified examples that illustrate specific points. (There are many computer companies with unusual names, so selecting fictitious names was not as simple as it might appear. My apologies if I used a fictional name that is actually real.)

"Vendor" refers to a company that either manufactures and sells hardware or a software company that authors the software that is sold. Resellers of any sort are not vendors.

"Channel" refers to the pipeline that brings the product from the vendor to the end user. For instance, when a vendor sells to a distributor who sells to a reseller who sells to the end user, the distributor and reseller are the channel for the vendor.

"Market" refers to the collection of individuals or companies that might purchase your product. An individual does not need to purchase your product to be part of your market. However, he does need to satisfy the definition of what your market looks like. If you define your market as lawyers for steel companies, then Jane Barrister is part of your market if she is the general counsel for Federated Steel, even if she is not aware of your product. She has satisfied your definition. A "market segment" is a market within a market that is defined more narrowly. In this book, I often use the word "market" in place of market segment. (This is common usage.)

In financial tables, a number in parenthesis is a negative amount (a debt or a loss). For example, ($4000) means a $4000 loss. This notation, though it's unfamiliar to engineers, is standard accounting practice.

# *Acknowledgments*

If you have ever been involved in software development projects, you know the great amount of time and effort required to produce a superior product quickly. Well, as I have just found out, writing a useful book takes the same type of devotion, time, and effort. It's a team effort from start to finish. And I have been lucky enough to have a great team to work with on this book.

The information contained in this book is based on fact and experience. I was able to broaden my own experience by consulting many people who have been active in the computer industry, including George Abbott, Jay Brotman, Jerry Chichester, Gary Collinsworth, Steve Eskenazi, Don Geckle, John Hooper, David Isenstadt, Dave Kosoglow, Mike Linton, Bob Ostrander, Karen Marini, Len Polk, Terry Rupp, and Winnie Shows. Whenever I needed in-depth knowledge in specific areas, this team of people provided information and guidance.

Then there are those who went way beyond the call of duty: those brave souls who subjected themselves to prereleased versions of the book as technical reviewers. Many thanks to John Brown, Kristi Clark, Paul Clark, Bob Davidson, John Dockery, Jerry Keane, and Gregg Reed. Not only did they let us inside their minds; they allocated large chunks of their valuable time to make sure that what I wrote was accurate, relevant, and insightful.

A number of other people have worked with us to provide the foreword and many examples scattered throughout the book: Nan Borreson, Philippe Kahn, Diana Pohly, David Thompson, and Joy Warner.

The book probably would not have happened at all without the coaching and teaching of Mike Loukides. As editor of the book, Mike gently led me in the right direction, fixed my most serious blunders and, along with Tim O'Reilly, showed me how to get the most out of writing a single work of this magnitude. Tim also contributed many examples from the history of ORA, and provided many insights on how to strengthen and focus the book.

O'Reilly's production and design staff deserves extra credit making this book shine. In the art department, Chris Reilly did the artwork; Jennifer Niederst designed the book's interior; and Edie Freedman created the cover design. In the production department, Chris Tong wrote the index; and Leslie Chalmers, Kismet McDonough, and Mike Sierra did the final editing, and made sure the writing was something we could all be proud of.

Finally, this book would not now be a reality without the support of my wife Anita and my children Daniel and Jaqueline. I thank them for urging me on and for not getting too upset during those nights and weekends that I was locked in my office working on this book.

## *To Get in Touch With Me*

Please feel free to send me comments on this book, ask to be on our mailing list or contact me for other reasons. My Internet e-mail address is radin@ora.com. My CompuServe address is 73234,3712. You can also use the contact information at the end of the book.

Don't keep this book to yourself. If there are others in your organization who can benefit from the information within, please let them know about it. Tell your marketing people, investors, or associates at other companies. The more productive the people you do business with, the more likely you are to profit.

# PART 1

# Marketing Strategies and Tactics

# Ingredients for Success

Throughout the industrial age, shrewd individuals have turned technology into money-making products—Thomas Edison and the light bulb, George Westinghouse and the radio, Henry Ford and the automobile. But at no time in history has opportunity been as readily available as in recent years in the computer industry. According to Jeffrey Tarter, publisher of *Softletter*, worldwide software sales for personal computers alone surpassed $20 billion in 1993. And that's just part of the total software market. Consider some recent success stories:

- Scott Cook, founder of Intuit, Inc., has sold more than 4.5 million copies of his Quicken financial management software. In 1992, Intuit earned $5.2 million on revenues of $84 million.[*]

- Douglas Carlston, founder of Broderbund Software, has sold more than 2.5 million copies of his Carmen Sandiego games since originating them in 1985.

- While IBM mainframe sales tumbled, Andrew (Flip) Filipowski's Platinum Technology's profits grew dramatically to $9.3 million for its mainframe database enhancement software.[†]

The biggest success story of them all is Microsoft's Bill Gates (or is that Bill Gates' Microsoft?). In 12 years, Gates built Microsoft into a company with higher net value than General Motors, Boeing, or Kodak. Today, his software is used on over 120 million systems worldwide and his personal fortune is in excess of $7,000,000,000.

What did these software entrepreneurs possess that catapulted them beyond the rest? After all, there have been thousands of software companies that have produced excellent products but still lost money, eked out meager profits or never made it out of the blocks at all. And many of the failures came from

---

[*] *Intuit Preliminary Prospectus*, February 3, 1993.
[†] "Controversy, Theater Serve Platinum's 'Flip,'" *Software Magazine*, May, 1993, page 117.

individuals or teams that have been successful in other endeavors. Lotus Development Corporation spent millions of dollars developing the still-born Jazz product in 1984. Javelin Software Corporation developed a spreadsheet product rated by 60,000 users as better than Lotus 1-2-3, but it never caught on, while 1-2-3 became one of the most successful products in history.

It happens all over the computer industry. Even the highly successful Digital Equipment Corporation meets failure at times, as it did when it introduced the Rainbow PC. DEC took it off the market after a short time of lackluster sales. More recently, DEC has had to restructure its entire business to move with the changing market. Its major challenge (like that of the other traditional industry leaders) is to move from a world of proprietary systems to a world of open system architectures. That's not easy, even for the best run organizations.

In the real world, it takes more than a great product to grant success. It takes a full complement of ingredients that, when combined under the right conditions, permit entrepreneurs to capitalize on their creations.

This book is about success—not to envy, but to emulate. If you have a software product idea, you will learn how to build a successful company around it. If you currently own or work for a software company, you will find information to help you reach your next plateau. This book is not about starting a company and "cashing out" with an IPO (initial public stock offering). It covers the traditional path in which you develop a marketable product and make your money in daily business operations. Before we get into the details of the individual chapters, let's examine the characteristics that are common to most highly profitable operations.

## *Finding a Path to Success*

In the computer industry change is the norm. Things can happen so fast that participants must scurry to keep pace. Innovations are quickly made obsolete by newer innovations. This climate of rapid change often means that software companies must establish new paths to survive. Yet there are no maps. As the leader on an innovative course, you walk alone. In the early eighties, Apollo Computer broke away from the pack to become the first workstation company, a position that earned it accolades and profits for several years. However, because Apollo was setting the course for workstation class machines, it should have set the course in the direction the users wanted to head—and users wanted open systems. (Users didn't know it at the time, but that was what they were looking for.) With its proprietary operating system, Apollo's road became a dead end. Sun Microsystems laid a new direction by touting industry standards, open architecture, and UNIX and, in the process, overwhelmed Apollo, the early market leader. By creating its own path, Sun soared to extraordinary success.

Even when you take the road most traveled, you may encounter unexpected obstacles. The sheer amount of innovation in the industry quickly makes standard practices *passé* so that historical outcomes become an inaccurate predictor of what will work in the future. Important industry changes, like the movement from text-based software to graphical interfaces, from mainframes to client/server networks, and from single processors to parallel processors, can add new road blocks and create new opportunities for software vendors. The changes can happen subtly over a few years, or there can be a revolution in which your market suddenly caves in or explodes.

Then there's the extremely important issue of whether you are developing technology or running a business. While operating a software company certainly requires both skills, rarely does the technology drive the business. Usually, the business (or more accurately, the market) drives the technology, a fact that can be easily hidden from somebody who spends the majority of his waking hours developing software. Those who put business decisions first are more likely to be the long term players. If nobody wants your product, or if you cannot generate enough revenue to compensate for costs, you won't last long. Ask David Gelernter, the developer of Linda, the parallel operating environment. In watching Scientific Computing Associates' efforts with Linda, he observed that they became more successful after they let marketing creep into virtually every area of the business, including product development.

The moral of the story: operate the business first and use your technology to support your business efforts. If you're not willing to do this, put somebody in charge who is.

## *Your Personal Challenges*

Commanders of companies in a fast-paced industry are faced with many personal challenges. If you're successful, you will find competitors aiming to shoot you down. If unsuccessful, you must face your own ego (a tough task). According to Guy Kawasaki, former Apple manager, running your own business takes a strong sense of security and the ability to cope with many unforeseen circumstances.[*]

You must also be willing to put in long days, at least in the initial stages of your business; there are always more things to do than there are people to do them. During your first two to three years of business, expect to work sixty to eighty hours per week with few (if any) vacation days. Hopefully, within a few years,

---

[*] Guy Kawasaki, *The Macintosh Way* (Harper, 1990), page 31.

your work week can be shortened to fifty hours, and you might even get to enjoy a week or two of vacation.

Most of all, you will need an undying drive to succeed. You may find yourself in situations in which you have absolutely no experience and must make immediate decisions or take immediate actions. You'll face obstacles that seem insurmountable, but must be oversome anyway for survival or prosperity. You'll survive on your wit and willingness to make things happen. In the early days of WordPerfect, Allan Ashton and Bruce Bastian found that the market was so saturated with other word processors that they were unable to convince corporate buyers at Computerland to purchase their new software package. So they personally visited individual stores in California and Georgia to drum up support for their product. Their extra effort began the string of successes that would place them among the richest people in the United States.

## *Your Management Challenges*

As leader of your organization, you deal with management issues that affect you, your employees, and your customers. How you handle these issues directly impacts your ability to flourish.

Most successful companies have a visionary. On the grand scale are the visions of DEC's founder, Ken Olson, who realized that mainframes could be supplemented or replaced by departmental minicomputers, and Apple's founder, Steve Jobs, who envisioned "the computer for the rest of us" that became the Macintosh. Olson's vision and leadership led DEC to become the second largest computer company in the United States. Jobs' vision became a part of Silicon Valley legend, and transformed the notion of a garage from a place to park your car into a place to build a business. Your vision doesn't need to be as grandiose as those of Olson or Jobs, but it should be concrete so that you can communicate it to your team sparking them to make your vision reality.

Always remember: nobody makes it alone. Most of the corporations on the Inc. 500 (the fastest growing small companies in the United States) were started by more than one person. In addition, the competitive climate forces software companies to extend their teams beyond traditional boundaries to form coalitions with hardware vendors, resellers, and other software vendors. It is imperative to know how to build a team and function effectively within the team atmosphere.

Even if you start your company by yourself, you will need help; one person can't be everything. No individual has all the expertise and experience needed. At some point, you will need to figure out what experience you're lacking, then explore ways to fill in the gaps—by finding partners, employees, or consultants who have what you lack.

Don't forget to include your customers in your team. They do more than hand you money for your product. They provide you with important marketing information, test your products for usability, and help you obtain additional customers. The best way to take advantage of customer input is to believe that your customers are intelligent, rational human beings. If you do, they are likely to prove you correct. I learned this early in my career from Joe Fridy, a systems analyst at Alcoa, who realized the importance of building a collaborative relationship between vendor and buyer. He found that most vendors assumed he must be coerced into buying their product, when, in fact, a collaborative relationship better suited his needs. Not only did he want a product, he wanted a working relationship with the company.

You'll undoubtedly see, as you read through this book, that most of your business tasks must be juggled concurrently. Be prepared to solve some tough problems. For example, how do you manage difficulties in timing between production and marketing? It's easier to sell a product that you can demonstrate, but if you wait until release to start selling, you won't sell much when it's first available. And how about pricing, which depends on your costs, but you often don't know your costs until after the product has been on the market for a while. And customer support requirements are based, in part, on how good your documentation is, but you often don't know what problems the customers will have running your software, so you can't always include the issues in your documentation. The list goes on. Be ready to handle multiple issues simultaneously (from all aspects of the business). That's how they'll come up.

## *Necessary, but Not Necessarily Sufficient*

There is a common misconception that a great product makes a great company. Certainly, having a viable product is an important contributor to financial success; however, it is not enough. Javelin wasn't successful, even though they developed a superior spreadsheet product; yet many of IBM's products have been successful, though they are rarely first to market, or best of breed.

Product aside, other contributors to success include effective marketing, cost controls, assembly and shipping, distribution, and customer support. You must address each. If the prospect cannot find your product, he can't buy it no matter how great it is. If you cannot convey to him why he should use it, he'll never try it. If you cannot package it and ship it out the door, you will never get paid for it. And if your costs are too high, you will lose money—even if revenues are high.

Although you may want to concentrate on developing the best product in the world, you will be challenged to balance product development with business efforts. A good hurdler clears every hurdle to win. You will be in good company if you balance your attack: the most successful entrepreneurs and business people recognize the multiple challenges and vigilantly strive to meet them. Venture capitalists refrain from investing in companies that lack seasoned management or viable marketing plans. Good corporate officers keep unnecessary costs down: Bill Gates flies coach when he travels on Microsoft business.

The product does need to be good. But good is defined by the market. It must fill a need for the user. It could be a breakthrough product like Lotus 1-2-3 and NASTRAN were over a decade ago, or a fill-in-the-gap solution like the Grammatik grammar checker. It can even be similar to other products on the market (although you do have a distinct advantage if your product can be differentiated from the pack). But as important as a good product is, be forewarned: Many superior products fail if their owners and authors forget to handle the other aspects of the business.

## There Is No Universal Truth

There is no one path to success. As you read this book, you will think of companies who have succeeded by charting a different course than what I recommend. The key is to look at the situation that faces you, and tap your own experiences. Then temper them with the experiences of others. We can only catch glimpses of the road ahead. If we can radio ahead for navigational help, we will do better. That's the aim of this book: to share the experiences of companies and entrepreneurs to increase your chances of success. Even if you only learn a little bit, you can prosper because that incremental knowledge might facilitate a new method or action, which, in turn, might lead to large monetary gains.

## Luck Doesn't Hurt

Finally, since you cannot control the world around you, look out for opportunities and take advantage of any breaks that come your way. Being in the right place at the right time has provided leverage for companies such as Mergent Corporation, which used the Michelangelo virus scare of 1992 to elevate sales for its system security software. Luck, in large part, is good planning properly executed.

# A Market-Oriented Approach

Are you market oriented? If so, you put the needs of your market front of all other factors. You build your business around satisfying your customers' needs. All other activities follow. First, of course, you must understand who your market is.

## *The Michael Jordan Market Model*

Michael Jordan does amazing things with a basketball.[*] His feats are so spectacular that people are willing to pay to see him work. Imagine somebody entering *your* office to watch you type commands into your terminal—and paying for the privilege. Even in his retirement, Michael Jordan is paid extraordinary sums of money because his entertainment value is in demand. The National Basketball Association and the Chicago Bulls knew this. So they purchased the rights to Michael Jordan's basketball playing time, packaged it, and marketed it to the prospects most likely to buy tickets: basketball fans. Nike, Quaker Oats and Hanes recognized his value as a spokesperson, so they purchased the rights to his image and continue to benefit by it—because the public still wants a Michael Jordan.

The Michael Jordan Market Model is the classic example of a market-driven approach. Figure out where the market is and what it wants. Develop a good product that satisfies the customers. Show them why they should pay for the product. Keep them happy. And get rich.

It works the same way in the computer business. Companies that are market driven—oriented toward satisfying the needs of the customer—are more likely to succeed than those that ignore customers' demands. Many software companies get this backwards; they're driven by engineering and think people will buy their product because it's neat, innovative, and has great features. This is a

---

[*] This is an update of the traditional Wilt Chamberlain model of economic behavior, which was standard fare when I was in business school.

recipe for failure if your technology blinds you (as it often does) from what the customers really want.

# *Henry Ford's Secret of Success*

It's 9 p.m. Friday. You're in your office staring at your monitor, trying to fix a bug in a software module that you have been working on for months. You've been hacking away since 7 a.m., with only a few short rest breaks. Your eyes are bloodshot. Your left leg has fallen asleep, and you can't wait to get home to rest. No wonder you don't have time to look at your market—the collection of individuals who *might* buy your product.

That's no excuse. You *must* look at the market. It pays your bills. Every time John Q. Enduser buys your product, he provides money for salaries, phones, rent, and profit. In a strangely disconnected way, that makes him your boss. How can you satisfy the boss when you don't even know what he wants? Henry Ford once said, "If there is any one secret of success, it lies in the ability to get the other person's point of view and see things from his angle as well as your own."* In essence, this man, known best for his automation techniques, not his marketing savvy, says the secret of success is being market driven.

To be truly market driven, every action you take must be driven by your vision of who your end users are and what you can do for them. You need to ask four important questions:

- What are users trying to accomplish?
- Are they having any problems doing it?
- What methods are they using now?
- Can you offer a better way to solve their problems?

In recent years, businesses of all types have been installing relational database products (ORACLE, Ingres, Progress, Paradox, etc.). The problem is that divisions and departments would choose their own software without concern for corporate requirements. The result: a myriad of incompatible databases. Recognizing the problem, David Assia of Magic Software seized the opportunity to develop a fourth generation language (4GL) that would allow users to access the multiple databases already in use.

Throughout the industry, many companies have succeeded by understanding what people were trying to accomplish, and by designing solutions to real problems. Robert MacNeal and other engineers had helped NASA develop NASTRAN, a finite element analysis (FEA) package that analyzed stress,

---

* Dale Carnegie, *How To Win Friends and Influence People*, (Simon & Schuster, 1936), p. 42.

vibration, and heat transfer characteristics of NASA spacecraft. Recognizing that other industries—notably automotive and aerospace—could use FEA to solve similar problems, MacNeal formed MacNeal-Schwendler Corporation to refine and market NASTRAN, which was already in the public domain. Similarly, John Swanson formed Swanson Analysis Systems, Inc. to produce and market FEA software similar to what he had developed as an employee of Westinghouse Electric. Like Ford, these successful software entrepreneurs put themselves in the other person's position to find and solve his problem.

Even if you spend most of your week in your office, get out to view the market. Understand its problems. Offer a better alternative. In other words, be market driven.

## *What's Your Opportunity?*

Market opportunities exist whenever a group of individuals with common attributes (a market or a market segment) perceive a discrepancy between an existing or expected condition and the way they want things to be. For instance, John wants to spend more time with his family, but he can't because he must work 7 a.m. to 9 p.m. to get his work done. An opportunity exists for someone to create a product that will help John do his work in 75% of the time. He'll buy it to gain more family time. There may be thousands of people who also need to compress the time it takes to do work similar to John's. By providing a single product that will be purchased by all these people, you seize the opportunity.

In the workplace, there are four conditions that determine whether an opportunity exists:

- Things are fine. There are no problems.

- Things are bad. Help is needed.

- Things are fine now, but a surge in work load is expected.

- Things are fine now, but a decrease in work load is expected.

To find your opportunities, look for situations in which condition 2, 3, or 4 exists. The more companies or individuals who fit into these three categories, the greater the opportunity.

If things are fine, there is no opportunity. No matter how good your product is, it is a solution in search of a problem—and the problem does not exist. When I was marketing CADD systems for Auto-trol, I found a class of prospects that had already automated. Instead of using CADD, though, they "automated" by cutting and pasting paper. These people were already getting three times the productivity of manual drafters and they didn't feel that they needed to spend $100,000 or more to do the same thing electronically. There was no opportunity.

On the other hand, you have an opportunity when your prospective users feel they have a problem. Most large corporations, for instance, have facilities management departments that assign space to other departments, lay it out, and keep track of furniture and equipment. They constantly produce drawings that show how furniture is arranged in rooms. Every time the furniture is rearranged or a department is moved, a new drawing is made—a perfect application for CADD. It is much quicker to arrange furniture and equipment electronically than it is to do it on paper, especially when the electronic database associated with the CADD drawing can also help track inventory.

Expectation levels fuel opportunity, too. Suppose the economy is expanding; new buildings are being designed in record number. The expansion is so great that good designers are in short supply. Architectural firms would have to find ways to meet their deadlines even though they may not have enough staff. Even if the situation is not yet dire, the firms will move to buy productivity enhancement software before the real problem hits. Likewise, if the market expects conditions to worsen, prospects will look for ways to decrease cost or get into new businesses, hopefully avoiding layoffs.

While my examples focused on how discrepancies between capacity and work load can generate opportunity, there are other types of discrepancies that create it, including: quality, cost, ease of accomplishing a specific type of task, and ability to do something that currently cannot be done at all. Your mission, as a marketing strategist, is to identify the opportunity, then seize it by developing and marketing a product that solves the customer's problem.

Borland seized its opportunity when Lotus Development, then the unchallenged leader in spreadsheets, decided to split Lotus 1-2-3 into two separate products (using separate version numbers). One product was fully functional; the other cost less. Perplexed spreadsheet buyers had to choose between functionality and price—and they viewed that as a problem. Borland viewed it as an opportunity. It gave users both, by aggressively pricing a single, full-function version of Quattro Pro.

Market opportunities are created every day—whenever a new problem flusters the individuals in a market. What's your opportunity?

## Pinpointing Your Market

A few months ago, the business manager of a small software company approached us at Marketing Masters to help her launch a new product. Her team had already developed the product, named it, and put it into alpha test.

They figured it was time to roll it out, and wanted us to put together a marketing campaign. But in reality, marketing is more complex than simply making your customer aware of the product; it involves matching your product and sales pitch to your market's needs. Therefore, we took a slower approach: we suggested that our client start by talking to potential users to get a feel for what would attract them, instead of just going after them. It's a good thing we did. The users didn't need the product. After a few conversations, we found out that the product, although well designed and coded, was filling a need that did not exist.

This is not an unusual situation. It's difficult to get into the minds of the people that you expect to use your product—especially if you don't directly ask them whether they need it. Sometimes software has been developed to meet your own requirements; perhaps your company needs it to automate a specific function for which there is no off-the-shelf software. So you develop the software and figure that other people can use it too. However, not everybody has the same requirements as you. Even if the requirements differ slightly, your software might not be adaptable to the needs of others. So they won't buy it.

That doesn't mean it's not marketable. It may mean that you simply must find your market. Are there other people that have needs just like yours?

In the case of Marketing Masters' client, the answer was yes. But it was not the market originally expected. In fact, only a small portion of the product was needed to satisfy the most important demands. So the product was reworked to be marketed in pieces. The first piece is already being accepted by the revised market. The follow-on pieces are not yet ready to be marketed. When they are, they will be marketed to different groups of users.

Identifying your market often takes a lot of work. You need to figure out who has the need, what it is, how many people are in the market segment, and what it takes to get them to buy. Some of this information is available in written or electronic form. Other information can be gathered by contacting the people that you think are likely candidates, as well as the people who influence them. Then you will need to process the information with common sense.

When looking for information about market size, spend time at your local library. Its reference section probably has a number of volumes that provide demographics. Some libraries even have CD-ROM disks or electronic services; if not, you can subscribe to commercial services that provide this information. How you slice the information you collect depends on your product. If you plan to market a computer quiz game about flowers, you can probably find out how many horticultural societies there are, where they are located, how many members they have, etc.

To find out about trends or competition, examine trade magazines and industry reports; attend trade shows; speak with associates and consultants. Don't forget to look at what's happening around you. That's where the market is.

To ensure that your product fills the needs of the market, speak with people who would be in your target market. They're the best people to tell you whether they want the product and what it would take to get them to buy it.

Sure, there's a significant amount of work involved in collecting the market information you need, but doing it will help you develop a more marketable product. And not doing it may doom you to failure. Given the alternatives, you're better off doing the extra work to make sure that your development effort is not in vain.

## Focusing Effort To Dominate Your Market

If you pick up a stone and toss it into the ocean, you will make ripples. The ripples will radiate out from the spot at which your stone enters the water and after a moment or two, disappear. They disappear quickly because they are dominated by the other forces in the water, such as waves and tides. Suppose we do the same thing in a lake or pond. The stone will still create ripples, but this time they seem stronger and last longer than they did in the ocean.

The marketplace behaves similarly. If you throw your product wildly into the broad market, your efforts will go unnoticed or disappear quickly. If you aim carefully at a smaller target, you will make a bigger splash. That's market segmentation.

Lexus doesn't try to appeal to all car buyers. It goes after people with high incomes who are willing to pay for a luxury car. Toyota, the company that owns Lexus, aims its Tercel at buyers who are more price sensitive and want basic transportation. It has segmented the market in its attempt to become the dominant automobile company in each segment.

If I ask a desktop publisher about NASTRAN, the leading Finite Element Analysis software (FEA), she'll probably tell me that she has never heard of it. Likewise, PageMaker and Ventura, the desktop publishing packages, are not well known among mechanical engineers, the most likely users of FEA.

It's much easier to sell your product if you approach the market by segmenting it. First determine who is most likely to buy your product. Then ignore everybody else. Focus all your attention on solving the problem of your target segment.

The benefits of segmentation are enormous. Your product's advantages will more closely align with the needs of your users, making it more marketable. You will be able to concentrate your marketing dollars, making it less costly to sell your product. And your message will reach real buyers more often. You increase selling potential while decreasing marketing costs, making your entire operation more profitable.

If you become the dominant vendor, you will make it more difficult for competitors to enter the market. Suppose you became the dominant player in your segment and a new competitor tries to enter that market. Every time your competitor tries to make a sale, the prospect compares its product with yours. Since you have designed your product to suit only this segment, your product meets user needs better, thus barring your competition from entering. It's also more expensive for your competitor to enter the segment because he has to (1) develop a better product, (2) find ways to gain access to prospects by sales force or distribution channels and (3) convince the prospect that his product is as good as or better than yours. As the leader, your product is more readily accepted.

No company has executed the segmentation strategy better than Intergraph. When it started (as M&S Computing), it developed a CAD system that was aimed at organizations that do mapping. Its handful of salespeople called almost exclusively on mapping accounts until the company became the leading vendor of CAD systems for mapping. It then targeted architecture and engineering (A&E), a complementary segment. (Many companies do work in both areas.) The added benefit of choosing this segment is that the dominant CAD vendors were concentrating on other market segments. This left only small competitors in Intergraph's way. Time and time again, Intergraph would enter a market segment, become the dominant player, then keep its current resources intact to maintain its hold on the segments it owns while it attacked an additional complementary market. It developed special products to optimize its basic CAD system for each market, and it added additional targeted salespeople to go after the new markets so not to lose momentum in its existing markets. Intergraph is now a Fortune 1000 class company.

You might feel compelled to stray from your target market because you see additional opportunities in other markets. Be careful. As you move away from your original target, you lose focus, which may lead to loss of dominance. Just as the ripples from your stone get smaller as they get farther from the point the stone entered the water, you lose impact on your market as you move further from your sphere of influence. You should not begin to market to a new market segment unless you have enough funds (like Intergraph) to enter the new market without taking resources away from your original one.

When Lotus began to market products other than Lotus 1-2-3, it suffered a string of losers including Jazz, Magellan, and Symphony. Even though the quality of the products were high, they did not catch on in the market. Worse,

Lotus lost its focus on its core product, 1-2-3. It took years for Lotus to gain momentum with other products (notably Notes, AmiPro and cc:Mail). But it has faltered in the spreadsheet market where it faces consistent fierce competition from Microsoft and Borland, each with a respectable share of the market. On the other hand, Silicon Graphics has been wildly successful by concentrating on its core market. Even though SGI's UNIX workstations can be used for many applications, SGI focuses its efforts on visualization oriented scientific-engineering applications.

These examples and many others from the industry clearly show that it is better to dominate a smaller market segment than to be a little ripple in a big ocean.

## Ways To Slice Your Market

The key to segmentation is to identify a set of users that have common problems, needs, and buying criteria. Table 2-1 offers some examples of segmentation criteria that you can use. You can also define your own.

*TABLE 2-1: KINDS OF MARKET SEGMENTATION*

| Segmentation Criteria | Examples |
| --- | --- |
| Platform Type | DOS, Mac, SCO UNIX, HP-UX |
| Application Type | Word processing, education, entertainment, manufacturing, scientific |
| Organization | Corporate, government, schools, libraries, home/ office |
| Industry | Automotive, petroleum, insurance, real estate |
| Geography | World-wide, Japan, North America, Germany, New England |
| Performance Requirements | Interactive, batch, long-term batch (several-day turnaround) |
| Department | Human resources, order entry, marketing, finance, shipping |
| Age | Elementary school, adult (particularly useful for education and entertainment software) |
| Work Habits | Mobile user, occasional user, frequent user |

| Segmentation Criteria | Examples |
|---|---|
| Computer Knowledge | Novice, intermediate, expert |
| System Configuration | Network, stand-alone, remote |
| Problem Type | Needs more functionality, needs more performance, needs easier user interface |
| Price | Inexpensive, entry level; premium-price, feature-rich |

# Marketing's Four P's

Your market segment is actually a collection of individual prospects with similar needs. Even though we lump them together for discussion purposes, each individual decides whether to buy your product based on his or her own needs and circumstances. It's in your best interest to make information readily available to assist the potential buyer in making that decision. The best way is to address the four "P's" of marketing: Product, Price, Place, and Promotion. If you address each one, you might be successful. If you skip any one, you can seriously undermine your efforts.

*Product*

Does your product address the needs of the prospects? Does it solve a problem that they will pay money to solve? Have you put it together in a form that they can use?

*Price*

Does the price of your product coincide with its value to the users?

*Place*

Where will users go to purchase your product? Have you set up distribution channels that they can access? When they decide to examine or buy, do they know where to go?

*Promotion*

Have you set up a way to communicate with prospective buyers? Have you determined the best way to present the benefits of your product? Is the presentation of benefits both easy to understand and stimulating?

Figure 2-2 shows a four-section pipeline through which liquid flows. The maximum amount of liquid that can flow is determined by the capacity of each section. If you keep all four sections clear, the liquid flows freely. If one section is clogged, the flow stops. This is analogous to your sales and marketing effort. As long as you address all four P's, your product can flow smoothly to your customer, and sales will happen. If any P is left unaddressed, it will hamper your

***FIGURE 2-1:*** *You Must Address All Four P's to Successfully Market Your Product*

effort. In addition, just like you need to point the pipe at the vessel you want to fill, you must aim directly at the appropriate market segment to sell your product to the prospects there.

I'll address each of the four P's of marketing separately in later chapters.

# Designing To Meet
# Market Demands

Designing an intellectually appealing product is fine as long as the product also meets the needs of the market, and is sellable. No product does anybody any good if it sits on the shelf without being used—or worse yet, never gets to the user's shelf because it hasn't been purchased. Before you design your product, uncover what the user needs and wants. Then design it in.

## *Keep That Customer in Your Mind*

Apple's PowerBook and IBM's ThinkPad are the two most successful portable computers ever. Hundreds of thousands of each product have been sold into a market segment that is crowded by many competitors. IBM and Apple have tightened their grips on the number one and number two position in the personal computer market, in large part due to the strength of these products. But what exactly powers the sales of PowerBook? What thoughts make users buy the ThinkPad? In both cases, sales are brisk because the products were designed with the customer in mind.

At Apple, the PowerBook design process began when designers studied how users operate other notebook computers. They found that users often tried to use their portables where mice were inconvenient and space was at a premium. Realizing that most competing models were shrunken versions of desktop computers, Apple's design team set out to redesign the portable computer so it met the needs of the mobile user. Their solution now seems so simple: replace the mouse by a trackball, thereby eliminating the need for table space for the mouse; push the keyboard closer to the screen to save space and create a palm rest; and place the trackball right in the middle of the palm rest so either thumb can reach it. With these few small ergonomic changes to the standard concept of portable computers, Apple's design team made PowerBook a flexible, easy to use mobile computer—different from the rest. But they would not have been able to do it if they had not put the user's needs first.

Similarly, IBM differentiated the ThinkPad from other portable computers by designing the product to meet the needs of the user. In this case, though, it did it by "borrowing" technology that was being developed for other IBM products. The most noticeable market-oriented feature of the ThinkPad is the TrackPoint cursor control. ThinkPad designers, in their efforts to put together a user-oriented machine, located this tiny pointing device (it looks like the eraser end of a pencil) in another IBM lab that was designing a desktop machine. They recognized that this tiny cursor control could revolutionize IBM's next portable PC by making it more user friendly.

When you keep the user in mind during product design—whether it's hardware or software design—you will find new ways to differentiate your product from your competition.

# *Building Your Product To Satisfy Market Needs*

The first step in product design—even before the technical specification—is to determine what the market needs. You must step back, imagine a "typical" end user, and try to figure out what problems he has. Then develop your product around the single notion that you will solve his problem. In the last decade and a half, I have seen many prospects make purchase decisions about software and systems ranging in price from a few dollars to a few million dollars. In virtually every case, the winning vendor's product satisfied three criteria: function, safety (a.k.a. risk avoidance), and personal fulfillment.

### *Function*

Function is the easy one. The prospect always tells you the functions he needs. Many times, he even rates the importance of specific features: "I want fluid analysis software that runs on IBM RS/6000, allows me to model using non-rectangular geometry, is accurate within 2% of real world conditions, and can complete my job within four hours. If it doesn't run on an RS/6000, I can't use it." Functional definition is pretty cut-and-dry. There is little emotion attached.

### *Safety*

Not every prospect voices his concern for safety, though most use it to determine whether to purchase a product. The real issue is whether the product jeopardizes his job or his ability to reach some important goal. If the prospect sees your product as a risk, he won't buy. Figure out what risks are of concern to your target market. Then design your product to reduce those risks. If your market is conservative (e.g., accountants), new technology might scare them; a product that is based on "bleeding edge" technology might be difficult to sell.

Engineers, on the other hand, are more likely to be worried about the risk of an obsolete product. They won't feel safe using anything but the latest software. If your product will only be used occasionally, command-driven software will intimidate users. Consider a menu-driven structure or a graphical interface instead.

### *Fulfillment*

The need for personal fulfillment is almost never acknowledged (except in games and educational software), but it is there in virtually every case and can reveal itself in a few ways. First is the need for a personalized product: one that the customer thinks is a pleasure to use because it was written to meet his needs. Here you indulge your customer's desire for fulfillment by making him feel that your product was written "just for him." Perhaps it's easy to use or fun. He might even be able to brag about using it to coworkers.

Additionally, most people want to be recognized by their boss for a job well done. In most cases, the boss doesn't care which software is used. He cares about the results his staff can get from the software, measured according to his department's own scale: better designed aircraft, more transactions processed per day, lower cost or some other measure. You can make your customer a hero by selling him a tool that meets his operational needs. His boss gives him credit for selecting the right tool and using it to impact his organization. When he becomes a hero, you become a hero too—and your sales skyrocket.

Any time you, the software vendor, satisfy all three needs (function, safety, and personal fulfillment), you gain a competitive advantage. Look at the incredibly successful debut of Lotus 1-2-3. It was introduced at a time when most financial workers were using paper spreadsheets. (A few were already using VisiCalc; but most financial types had not yet heard about it.) Lotus 1-2-3 sped up the task of financial analysis. And since it was based on a paper spreadsheet paradigm, the user was able to apply concepts that she already knew. That's the function. Using 1-2-3 was safe because it allowed the user to back her business decisions with detailed analyses. With a few simple changes to data in a few spreadsheet cells, she could examine alternative scenarios. As important was the satisfaction that she got by using the software. She became the computer expert in her department and impressed her boss with a thorough analysis of business situations. Lotus 1-2-3 was her miracle.

So when you set your product specs, make sure that you have satisfied the functional, safety, and personal fulfillment issues of the person that you want to buy your product.

# A Decisive Advantage Is the
# Only Advantage

Many people think that Procter and Gamble makes its products successful by spending a lot of money on advertising. According to Howard J. Morgens, former chairperson of Procter and Gamble, "It all gets down to the fact that if you have got a good product, you can be successful with a reasonable marketing expenditure, but if your haven't got the product, the surest way to go broke is to pour your money behind it."[*]

That same notion is shared by many high tech executives. Your product is the core of your business. So, what constitutes a good product? It's not being the best at everything, because that would be nearly impossible. More likely, it's being decisively better on at least one thing.

Parametric Technologies has taken the mechanical modeling market by storm. Its Pro Engineer software goes beyond boolean algebra oriented CADD systems. Although other CADD vendors have implemented boolean models, Parametric has given Pro Engineer a set of utilities and an interface that greatly differentiate it from the others. Parametric Technologies has been able to grow at an average rate of about 100% per year.

Digital propelled its way to the top of the computer world because it offered a departmental computer instead of a corporate computer. Its PDP systems (and later its VAX systems) put the compute power in the departments that were previously being serviced by corporate computers in the MIS departments. IBM could not respond because it was tied closely to the MIS department. If IBM started to sell to end users, it would risk losing its support in MIS. DEC's primary advantage was decisive: local control for the departments, and computer autonomy. It freed users from MIS control.

Freelance Graphics for Windows drastically decreased the time it takes to lay out and print a high quality presentation with text and graphics. While other presentation graphics programs made users build their presentations, Freelance came with prebuilt masters. The user need only substitute his own words and graphics.

Each of these products made large strides in function, rather than superficial improvements. Your product, too, must stand out in one area. As you will see in the following chapters, your product is more than the software. You can make your decisive advantage in areas such as support, delivery, and price.

---

[*] John S. Wright, Daniel S. Warner, Willis L. Winter, and Sherilyn K. Zeigler, *Advertising*, fourth edition (McGraw-Hill, 1977), page 81.

However, you should build a decisive advantage into your software whenever possible.

# *Seizing Opportunities*

*"The whole of science is nothing more than a refinement of everyday thinking."* —Thomas Edison

There are product opportunities everywhere. Many of them may seem trivial to you, but may be important to your market. Word processing packages, spreadsheets, engineering analysis systems and other horizontally-oriented software (software oriented toward a function that covers a broad range of users) cannot be all things to all people. This creates an opportunity for you to fill in the gaps.

Frank Hainze, President of MicroLogic Software, found such an opportunity. He felt that users wanted to be able to make their words stand out on a page, so MicroLogic introduced True Effects, a software package that adds special effects to TrueType fonts. He has sold thousands of this small (less than 1/2 MByte), inexpensive (less than $50) product.

When it comes to finding opportunities, no idea is too trivial. Spell checkers, button bars, mouse enhancers, and other utilities fly off the shelf at software stores. These fill-in-the-gap opportunities exist in all parts of the industry.

## But I'll Ruin Sales of My Other Product

The software market is like any other: good products are eventually replaced by better ones. If you don't introduce a product that makes your old one obsolete, someone else will. So, to stay in the market, you have to risk surrendering your current product to any improved one, a concept known as self-cannibalization. Companies that improve their products prosper; otherwise, they become victims. Better to eat than be eaten.

When you're the leader in your segment and have commanding market share, you might feel compelled to worry about cannibalization between products. You'd have a lot to lose if you make a mistake. That's what kept IBM from jumping into minicomputers when DEC came along...and desktop systems when workstations and personal computers first gained favor. WordPerfect and Lotus also had a lot to lose when Windows came along to threaten their DOS products. They both lost a significant amount of business to Microsoft, who beat both companies to the market with competitive Windows applications. Word for Windows captured many word processing sales while Excel attracted Lotus 1-2-3 prospects. Both WordPerfect and Lotus introduced Windows products, but not until after the damage was done. Neither company is dominant anymore.

When you aren't the leader, there is no choice but to improve your product consistently, whether it cannibalizes your current offering or not. Even as you cannibalize your own sales, you will gain more from the sales you get from the leaders. Let's suppose your original product has a 10% share of the market while companies A and B hold 60% and 30% respectively. Now, let's suppose that you introduce a new product that steals market from all competitors evenly (including your own) to gain a 10% share. It gains 10% of your first product's share (10% × 10% = 1%), 10% of company A's share (10% × 60% = 6%) and 10% of company B's share (10% × 30% = 3%). Your first product has lost 1% of the total market, but you have gained 10% for the new product. You now sell 19% of all units sold (9% attributed to the old product, 10% to the new). Market shares for companies A and B will shrink to 54% and 27% respectively. You have cannibalized your own sales, but have increased sales tremendously at the leaders' expense.

Hewlett Packard's Boise Printer Division doesn't worry about losing sales to itself. It consistently improves its products, often making its older products obsolete. The HP LaserJet III, for instance, added a resolution enhancement mode to its page description language that the Series II did not have. The LaserJet IV, in turn, quadrupled resolution over the III. The net result of HP's self-cannibalization is that it keeps raising the bar. Other printer manufacturers must keep up with HP's printer capabilities just to have viable products. HP sells more laser printers than the next nine largest competitors combined.

To see self-cannibalization work to perfection, look at consumer goods. You can't even walk down the supermarket aisle without seeing at least a few "NEW" or "IMPROVED" claims. Some are minor improvements that may get new customers to try a product. Others are major innovations (such as freeze-dried coffee or ultra-concentrated detergent) that create whole new product categories.

In software, you can't afford to miss opportunities just because you're worried that you may steal sales from yourself. Losing to yourself is not a nightmare. Losing to your competitor is. Make your product the best it can be. Then make it better. Repeat the process.

## Choosing Between a Product and a Product Line

Every time you introduce a product in addition to the one you're currently selling, you add complexity to your business life: your marketing changes; you must carry multiple types of inventory; product support becomes more difficult. Your costs go up too, and rarely go down, even when you expect them to.

Therefore, you should think twice before you expand your product line. As Mark Twain said, "Put all your eggs in the one basket and—watch that basket."

A new company should start with a single product. Build your business around that product and make it profitable. When your first product is self-sufficient it's time to expand to a second. Use the profits from the first to fund your next. But don't take your mind off the first product; if you do, you may lose your market to competition.

The best products to add are those that complement your existing product. Perhaps the new product can be sold to the same market as your current product. Maybe they can share distribution channels or even technology. Intergraph supplements its core CADD system with add-in applications modules. This lets them enter new markets with the same underlying CADD software, but keeps the software targeted at the key prospect groups. Borland and Lotus both use common code among products within their own product lines. Avery Dennison uses its software packages to spur sales of its paper office products.

Don't let my implementation suggestions keep you from brainstorming about additional business opportunities that can be based on complementary products. You want to be ready to take advantage of market opportunities—especially when you have a superior product. Just don't jump into additional products unless you're ready and able.

If in doubt about whether you should be developing more than one product, ask yourself a few questions:

- Do we have the expertise to make a product that will be competitive?

- Do we understand the target market and what it needs?

- Is it complementary to our current product—in terms of either market, technology, or distribution?

- Will we lose focus on the first product when we develop or market the new one?

- Do we have the cash to support both products?

- Are members of our staff underutilized? (If you are paying for them, you might as well keep them productive.)

- Will the net result of having two products on the market be worth the effort?

In short, look at your situation to determine whether additional products make sense. If so, develop and market them. If not, concentrate on your current product.

By the way, when you port a software product to a new platform, you undertake many of the requirements of a totally new product. You'll need to support both products, keep separate equipment, and probably market to different users. Ask yourself the same types of questions when you consider a new port as your would when you consider a totally new product.

# *Offering Source Code*

The heart and soul of a software company is the intellectual property embodied in its source code. Your entire business life is wrapped into that one item. Should you give access to others? That's been the subject of intra-company debates for decades. Few PC software companies do it. It's a bit more common for UNIX software companies, but still somewhat unusual. That's because you risk your entire business when you put your source code in the hands of others. If you let somebody outside your company have it and they give it to a competitor or include it in their product without paying you, you might lose a great amount of profit. Or he might destroy your credibility by presenting your product unfavorably. Yet there are some valid reasons to offer source code to outsiders.

Many software vendors provide source code to hardware vendors, who can port the code to their own machines, and, thereby expand the market for the software. At Multiflow Computer, for instance, we would often receive source code from software companies so we could port the software and tune it to run faster on our minisupercomputers. We had to sign non-disclosure agreements to protect the property rights of the authors. Because moving from one operating system to another requires you to recompile on the target system (as a bare minimum), letting the hardware vendor do it often reduces the software vendor's equipment and staffing needs. PC software vendors have less incentive to release source code. Hardware is relatively cheap, and virtually all vendors maintain 100% compatibility with standards. If vendors want to port from DOS to Windows or OS/2, they can even use a single system to do the port.

Real World Corporation has taken the plunge by selling its source code to third parties. Customers integrate Real World's software into their own products. By doing so, Real World Corporation has attracted over 800 VAR's (value added resellers—see Chapter 5) and integrators who now sell products that use Real World as their core software. It hasn't been without risk, though. According to Doug Weishaar, VP of Market Development at Real World, once you release source code, you no longer have control. For Real World, that hasn't been a severe problem, but occasionally it causes concern. A few years ago, one of its resellers went out of business, leaving 100 users without a service organization to respond to problems. Knowing that leaving customers without support would hurt Real World's reputation and might force Real World to pick up support for code that was altered, the company acted swiftly by arranging to have a different reseller support those users.

When you supply source code, you're really giving your customer (whether a reseller or end user) the ability to change the software. That cripples your ability to support it. Furthermore, whenever other companies resell your software, you are taking the risk that one or more resellers will not move to new versions as you develop them. So you might need to maintain support staffs for older versions in addition to the staff that supports your latest versions.

If your intention is to provide an open architecture that allows the user to customize your product, you might profit by providing customization tools instead of source code. This lets users customize your software to meet their needs, but does not leak your intellectual property. It also allows you to maintain better control. You decide what information can be changed, how it can be changed, and when your customers and staff migrate to new versions. There are plenty of precedents for building such tools. PC programs such as Paradox, Lotus 1-2-3, dBase, and WordPerfect have macros. PDA Engineering's Patran, which runs on UNIX-, VMS-, and MVS-based systems, has its developer's toolkit. SGI even provides graphics libraries to the industry (including competitors) allowing the industry to use the libraries as a *de facto* standard."

## *The Target Is Always Moving*

Your target is moving. But that is what creates the opportunity; your competitor's target is moving too. The key to prosperity is to aim where the target will be tomorrow, not where it is today. Consider the arcade game where you shoot an air-gun at a moving duck. If you shoot directly at the duck, you miss. If you shoot in front of it, you might hit it. Playing the market is similar. As the market moves, you have to adjust your aim. If you only try to beat today's product capabilities, you will miss the market, because tomorrow the target is farther away.

As Mark Tavill, Mentalix's VP of Sales and Marketing, says, "Be prepared to make quick changes to react to the market. Figure out what the opportunity is. There may be a window because of somebody else's mistake." Mark was at Borland when it seized an opportunity by marketing a single, low-priced comprehensive spreadsheet to compete with Lotus, who had split 1-2-3 into two products. Borland's Quattro Pro spreadsheet became a contender in the spreadsheet wars, and now commands a significant market share on a consistent basis.

## ☞ *More Thoughts About Product Design* ☜

1. Choose a platform based on market needs, not what's easiest to program or cheapest. If you don't have expertise in the platform the market wants, find someone who does.

2. Don't commit to ports until you know what you're getting into. If your system runs on UNIX and a customer asks you to port it to the Macintosh (or *vice versa*), make sure the market will support the cost of the port. It's often not practical to port for a single customer. But in some cases, the new market may be bigger.

3. Keep your product up-to-date with the latest operating system release. That's where you will be getting the most new users; new entrants to the market will buy systems with the latest software.

4. If you are trying to woo customers from other vendors, make your software compatible with theirs. Accept their file formats. Make it easy for the other product's users to learn yours, perhaps by using similar command (or menu) structures. Don't cross the legal line by plagiarizing. If in doubt, contact your lawyer.

5. Take advantage of standards like X Windows, POSIX, Microsoft Windows, and MHS. Your MS-Windows-based product can use Windows' print drivers instead of your own. You'll reduce your development workload and keep closer to the market. Every time Microsoft upgrades its drivers, yours are automatically upgraded.

6. You're not the only one with a great idea. Take advantage of other talent out there by licensing outside software to use in your product. It reduces design time so you can take advantage of market opportunities.

7. When choosing your product, concentrate on areas in which you have a strong background. You'll meet competition in every part of the industry. If you have extra knowledge, you have an advantage. Go with your strengths.

8. Timing is important. Sometimes a market opportunity forces you to release a product without full functionality. Don't miss your chance because you want a perfect product. Make it as good as you can within the window of opportunity. Then, if it's good enough to win business, release it. Add functionality to later versions.

As you keep your fingers on the keyboard, keep your eyes and ears on the market so you can spot trends. How many of us actually spotted trends such as client/server, open systems, or graphical interfaces when they first started to appear? Those that did became important players. Significant trends are still trying to work their way out. UNIX vendors are uniting behind the COSE flag. Windows NT, UNIX, and S2 are fighting it out for ownership of 32-bit computing. There will be many new applications for CD-ROM, interactive video, email, and workgroup computing.

In the background, thousands of software vendors are designing products to take advantage of the next trend—even as they try to introduce products today. You should be one of those vendors. Watch the market. Figure out where it's going. Then make your software meet the needs of future markets—not today's.

# Pricing Strategies

Your product's price is second only to its user benefits in defining who is willing to purchase your software. Choose it wisely; it won't be an easy decision. It may be one of the most confusing decisions you must make as a business person. There are so few rules. Here, we offer a few guidelines.

## *The Age-old Pricing Problem*

When the first successful high-tech entrepreneur invented the wheel, he had a problem. He didn't know what he should charge for his new device. It was a state of the art technology that would fill the needs of a large market. But he did not know what people would be willing to pay for a set.

Thousands of years later, we still don't have the foolproof answer to the pricing question. Millions of high tech inventors before us have faced it. We can refer to their experiences, but we don't really understand why one price "works" and another doesn't. We even have enough compute power on our desks to calculate massive pricing algorithms in moments. Then why does pricing seem so erratic?

Consider these situations:

- In 1982 the list price for Lotus 1-2-3 was $595. In 1993, you could have bought Lotus' Improv spreadsheet package for $99.

- Corporate licensees of virus protection products from McAfee Associates pay anywhere from $3 to $30 per license (single CPU/two-year term). That's a 900% difference for the same product.

- Large deviations occur in other industries, too. If you call American airlines at 9:45 a.m., the reservation agent may quote you a price of $550 for your flight from San Jose to Boston. Call again at 10:15, he'll tell you it's $1100. Try at 1 p.m., you will pay $345. Try at . . . (I think you get the picture.)

The large variations happen because the majority of the cost of developing and marketing software is fixed (much like airline ticket cost). Therefore, companies have a great deal of latitude in determining their pricing structures. (We'll explain more later. Combine that with the quickly changing competitive climate for computer products and the fickle nature of buyers, and the end result looks like confusion. (Some of us prefer the term "free enterprise.")

The fact is, software prices are based on a few pieces of hard information combined with a great deal of intuition; the bulk of the decision rides on intuition. Suppose your software makes it easier for a salesperson to complete a proposal. You can probably ascertain how many people do proposals. But figuring out how many will be willing to buy at price *x* or price *y* is more difficult. It requires guesswork. So does figuring out how the competition will react to your price.

Okay, so software pricing is hard. It's more art than science. My best pricing advise is: base your price on your best guess about what the market will bear; then make sure you can live with this price. You will do okay. After all, you're probably aiming at a target market that you know pretty well. And, by the way, don't worry if you choose the wrong price.

## *The Price Your Market Will Accept*

The most significant factor in determining your price is actually out of your control: your market determines what you can charge for your product. Millions of people are making purchase decisions every day. Each one has a certain sensitivity to price. He or she is willing to purchase a particular product or type of product at one price (say, $199), but not willing to buy at a higher price. If you set your price at $499, you will return home with your product still in hand and no money in your pocket.

To sell your product, you must determine the highest price at which your primary market will purchase your product in sufficient quantity to meet your revenue and profit goals. You will need to understand the value that the customer places on your product, otherwise known as the price the market will bear.

Value is somewhat subjective. Jane Smith, decision maker at January Corporation, may be willing to buy your product as long as your price stays below $7500, while Fred Jones at February Corporation may be willing to pay as much as $10,000. The differences may be attributed to other alternatives that each buyer has available, how they compute the value of a product, or some other intangible factor.

# What's the Value of Your Product?

The best way to determine how much value the end user places on your product is to find out how much money he will save by using your product, compared to his current practice. Then price your product at the highest price that still allows the prospect to save.

Drafters using Computer Aided Drafting software (CAD), for instance, can produce a finished drawing five times faster than drafters who use pencil and drawing tables. If a prospect typically uses 500 staff-hours per year to do manual drafting, and it costs $50 per hour, she is spending $25,000 per year. By letting her draft at five times the speed of manual methods, your CAD software would save her $20,000 in annual staffing costs.

Similarly, you may have a PC-based product that can replace dedicated minicomputer software. Let's say that your prospect is paying $2000 per month for a maintenance contract on his current minicomputer (dedicated to that application). Being able to replace his minicomputer with an inexpensive microcomputer will let him decrease his maintenance cost by $24,000 per year. After paying $4000 for a microcomputer and peripherals to run your software, he has $20,000 to spend on your software while breaking even.

Sometimes you need to look at seemingly unconnected issues to find the savings. For example, the traditional method of constructing bridges is to pour extra concrete or use extra steel to "over-engineer" the bridge so it can withstand stress. If a design firm really wants to decrease the cost of building the bridge, it tries to decrease the amount of raw materials. To understand how to reach this goal, the design firm might try to use finite element structural analysis (FEA). By using FEA to clarify exactly how much load the bridge can withstand, engineers can be more confident that their designs will handle the expected amount of traffic, thereby reducing the need to over-engineer. This can save hundreds of thousands or even millions of dollars on average-size bridges.

The same type of value computation can be applied in the other direction, too, to figure out how much the user will *gain* by using your product. An automobile company would be interested in any product that can help it reduce the total amount of calendar time it takes to design its cars. Each extra month of sales on the front end can mean millions of dollars of extra revenue—revenue that would otherwise have been lost to its competition.

If you enter into a market that already has a similar product, the value of your product may be perceived by the market as similar to that other product (or if there are many, to the market leader or to the product that most closely resembles yours). This gives you a baseline for comparison and allows you to vary your price in either direction based on intrinsic advantages or disadvantages of your product. More on this later.

In the absence of quantitative measures, select a price that seems fair. If your product is revolutionary, you may have no choice. The original UNIVAC, the Xerox copier, and VisiCalc are all products for which pricing models had to be developed with little empirical background. Again, you are left to your own judgment, because fairness is subjective. Jane Smith and Fred Jones may have different opinions about what a fair price might be for your product.

## Price Should Reflect More Than Technology

Don't be fooled into thinking that your price is determined purely by the software itself. It isn't. People are willing to pay premiums for value associated with intangible benefits that they receive along with the software program. Although these intangibles are difficult to price, they are clearly important. Conversely, buyers expect to pay less when a good piece of software isn't enhanced by these other valuable ingredients.

The most obvious enhancement is a good support policy. WordPerfect is consistently rated among companies that best support users. Its flagship word processing package commands a higher price than its competitors.

Even if your software is simple, you can charge more if the alternatives are costly. However, this situation usually doesn't last long. When other software companies notice that you're selling a lot of product for a high margin, they'll flock to your market with competitive products to get in on the action. This will depress your price or reduce your share of the market as the competitors undercut your price to win deals. Unless . . .

The most effective way to keep your price high is to establish a proprietary position by owning a patent, using a technology that provides benefits difficult to duplicate, or owning a commanding market share in your segment. For example, ACT! commands a premium price because it is the preferred contact management tool for sales executives.

Many new technical entrepreneurs are amazed to find out that they can boost their prices when their distribution is better than their competition. But it really shouldn't be surprising. If Mary Lincoln calls her neighborhood software store to buy software (she knows what application category, but doesn't specify brand), and if the store only carries one product of its type, she'll probably buy it, even if it costs more than another product that the store doesn't stock. At that store, at that time, there is no competition to cause price reductions.

Even as good distribution helps, sometimes overdistribution erodes the street price of your product, as your resellers lower their prices to compete with one another.

How many times have you heard that IBM is never the low-priced vendor? That's because the company has traditionally been able to command a premium price by including intrinsics such as good support, proprietary position, excellent availability, and decreased risks. Even though it has recently become aggressive with its pricing policy in certain product lines (notably its PC products), it still charges a premium for those products that are not commodity oriented. You can too.

## *The Price You Will Accept*

If you imagine the price that the market is willing to pay for your product as the ceiling in your range of possible prices, your cost represents the floor. That is, you want your price to be low enough so the prospect will buy your product, but high enough so you can cover your costs plus make a reasonable profit. So you also need to use quantitative methods to determine how profitable you can be at various price and quantity levels.

There is an old cartoon in which a salesperson brings a discounted deal to his boss and says, "I know that we lose $30 per unit, but we'll make it up in volume." As silly as it sounds, software companies can often make money by selling large numbers of licenses at prices below the cost associated with low quantities. You see, the cost structure of your firm determines whether you can make a profit. And the typical cost structure of a software company is highly skewed toward fixed costs, so increased sales quantity often means dramatic decreases in cost per unit. To illustrate, let's start by defining a few terms:

*Fixed cost ($f$)*

A cost that you incur whether or not you sell a single unit. To figure out your fixed costs, look at your monthly bills or checks. If there is any expense that you pay consistently, it's probably a fixed cost. Examples include personnel, basic phone service, rent, and some taxes. Most development expenses are fixed costs. Janet, the programmer on your staff, gets a paycheck every week. Whether you sell 50 copies of your program or 5 million, she still gets paid a fixed amount. Her paycheck is a fixed cost. Your total fixed cost is the sum of all of the individual fixed costs. (See Chapter 15, *Prospering By Keeping Expenses Low*, for more details about cost structure.)

*Variable cost (v)*

    A cost that is incurred every time you produce, ship, or sell a unit. To figure out your variable cost per unit, add up the cost of material that is included in each customer shipment. Then add the cost of staffing and additional out-of-pocket expenses related to putting the product into a shippable form and sending it out. If you incur other out-of-pocket expenses with each unit (i.e., travel cost for your installer to get to the customer), add them too.

Your total cost equals your fixed cost, plus the cost of all the units you produce:

$$c = f + qv$$

where c is total cost, and q is quantity sold. For simplicity, we'll assume that you sell all that you produce. Figure 4-1 shows the equation graphically.

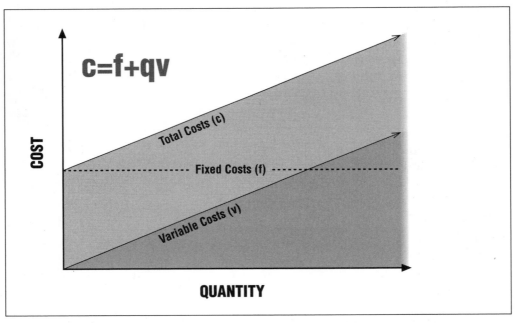

**FIGURE 4-1:** TOTAL COST EQUALS FIXED COST PLUS VARIABLE COST

Let's say your total fixed cost is $400,000, your variable cost is $15 per unit, and your expected production quantity is 50,000 units. To break even, you would need to bring in $1,150,000. Then, by dividing $1,150,000 by the number of units you sell, you can determine that your average selling price must be at least $23. But that doesn't allow for any profit. It simply states your break-even price for 50,000 units. If you require $300,000 in profit, add that to your fixed cost. Your *minimum* selling price then becomes $29.

Since you are attempting to determine the minimum acceptable price, you must be sure to include every single cost. If you miss any significant cost—including your own salary—your floor is no longer correct. You may lose money because you underestimated your break-even point.

## Can You Make Money at These Prices?

Cost-based pricing tells you more than how low can you go. There are three types of cost analyses that can give you plenty of information to help you with your pricing decisions:

1. Determining the lowest price acceptable based on expected sales (which we discussed in the previous section).

2. Finding the break-even quantity: the number of units you must sell at a given price to reach your profit goals.

3. Figuring out whether you make enough money at a particular combination of price and quantity to warrant bringing the product to market.

Your break-even quantity can be found by identifying the point of intersection of your cost and revenue curves (see Figure 4-2). You already know your cost equation ($c = f + qv$). Your revenue equation is:

$$r = pq$$

where r is your revenue, and p is the price you receive per unit. The resulting equation that shows the break-even quantity is:

$$q = \frac{f}{(p - v)}$$

You need to sell at least q units based on the price you set and your costs (fixed and variable). If you increase your price, your break-even quantity decreases. If you decrease price, you need to sell more units to break even.

Again, let's assume your fixed costs are $400,000 and that your variable costs are $15. If you set your price at $20 you must sell 80,000 units to pay your bills (not including profit). At $40, you would only need to sell 16,000.

To determine whether it's even worth your while, estimate how many units you will sell. If this satisfies your sales volume requirements, compute your expected profit at that quantity. (It's the vertical distance between your revenue and cost curves.) If it is high enough, that is, if your revenue minus your cost is greater than the minimum amount of profit you will accept, go for it.

In our example, suppose you require a profit of $300,000, and believe you can sell 40,000 units if your price is $40. Your expected revenue is $1,600,000 (40 ×

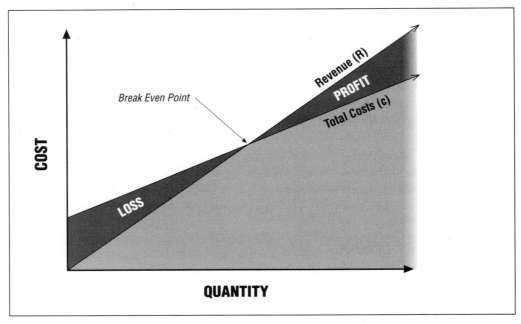

**COST**

Break Even Point

Revenue (R)

PROFIT

Total Costs (c)

LOSS

**QUANTITY**

*FIGURE 4-2: FINDING YOUR BREAK-EVEN POINT*

40,000). Your expected total cost is $1,000,000 ((15 × 40,000) + 400,000)). The resulting $600,000 profit potential is greater than your $300,000 threshold and is, thus, acceptable.

An important consideration of cost-based pricing analysis is the amount of your fixed cost and what you do to change it. Much of your fixed cost is *sunk*. You have already committed it and cannot change it. You cannot fire programmers, break your lease, or do without telephones. But you can determine how much you spend on marketing. Marketing expense is usually one of the largest fixed components of cost, if not the largest. For a PC software product that sells for $50, $500,000 of marketing expense (which is not a lot by today's standards) spread over 50,000 units is $10 per unit—a whopping 20% of the selling price of the product.

This is important for two major reasons. First, some entrepreneurs tend to discount the impact of marketing costs on price by considering them variable costs instead of fixed costs, figuring that if the cost is controllable it's variable. An expense doesn't have to be variable just because it's controllable, or vice versa. For instance, if you decide to add $5000 for advertising, it must be factored into your analysis as a fixed cost. If it results in ten additional units being sold, your added cost per unit is $500. If you sell 100 additional units, though, the cost per unit drops dramatically to $50. Even though you can decide whether to add the money, the amount you're spending isn't proportional to the number of units you sell. If it was, the cost per unit would not change. So make sure you put your costs in the right category.

Second, some managers decrease marketing expenditures to help decrease their break-even points, but they don't change their revenue projections to reflect the weaker marketing effort. For instance, if you eliminate a 40,000 piece mailing to cut $20,000 from your fixed costs, you would expect a decrease in revenue. If your normal response to a mailing is 1%, you would potentially lose 400 customers. At $50 each, you would decrease your revenue by $20,000. The net result does not save $20,000; it breaks even. The real point here is that you should make sure your analysis takes into account the interactions between the various revenue and cost factors when you do your cost-based pricing analysis

## The "Gotcha" of Cost-based Pricing

You might feel inclined to use cost-based pricing as the main instrument to set your price. It's so much easier than figuring out what the market will bear. The information is easier to obtain and its unquestionably quantifiable. This could be the biggest mistake of your life!

Buyers don't care what you have to pay to provide your product. As far as they're concerned, you ship them a floppy, CD-ROM, or tape and some manuals. They cannot see the amount of effort that you have put into developing the product, nor the expenses of marketing it. They will pay what they will pay.

Besides, in a competitive market, someone else may have a similar product, but a lower cost structure. Perhaps your competitor bought their product cheaply from a company that was going out of business, rather than developing it themselves. Or they might use inexpensive off-shore labor. No matter what the reason, if your competitor has a lower cost structure and is willing to accept the same return as you, they can afford to beat your price. (The same holds true if it has the same cost structure and is willing to accept a lower return.)

The only company that can use cost-based pricing as a competitive weapon is the company with the lowest cost structure of all the competitors. Since you don't know anyone's cost structure but your own, don't fool yourself into using cost-based pricing as a competitive pricing tool. Use it only to evaluate your market-based prices and the sanity of participating in the market. Make sure your pricing analysis thakes into account the interaction between the various revenue and cost factors.

# *Approaches to Pricing Decisions*

The way you use market and cost information to set your price depends on the way you want to do business, your long-term goals, and the idiosyncrasies of your segment. You can skim the market, penetrate it, or split it to suit your goals.

To obtain maximum short-term profits, you would use a skimming strategy in which you charge the maximum price that you can get now to accumulate as much profit as you can quickly. In the absence of direct competition, this is relatively easy to do. Set your prices high and sell to those who are willing to pay that high price. Then, when you exhaust the market at that level, or when a competitor enters the market, you can lower your price to reach the next level of buyers. This procedure is repeated until the price of your product is within the reach of all possible buyers. The computer industry, on a whole, operates with this type of model. As time goes on, prices decrease, broadening the number of computer users. Early spreadsheet programs had list prices approaching $1000. Then prices dropped in stages. Most users now only pay a few hundred dollars.

In the long run, however, you might be better off increasing the market early or amassing a commanding market share. In this case, you would use a penetration strategy in which you set your price to spur sales to new users. Since your price is somewhat lower than a skimming price, your profit per unit is lower, but so is your cost per unit since your fixed cost is spread over more units. You still need to be on the right side of the break-even point to maintain profitability with this strategy. But you would not necessarily attempt to be as far right of breakeven as you would in skimming mode. For example, to accumulate market share for its $400 Access database package, Microsoft introduced it for a limited time at $99. More recently, Borland set the introductory price for Quattro Pro 5.0 for Windows at $49.95 to build market share. Within 60 days of release, Borland sold 500,000 units.

Some products can be repackaged to sell at different prices to different market segments. The usual way to implement this strategy is to develop product lines that include products appealing to different types of buyers. The current street price of ACT! is about $260. 1stACT!, a subset of ACT!, gets around $50 on the street. Similarly, Central Point Backup is part of the $100 PC Tools package from Central Point Software and is available separately for about half the price. Many engineering software packages, like FIDAP, the fluid analysis program from Fluid Dynamics International, are priced differently depending on whether the user runs them on supercomputers, mainframes, minicomputers, UNIX workstations, or personal computers. If a person is willing to pay for performance, he will do so.

# How To Price When You Don't Sell Direct

Not every software vendor does business directly with the end user. In many cases, the vendor reaches the user through distributors, resellers, or OEM channels. (An explanation of various channels can be found in Chapter 5, *Your Conduit to Your Customers.*) Doing business through these channels changes the manner in which you price because you have even less control over the price the end user pays.

Jane O'Hara of March Corporation wants to buy two different types of software. The first is a quantum chemistry package that will be used by her firm's scientists on the local minisupercomputer. The second is a flat file database program that she will use on her standalone PC. Jane purchases the chemistry software directly from the company that developed it, negotiating the price with the salesperson and officers of that company. For the database, she runs down to her local computer store and picks the database package off the shelf. In the second case, the vendor has no knowledge of the price she paid, nor that she even purchased the software (until she registers it). If the vendor does not know she is buying, how can it control the price?

First, the value to the user is the same whether she buys directly from you or from somebody else. It's the same product. So you already know the highest price that the market will bear. You also know the lowest amount you are willing to accept. Those upper and lower barriers remain relevant. Now, however, you must split the revenue with your channel—either a reseller or a reseller and a distributor. And you must allow them enough margin to meet their goals too. After all, you have delegated the sales function and its associated costs to the reseller. So you are obliged to give them some of the profit.

The normal method is for you to set a suggested retail price (SRP), then offer your channel partners a discount based on volume.[*] It may range from 30% to 60%. Your reseller buys from you at discount, then sets its selling price based on the market conditions and what it needs to make its profit goals. Often he discounts the product from SRP to a price that is known as the street price (usually 10% to 25% lower than SRP).

The magic of distribution channels is that you can sell more units without investing in a costly direct sales force. Selling through the channel increases your unit sales volume, thus, decreasing your cost per unit by spreading your fixed costs over more units. It also decreases your sales administrative expenses because each sale consists of multiple units—sometimes thousands of units. So

---

[*] That's *suggested*, not *required*. See the section "Keeping it Legal" later in this chapter.

you can afford a wholesale discount because the channel improves your cost structure.

If more than one reseller tries to sell your product to the same set of prospects, your street price will go down because they are selling essentially the same item. Price may be the only way that the resellers can differentiate themselves. In competitive markets, street price often hovers around 75% of SRP. If your channel can make money at these prices, you're okay. If not, you will need to lower your price to them. Again, the market takes control.

Jane at March is a shrewd buyer. She has done her homework and has identified the specific product she wants. Instead of running down to her local computer store for the database software, she picks up the phone to get prices from six different resellers. Then she buys from the least expensive dealer.

## Pricing for High-Volume OEM Deals

Macpaq Business Machines is looking for ways to differentiate its systems from the other PC vendors. So its vice president of marketing meets with you to discuss how to include your software on the 100,000 systems it ships each year.

OEM deals—arrangements in which your software is included under the covers in another product—are scary to many developers because the percentage of SRP that you get is often extremely low; sometimes only a few percent. But that's not important. The key is that they are profitable. It doesn't matter that your retail product sells for $99 to the end user. He won't buy thousands of copies at that price. On the other hand, if you can sell a copy license for 200,000 copies to an OEM at $2 per license, you receive $400,000 in revenue. Your variable cost is much lower, too. Typically, instead of thousands of copies of software and documentation, your OEM deal involves only a single golden master copy of your product (object code), electronic documentation, and hardcopy documentation. Your total cost is roughly similar to the variable cost of a single unit. There are also non-financial reasons to close this deal: you will obtain prestige that you can parlay into additional business elsewhere; and you will gain a user base that you can potentially upgrade to full-cost versions of your software.

If the customer requires source code (and you agree to provide it), you can price the source code as a lump sum payment in addition to your unit price. A recent OEM deal for a Windows utility netted the authors around 25-cents per unit (600,000 units) plus $50,000 for source code. The $200,000 total purchase went directly to the software vendor's bottom line profit.

When selling to OEM customers, recompute your floor price to make sure you don't lose the deal based on irrelevant cost data.

# Offering Quantity Discounts

Aaron Irsay of April Corporation needs to buy a utility package for 100 UNIX workstations in his department. He's your dream end user. There are 200 workstations at his site, and four other sites at April Corporation just like his. That means growth possibilities. Best of all, he plans to purchase his software from a single vendor. Should you give him a discount?

Yes, unless you want to lose his business, because your competitor will probably offer one. Even if you do give a substantial discount, you will still wind up far ahead. Consider the following possibilities:

- Aaron has a staff of support people whose sole mission is to help April's computer users make proper use of their systems and applications. One of them will be assigned to your application to act as first line of support for user questions and problems. The majority of the time, your support staff will only need to answer questions from him, instead of questions from 100 novices.

- Depending on your application, you may be able to double the number of licenses at his site, then parlay the installation into the four remaining April sites. Your total growth potential is ten times your initial installation.

- To make version management easier, Aaron will probably want only one copy of the software that he can issue to his users. He'll probably only want a few manuals that would be shared by all the users at his site. Because you don't have to reproduce your software and manuals, your real cost of each license decreases.

- Aaron will probably want a support contract, which may be incremental revenue for you.

- Your cost of selling many licenses to a single customer is much lower than the cost of selling 100 individual licenses to different companies.

If you have not yet put together a quantity discount strategy, this is the opportune time to do it—when your first big deal is on the line. You may even want to publish your discount schedule in your price list to facilitate use for other accounts. Start by estimating how your costs will change for this deal. Take into account the number of licenses, number of manuals, and expected support cost. As before, this provides a floor price under which you will not go. Then set up your discount schedule based on quantity. (See Table 4-1.)

**TABLE 4-1:** *TYPICAL QUANTITY DISCOUNT SCHEDULE*

| Number of Licenses | Discount |
|---|---|
| 1 | 0% |
| 2-5 | 5% |
| 6-10 | 10% |
| 11-50 | 15% |
| 51-100 | 20% |
| 100+ | 25% |

In "stair-step" or "plateau" discount schedules like the one outlined in Table 4-1, the discount remains the same for some number of units before increasing. One consequence of this schedule is that it increases the customer's incentive to buy at the next higher discount level. Suppose your list price is $5000 per license. If Aaron's company licenses 90 workstations, it would pay $375,000 after discount. But if Aaron chose to license 100 workstations now, he would be eligible for the next higher discount. For an additional $15,000 (enough for three workstations at list price), his company would receive an additional ten licenses. This might give him enough incentive to do so.

The quantities and percentages will vary depending on your application, your costs and the operating system or platform on which you run. UNIX software may peak at 100 licenses, while Mac software schedules may not peak out until 10,000 licenses. To ascertain which percentages are best for you, evaluate how similar packages on the same platforms are discounted.

Another useful pricing tool is site licensing, where the buyer pays one price to license all systems at his site—is also a useful pricing tool. If you make site licenses available, your prospect just may license more systems than under a standard discount schedule. If your $5000 package was discounted according to the example schedule above, Aaron would pay $250,000 for his 100 licenses. If you submit a site license rate of $300,000, he might decide to license every workstation immediately. His average license fee goes from $2500 per system to $1500—a substantial savings. You receive $50,000 additional short-term revenue.

Site licenses are also easier to administer to you and your customer: there is only one transaction instead of many; you don't need to keep tabs on which licenses are legal; and you have flexibility to install software on any system as the need arises.

On the negative side, site licenses are a bit dangerous because the close link between the amount of money spent and the number of licenses received is broken. If quantities change, one party might become displeased. Let's say you grant my company a site license knowing that I have 200 workstations. During the next 18 months, I lay off half my staff and disconnect 100 of the workstations. Suddenly, I'm not happy because I have paid twice the amount that I expected to pay on a per-workstation basis. Conversely, if I decide to add 200 workstations, you lose a substantial amount of license revenue.

Having a set discount schedule does not preclude you from putting together special deals for strategic prospects or when competition underbids you. You write your own rules when it comes to pricing.[*] In fact, many competitive situations have been won by software companies willing to deviate from standard price policy.

## Making the Price Fit the Situation

Remember Jane and Fred? Jane would buy your software as long as it costs less than $7500. Fred would pay up to $10,000. Wouldn't it be nice if you could get full value from both? That's $17,500 total. To do so, you would have to alter your price to suit various circumstances. With a little imagination, you can do it. Here are a few ways that others before you have done it:

- Set your price at the higher level, but negotiate on a prospect-by-prospect basis to win business from those who won't pay the full price.

- Vary your price by platform so prospects willing to pay for performance have incentive to do so. Prices for PC and Mac licenses can be set at one level; RS/6000, Sun, SGI, and other workstations at a higher level; Convex and Cray even higher. How you stratify your pricing is up to you.

- Charge according to usage. Several FEA vendors base their fees on a monthly cost (typically a few thousand dollars) plus a charge per CPU minute that the software was used during the month. This automatically relates value to each customer's amount of use and charges him accordingly.

- Sell different configurations depending on what the customer is willing to pay. Disable features for lower price versions or add services (such as special technical support telephone lines, software updates, or training) for higher-priced versions.

- Have a special upgrade price for current users. When Lotus 1-2-3 Release 4 for Windows came out, users of version 1.1 were offered a special reduced price of $129 for the upgrade.

---

[*] Actually, it only seems like you write your own rules; there are laws covering monopolistic practices, restraint of trade, etc., that limit your freedom. See the section "Keeping It Legal" later in this chapter.

- Offer a competitive upgrade price to get users to switch from other software. To entice users of AmiPro and WordPerfect to switch to Word, Microsoft offers a discount of almost $200.

- Offer trial licenses so the customer can use your software for a short duration at a reduced cost.

- Sell two licenses (or some other acceptable number) at list price, but provide an extra seat at no charge. This is effectively a 33% discount, but it doesn't break down your price structure—an important consideration if the customer will want to buy more later. If you simply gave the customer a break from your price schedule (i.e. a 33% discount off all three seats), you would have established your price permanently, at 33% lower than you want.

## Extenuating Circumstances

So far, we have made the assumption that you will attract more buyers if you lower the price. While true in most cases, there are people who won't buy your product if it's the least expensive. To them, price denotes quality—whether real or imagined. For that matter, most of us associate price with quality in some respect. We'd rather buy jewelry in Tiffany than in K-Mart. We'd choose Cadillac over Chevrolet even though the cars are often made on the same assembly lines using many of the same components. Test yourself now: even if you know nothing about the companies or products, which desktop publishing package do you think is better—the $50 PFS:Publisher or the $500 Page-Maker? Price communicates!

On the other hand, there are prospects who find the perfect software for their needs and then realize that their budgets don't cover the price or that they don't have enough ready cash. If you want their business, but don't want to discount further, offer them a rental. This lets them pay for the software in installments, either on an open-ended basis (that is, they pay a monthly fee as long as the software is installed) or for a specific period of time (that is, you let them stop paying after a prespecified sum is paid). A similar alternative is to "sell" the software to a third party who can lease it to the end user. If you decide to allow users to defer payments, add in an incremental charge to compensate for financing them.

# *Keeping It Legal*

As you watch the pricing dynamics of the software market, it's often easy to believe that there are no rules. However, there are several laws that govern pricing. The most important of these are the Sherman Antitrust Act, the Robinson-Patman Act, and your state and local regulations.

The Robinson-Patman Act forces you to treat competing resellers on proportional or equal terms. That means that you cannot give one distributor or reseller an unfair advantage over another in making a market for your product. You must provide similar prices for similar purchases. If you provide trade allowances for promotion or advertising, you must also provide them to competitors on equal or proportional terms. The key to obeying the law is not to treat all of your customers alike—simply to treat those who compete alike. If John's Computer Store of Milwaukee and Milwaukee Computer Sellers, Inc. purchase from you, you must offer them similar pricing, discount structures, and promotion allowances. That doesn't mean that you must give them the same price even though one buys 10 units and the other 100 units. You just can't give one a competitive advantage for a similar purchase. If you do, you might be sued; and you will probably lose. Here are a few suggestions to help you treat resellers fairly:

- Have standard programs for price, discounts and allowances. Put them in writing.

- Make these programs available to all competing buyers.

- Send copies of your program rules to your customers with sufficient notice that they can participate in discount and promotional programs.

Price fixing is illegal, and is governed by the Sherman Antitrust Act. In essence, you cannot restrict competition in your market, by colluding with your competitors or customers to determine price levels. Here are the main "don'ts":

- Don't get together with your competitors to determine the list price you will charge, discounts you will grant, or allowances you will give to resellers. Don't agree to change prices, either.

- Don't exchange confidential price data with your competitors.

- Don't "signal" your price by announcing it to see whether the competition will follow—then implement the new price only if the competition follows, otherwise keeping your old price.

- Don't rig your bids when you are in individual bidding situations. Don't compare bids. Don't make your bid identical or complementary to those of competing bidders. Don't repeatedly use unsuccessful bidders as subcontractors if you win the business.

- Don't coerce your resellers to adhere to your SRP (suggested retail price).

- Don't force your resellers to set their prices at specific levels to receive discounts or allowances.

- Don't sell below cost.

- Don't use "predatory pricing" tactics. Don't reduce your prices to a level so low that you will drive your competitors out of business.

Okay—so you don't think you have that much clout in your market. You might not. But if you are a leader in your segment, your competitors may think you have enough clout to restrict competition. That's enough for you to run into trouble. The best advice is to have a lawyer who understands these pricing issues and keeps you out of trouble. It's better to spend a few dollars to check your policies with your lawyer, than to spend lots of money when you need him to defend you later.

## *Price Comes Last . . . and May Change Often*

Once a company announces a price, competitors can react by increasing or decreasing their prices to meet the market; therefore, it is often beneficial to announce prices at the last minute. Consider IBM's strategy for announcing its price for DOS 6.1:[*]

> "While sources said that IBM will undercut Microsoft's pricing—possibly by as much as $10 per copy—the spokeswoman said that 'pricing has not been pinpointed. To say we're undercutting [Microsoft's] pricing is premature.'"

Smart company, that IBM. It waited as long as possible before announcing its price. That's because price is fluid.

For companies that sell to price sensitive buyers, a small price swing might affect a lot of revenue. Suppose, for instance that a decision to charge $100 instead of $99 for your software package would have no effect on sales. For a company that sells 100,000 units per year, the associated profit swing is $100,000. Of course you want the extra dollar. But if that one-dollar change pushes a mere 2% of your buyers toward your competitor, you have lost $200,000, double the amount that you gain. It's not worth the extra dollar.

There are many entrepreneurs in the software business who will change their price instantly to maintain market share or profits. There are just as many career marketing managers who will do the same thing to boost their careers. These are the people with whom you battle when setting your prices. Be ready to battle them fiercely and often.

---

[*] "IBM takes on Microsoft with a DOS of its own," *Computer Reseller News*, May 17, 1993, page 169.

# *So What Does It All Mean?*

While the rules of pricing are flexible, there are definite limits to what you can do with your price and still stay in business. Remember that you must price your product high enough to make financial sense. But market forces ultimately determine your price, not your costs. Therefore your attitude toward pricing must be flexible too: in initial selection and in constant fine-tuning. Be ready and willing to meet competitive challenges when necessary. At the same time, be willing to hold your ground if your product can command a premium. In either case, be willing to accept that the market will decide whether you have made the right choice.

# Your Conduit to Your Customers

How does your product get from you to your customer? The answer varies by product type and by your end user's purchasing habits. Certainly, a customer who is buying a complex engineering design tool has a different buying strategy from a customer for a Windows-based word processor. When someone purchases an engineering design package that costs hundreds of thousands of dollars, he examines every aspect of the software and the vendor; his purchase decision may critically impact his future and the future of his firm. If he purchases a single $200 word processor, he won't spend as much time evaluating it. While the engineering software purchaser may hold dozens of evaluation meetings before a decision is made, the word processor purchaser may make his decision on the basis of recommendations, advertisements, or magazine articles, without ever seeing the product.

Determining how a software vendor connects with its customers is what we call "building distribution channels." Next to product selection, development, and pricing, establishing an effective distribution channel has the most impact on a company's ultimate success. If you build an appropriate channel, the end user will be able to find and purchase your product easily. If you don't, the customer will have difficulty purchasing your product, and will buy someone else's instead.

You can choose from several types of channels: indirect channels such as retailer resellers, OEM's (Original Equipment Manufacturers), and VAR's (Value Added Resellers); as well as direct channels such as your own direct sales force, manufacturer's reps, or direct marketing (direct mail, telemarketing). In some parts of the software industry it's even common to sell through several levels of resellers by selling through distributors (see Figure 5-1).

When you choose indirect methods, you add an additional level of complication: your sales force and direct customers become one and the same. Not only do you have to give them the tools to sell your product, you have to convince them to sell it first. Some of them won't be interested in selling for you either.

They're too big, too busy, or carry other profitable products that compete with yours. So your challenge is two-fold: you must select the appropriate channel (or channels), then gain acceptance by that channel.

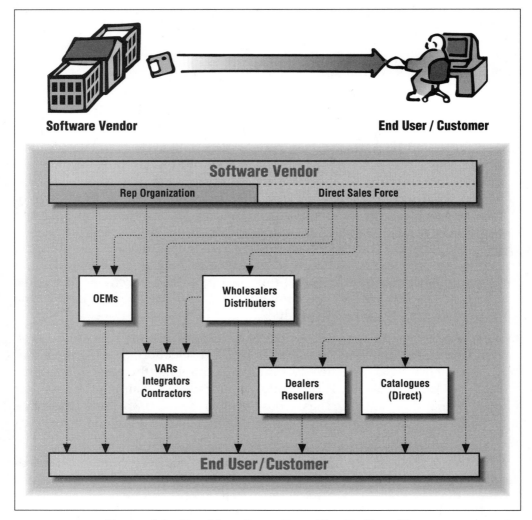

*FIGURE 5-1: THE MANY PATHS FROM YOU TO YOUR USERS*

# *Turning on the Right Channel*

Let's say your product is a $15,000 package that helps manufacturers on the shop floor. Your software runs on most UNIX workstations, including Sun, SGI, DEC, and HP workstations. A typical end user might buy five licenses for her facility (a $75,000 total purchase). Large companies might duplicate purchases for dozens of plants. Your package affects the heart of the end user's business—if it doesn't work, her plant must shut down, causing her large losses.

This is a classic example of a product that can be sold in person, either by the vendor or by a closely related company. The decision maker puts herself at extreme risk when she selects such products because (1) the product is expensive, (2) she needs long-term vendor support to ensure maximum uptime, and (3) if the system fails, she will be blamed for large losses at his company. She is likely to spend plenty of time to ensure that she is purchasing the right system. She will examine software packages from several vendors, and require demonstrations and references from other users. She may even ask her preferred workstation vendor for help making a selection.

In this case, your distribution channel should allow for direct sales. You might have your own salesperson deal directly with the end user, or you might develop a relationship with a VAR who can integrate your software with hardware to provide the end user with a complete solution. You would, in turn, support the VAR so he can support the end user. Since your average sale price is high, you can probably support a direct sales force.

If, on the other hand, your product is a utility package that runs under MS Windows and sells to the end user for $49, you cannot justify spending lots of time with each user. Even if your salesperson only makes $10 per hour, he would need to sell around one per hour (remember, he has overhead) to break even on selling cost alone. But the cost of sales is more that $10 per hour; much more, in fact. Jerry Keane, Vice President of Marketing and Sales at Universal Analytics, estimates that his cost of sales is $500 per hour (including staffing, prep time, travel, etc.). Even if your cost per hour is significantly less than Jerry's, you still wouldn't win if each prospect purchases a single $49 license from your salespeople. You'd lose money with every sale. So an outside direct sales force targeted at end users would be unacceptable. An end-user sales force could only work if it sold many units to each direct prospect—for example, selling site licenses for large installations.

But most of your customers may want a single unit at a time. If so, it's better to do what most vendors of inexpensive software products (and some vendors of expensive products) do: sell in quantity to a reseller who can resell your product to its customers. Selling this way consolidates the work that your team must do. There would be a single sale, a single shipment, and integrated billing—saving you much of the cost of distribution. Of course, you would share the profits with the reseller by allowing him significant discounts. (We are talking about any type of reseller here, including computer store, distributor, OEM, or VAR. The differences between them will become apparent later.)

When you choose an outside channel, you need to select one that complements your product, target customer, and price point. If you choose a channel that does not do this, you will simply waste your time and the time of your channel partner. Let's say you sign up an inappropriate VAR. Perhaps his other software products are used in offices, while yours is engineering software. Even though he agrees to carry your product, his chances of successfully selling it are slim. He doesn't know the engineering market, how to sell to engineers, or who the decision makers are. You both lose. Instead, find the *right* types of companies to sell your product, then show them that the buying habits of your end users coincide with the buying habits of their own customers. Now you have the match. Go help them sell.

Your final selection does not have to be a single channel. You can choose multiple channels if it makes sense. However, to penetrate each channel, you need staff (to sell them) and money (to support them). In the end, you still have to make sure you have selected the channels that are keyed to your product and market, and that you can afford to support these channels.

## *Breaking In Is Hard To Do*

There are tens of thousands of software companies chasing business from millions of computer users. There is obviously not enough time for each user to personally check out every software package. And since you have limited funds, you can only personally reach a small portion of them yourself to expose them to your product.

That's where distribution channels come in. You can sell your product to intermediaries who, in turn, sell it to the end user. You can reach more end users with fewer of your own staff while the end user can check out more software packages without having to hunt down and contact each individual vendor. But, with the large number of software vendors, even companies who resell software can't resell them all. So they're forced to choose between your product and someone else's. Sometimes, someone else means a large established company with a name that is almost a household word.

Large established software companies have an advantage when attempting to put a new product into a channel. They have company name recognition, large marketing budgets, and long-term contacts with the decision makers. Young companies with new products have to fight to get their products into a channel because they are often underfunded, have little knowledge of how to market to the end user, and are unknown by the channel's decision makers.

Established vendors win in the channel by relying on the momentum of their established products. New vendors must prove that their products will sell enough units at reasonable margins for the companies in the channel to risk carrying them. Your challenge is to prove your product can sell before you establish its distribution—the celebrated "chicken and egg" problem.

Let's look at the problem from the reseller's standpoint. He has limited shelf space, warehouse space, and time. You have just approached him to resell your $400 Macintosh-based software package. He senses that your package can satisfy a need in the market, but he realizes that many small software companies have gone under during the past year, leaving his customers with no support. Further, he examines your marketing plan and does not see you spending enough money to attract enough customers to ask him for your product. If you were him, would you agree to distribute your product?

To further complicate matters, he has just finished meeting with a Microsoft representative who showed him a new Mac application product that would compete with yours. He knows that Microsoft will be around in a few years because they have a proven management team, they're well funded and they have sales momentum. With only enough room to choose one of the two products, which one is he likely to select?

Okay, so it sounds difficult; it is. But it's not impossible. Let's look at the channel options that are available to you. Then, let's put together a plan to penetrate a channel, even when you have no momentum or prior sales record.

## Reaching the Masses Through Computer Resellers

The majority of software products for PC's and Apples, and an increasing percentage of software for other segments, such as UNIX, are sold through computer resellers. The resellers provide a direct link to the market without requiring the software company to invest in a large sales force or geographically oriented sales offices. Because of the lower fixed costs associated with external distribution, computer resellers are ideal for products with lower transaction values. There are thousands of resellers across the United States and the world, each with a different business model. They can specialize by market segment, geography, application, or any of a number of other differentiators. Sometimes they add value, other times they sell off-the-shelf. Superstores such as CompUSA constitute a growth segment. While the superstores move immense amounts of software, they do it at a very low margin, and it is next to impossible for a small company up to get these stores to carry its product at all. In fact, with the thousands of resellers out there and the plethora of products from which they choose, you have to be pretty aggressive and smart to cover resellers in a big way.

You can choose to sell to them directly. If you do, keep in mind that the big resellers have lots of barriers that keep small software companies out. They may require you to meet certain requirements for customer support, company size, co-op marketing dollars (the money that the vendor allows the reseller to spend on their behalf), or other requirements. The smaller resellers may each be able to sell only a handful of your products so you will have to cultivate many of these accounts, which in itself is a time-consuming, and thus expensive task. The majority of the product sold through resellers reaches them through indirectly via distributors.

Table 5-1 shows that, if you want to reach the large masses of PC users, you have to reach the retail resellers. If this sounds difficult, don't despair; you can put together a substantial mail order and direct sales business while you're preparing to penetrate the reseller channel.

**TABLE 5-1:** *PREFERRED SOURCES FOR PC SOFTWARE USERS**

| Source | Percentage of packages purchased |
|---|---|
| Retail/dealer/distributor | 76% |
| Mail order | 12% |
| Direct | 7% |
| Multiple Sources | 2% |
| Corporate | 2% |
| VAR | 1% |

* "Computer Intelligence," *Computer Reseller News*, July 1, 1991, p. 14.

## Distributors Sell Your Product Where You Cannot

One of the best ways to reach large numbers of resellers is through distributors—companies that purchase the product from the vendor, store it in a warehouse, and sell it to resellers. Distributors help you sell in quantity because they have direct links to thousands of resellers. When a reseller is interested in purchasing, it calls its distributor and purchases the products it needs, sometimes ordering products from several vendors at one time. This creates orderly processing: you sell your product in bulk; the reseller buys it in small quantities. Both your job and theirs are easier and more profitable. This isn't to say that resellers won't buy directly from software manufacturers; they do. But, as table Table 5-2 shows, distributors are their preferred source.

*TABLE 5-2: WHERE RESELLERS BUY THEIR PRODUCTS\**

| Source | Percentage |
|---|---|
| Direct From Manufacturers | 39% |
| Distributors or Super VAR's | 56% |
| Other Resellers | 5% |

\* "CRN Research 1991 Preferred Distributor Study," *Computer Reseller News*, Sept 2, 1991, page 15.

Selling to a distributor isn't fundamentally different from dealing directly with the reseller: both will ask you the same questions. However, distributors make their money by selling to the reseller at a higher price than they buy from you. Your profit is now split three ways. But the economies of scale that you get from the distributor, and from the entry into resellers make the split worthwhile.

When you sell your $49 package to a distributor, you will find that his requirements are similar to a reseller's. However, the economics are different. Distributors deal in large quantities. So a single distributor can affect thousands of packages each month. Let's say Distributor A can sell 10,000 packages per month. If he gets a 50% discount, you would be receiving $250,000 in revenue from him monthly—$3,000,000 per year. However, software does not sell itself, and the distributor won't do it for you. You have to create a demand or "pull" for your product so that it gets purchased from him.

This is where your marketing plan comes in. You will need to prove to the distributor that you will create demand, most often by placing advertisements in magazines. He will want to see the specific ads that you will run and the list of magazines and dates that you will run them. By the way, he won't take your word that you are running them. He will probably call a few of the magazines to make sure you have placed the ads.

You also have to help the distributor "push" your product through his pipeline by providing promotional dollars to help him sell your product to his reseller customers. This money might be used for direct mail, trade advertising, or seminars all aimed at resellers and large end users. Merisel, a leading distributor, does a series of seminars called Softeach to which it invites resellers and end users to view products that Merisel distributes. The seminars last several days and are manned by personnel from the vendors, each vendor demonstrating his own product and prompting the reseller audience to carry it.

Establishing distribution with key distributors is rough. You have to prove financial stability and you often have to show them that you have follow-on products to the one you are trying to sell. Distributors prefer to work with companies that are not one-shot wonders.

You can think of distributors as giant wind tunnels. They attempt to suck up as much product from vendors as possible and blow them quickly into the hands of resellers. Most distributors carry products that compete with one another. So when the distributor's customer calls him, he will fill the order, not try to talk him into a competing product. That's another reason that "pull" is so important. If the reseller doesn't ask for your product by name, the product will probably sit on the distributor's shelf.

As a new vendor trying to get into a distributor for the first time, you would be better off trying to establish a sales track record first. Then go to the distributor. We'll discuss how later.

## How Integrators Bundle and Sell Your Product

Integrators, like the famous Washington DC "Beltway Bandits" (consulting and service companies located in the DC area), include your product in a complete, integrated system that they design and build to end user specifications. Also known as a turnkey system (because the end user gets a complete system—all they need to do is "turn the key" to turn it on), these integrated systems are sold to government agencies, large corporations, or other end users who require a special purpose system.

When you sell to an integrator, you become part of a team. The integrator acts as a general contractor. It defines system requirements (the specification or "spec"), selects the products that will be integrated (either by developing them or buying them from other companies like yours), and assembles and delivers a finished "system." If you want to be part of an integrator's team, you will need to help the integrator win the business by providing a product that fits into its intended solution. You must also help the integrator reply to the part of the customer's written specification that would be satisfied by your product. It often takes a long time and a lot of effort, but can mean a lot of business if you win.

A few years ago, the United States Navy needed to develop maintenance systems that would be placed on each submarine to provide rapid access to instruction manuals. So, it asked several integrators to submit proposals. The integrators, in turn, evaluated software and hardware to include in their proposals. To become part of an integrator's team, the software or hardware vendor needed to convince the integrator to use its product. Once a vendor had done this, it had to help the integrator get the business by replying to the portions of the spec that dealt with his product, installing the product in a test system, and providing technical support. After all that, it was possible to be on a team that did not win the business. Worse, the process took several years, so it was almost impossible to cut losses by pulling out in the middle. Yet it made sense for many vendors to participate. The potential payoff was enormous: hundreds of systems were to be deployed, and there was really no other way to get the business. For the vendors on the winning team, victory would be several years down the line. That's when the bulk of the revenues would start to roll in.

This "delayed gratification" scenario, in which large investments of money and staffing must take place long before a large payoff, is not unusual when you deal with systems integrators. Each participant must be prepared to invest real money in hopes of a return later. In many systems integrator deals, there is a bidding phase, a proof of concept, and a full deployment phase.

1. *Bidding Phase.* In the bidding phase, the integrator solicits information about products available from outside sources, and often decides whether to buy the options or develop the "sub-system" internally. It relies on the potential subcontractors to provide information that can be used in the bid package and asks very detailed questions to make sure that it is choosing the correct subcontractors. The integrator may ask you to modify your software if it does not meet his specification. The bidding process is often long and arduous, and is not guaranteed to produce a sale. There's always at least one losing bid for each winner. (That's because the government and many corporations require competitive bids for large purchases.)

   If your software is unique, you may try to become part of several integrators' bids. However, there's more work involved. And some of the integrators may decide that you give them no competitive advantage because the other bidders will be bidding your software too. Your key task is to get on the *winning* bid and to support that bidder in every way you can to make that bid win.

2. *Proof of Concept.* The proof of concept stage is performed by the team that wins the initial bid. In this stage, the end user tests a single integrated system before duplicating it many times for full use. You will receive a small amount of revenue for this stage and will be required to support the system fully.

3. *Full Deployment.* The real revenue potential is in the full deployment stage. This is where the integrator uses the cookie cutter approach by duplicating the system many times for deployment on a large scale. By this time, the bugs are supposed to be worked out and the customer understands how the system works in a real world environment. It may be several months or even years from the initial bid to full deployment. Make sure you have other sources of revenue to tide you over.

Integrators are politicians in the truest sense. Their personnel take great pains to work with the customer as early in the cycle as possible, sometimes even suggesting systems or influencing specifications to give them a competitive advantage. Many of the larger projects, such as the billion-dollar Navy CAD/CAM project in the 80's, take years to define a specification as dozens of integrators jockey for position. So when you sell to integrators, be prepared for long lead times, large investments, great risks, and potentially large rewards.

## Becoming a Component in OEM Products

OEM's (Original Equipment Manufacturers or Original Equipment Market)[*] differ from integrators in the size of their target markets. Both types of companies will integrate your product into theirs for resale. However, while integrators sell many systems to a few customers, OEM's typically sell a few systems to many customers. OEM's do large-volume selling. If you can get them to include your software in their products, you will also benefit from their sales volume.

The end users of the OEM may never know who provided the individual parts of the system they receive. Therefore, they may not realize that your product is under the covers of the product they bought. To illustrate, let's look at items that are included in PC clones. All clones include disk drives, BIOS (basic input/output system), operating system, system board, and many other hardware and software items that end users buy as a complete package from the PC vendor. Normally, end users don't care who makes these items. They simply want a system that works, is well supported, and doesn't cost too much. So, they don't ask who made the parts. Do *you* know which BIOS is on the PC you use most often? I doubt it. How about your floppy diskette drive? Most users don't know and don't care, as long as it does what they want.

Other software companies may want to buy your software as an OEM product too. CorelDraw 3.0 includes modules called CorelPHOTO-Paint and Corel Show. In reality, these are bundled software from Z-Soft and AutoDesk. Lotus has bundled Sideways or Adobe Type Manager in various versions of Lotus 1-2-3.

OEM deals work well because everybody wins. The software vendor gets rapid penetration into the market and large cash inflows. The OEM purchaser gets to improve its product without having to develop new capabilities internally.

---

[*] Although the term OEM originally referred to the company that sold the product (i.e., BFGoodrich is an OEM supplier of tires to the automakers), it now refers to the companies on both sides of an OEM deal. If you sell your software in OEM quantities to another company, you're considered an OEM supplier, and you will consider your partner an OEM customer. It's confusing at first, but after a short time, you will be tuned in to what the speaker means by her context.

End users get more "bang-for-the-buck" because the products they buy cost just a bit more, but have a lot more capability.

In most OEM situations, end user support is the responsibility of the OEM, not the software vendor. In order to get a heavily discounted price, the OEM relieves you of the burdens of end user support, disk duplication, marketing, and distribution. Since the related costs go down dramatically, you can afford to offer a very steep discount. This situation works because the OEM is your customer, not the end user. The end user is the customer of the OEM, and (as I said) may not even know you exist.

To find OEM prospects, look at the products currently on the market and determine which could be improved by including your product's capabilities. Then approach the companies that own these products. They are faced with the "classic make-buy decision." If they want to improve their products, they can do it with internal staffing or by buying the technology externally, from companies like yours. It's your challenge to show them how your product can provide the capabilities they need quickly, inexpensively, and with less risk than if they develop the same capabilities internally. Additionally, you must convince them (if they have not yet recognized) that the capabilities of your product will make money for them, either by providing larger revenues or by making their product less vulnerable to competitive threats.

## Selling to Special Markets Through VAR's

Value Added Resellers (VAR's) are companies that purchase products from various hardware and software vendors, often bundling their own software, and offering their own training and support. They then sell their complete value added system to vertical markets. Concord Management Systems, for instance, sells to the construction market; Josten Learning to education; CompuData to non-profit institutions; and Insurnet to insurance companies. The VAR brings expertise and specialized systems to their clients as well as a single point of contact for support. If end users have questions or problems, they always know where to go. The key to breaking into a VAR is to have a product that supplements the capabilities of their system and is appropriate for their market.

The VAR concept is beneficial to you in two ways. First, as a dedicated software company, you can sell your product to them so they can include it in their value added product. Second, you might decide to complement your software with software or hardware from another company and become a VAR yourself. VAR's can be reached through specialty publications like VARBusiness.

# Using Your Own Direct Sales Force

Direct sales is the traditional method used by mainframe and minicomputer companies as well as many software companies in several segments of the computer industry. Until the past 10 years, virtually all computer related products were sold directly to M.I.S. departments by company salespeople. After all, the computer community was still relatively small; there were few vendors contending for the time of the decision makers, and each sale was worth hundreds of thousands of dollars. Vendors who could develop products were easily able to reach the decision makers who would purchase the new products as quickly as products were introduced. Under these conditions, a direct sales force is a rational, cost-effective method of making new customers.

But in today's marketplace, putting your own "feet on the street" to sell to end users is not always the best method. You need a relatively high-priced product—based on sales revenue per customer—to make any money because the cost of maintaining a sales force is so high. If each salesperson cannot sell around $1,000,000, you probably should use another method. Heck, when I was a sales manager, I wouldn't add a salesperson unless I felt he would bring in at least $2,000,000. There are so many other cost effective channels available today, it is difficult to justify end-user salespeople except for specialized circumstances.

Certainly, there are many software companies who have direct sales forces today. Some even thrive. ORACLE has an extensive sales force selling its relatively complex product to end users (at a high revenue per user). Lotus even uses direct sales for its PC software. But Lotus' sales force concentrates only on the high volume users; it uses other channels (distributors, resellers, etc.) for individual users.

If your product is extremely complicated or takes a long time to sell (9 to 18 months and ten direct calls), consider using a direct sales force, but only if the revenue per customer makes it worthwhile. If your product has a low price, is only sold in small quantity, and can be purchased quickly and easily, use other methods.

I'm not saying don't hire salespeople. If you can effectively sell directly, by all means, staff up to do it. If you can't, hire a few salespeople to work with resellers and distributors. You may even want one or two people who can focus directly on a select group of high-volume end user prospects.

WordPerfect found a way to use their "Regional Managers" effectively. They work with large end users to make sure that they are being productive with WordPerfect products and to find new applications for their products within their large accounts. This helps create a pull for WordPerfect through its channels. Yet, the salespeople are working with accounts that could each buy thousands of licenses of WordPerfect for DOS or Windows, Informs, or other WordPerfect Corporation products. Thus each account has revenue potential of hundreds of thousands of dollars.

### Manufacturers' Representatives and Software Publishers

There are many companies who "represent" small software developers by becoming their surrogate sales force. Usually, they carry complementary products that target similar users. For example, XChange, a software publisher in San Francisco, sells products that extend QuarkXPress, the publishing package. While XChange publishes a catalog and a newsletter, other firms use direct mail, live salespeople, or other methods.

The advantage of using external publishers and manufacturer's reps is that they often do the work for a percentage of the revenue. Even though it may be a large percentage—50% is not abnormal—they absorb many of the costs of marketing and sales. On the down side, your destiny is not under your control. If your publisher or rep does not do a good job, you don't get paid. A while back, I had hired a rep organization to help me sell scanners to the government. I chose them because they concentrated on technical publishing applications. Unfortunately, one of their complementary products was selling so well that they didn't take the time to learn and sell our complex product. After six months and little revenue, we agreed that they would never produce the amount of revenue that we needed and ended our relationship.

Manufacturers' reps are an effective way to build sales without the initial expense of hiring and training a sales force. Reps tend to be vertically focused, so they are somewhat knowledgeable in a particular market segment. Use reps when you can't afford to hire a direct sales force, when your product is somewhat complicated (and needs direct sales contact), and when distributors and resellers won't carry your product.

## *Marketing Directly Without Leaving Home*

When your own external sales force is too costly and you have not been able to break into the reseller channel, you can opt for direct marketing—using targeted databases to sell by direct mail or telephone. The cost per prospect contact is dramatically less than that of a sales force, and the number of people you can reach is much greater. You can even use charge cards to alleviate collection problems.

When direct marketing is your only method of getting business, your profits are highly dependent on how efficiently your programs work. If a 75-cent mail piece draws orders from 1% of the recipients, each order has cost you $75 to sell, not including the cost to process the order. That's not acceptable if your product only sells for $69.00.

You're dealing with large quantities, so every penny counts. So does every fraction of a percent in response. In the same example, if you could reduce your mailer cost by 15 cents and get 2% of the recipients to order, your cost of sales per order becomes $30 or 40% of revenue, a cost more likely to allow profit.

---

### ☞ *The Cost of Promotion* ☜

Simply stated:

$$cost\ per\ sale = \frac{cost\ per\ piece\ (or\ cost\ per\ contact)}{response\ rate}$$

This equation works—no matter how many people you contact!

This analysis might seem frightfully obvious, but every time I talk about it in a presentation, my audience starts scribbling furiously.

For some reason, many people hide this simple equation in more complex equations to figure out what their breakeven points are for each of their marketing programs. But you don't need to know quantities of contacts (mail pieces, phone contacts, etc.) if you know the approximate cost per contact and what percentage will buy.

---

Outbound telemarketing must be treated the same way. If it costs you $50 per hour for telemarketing, you need to sell around three units per hour to make a profit.

If direct marketing is part of your sales strategy, you need to make sure you can process the orders. If you accept orders by phone, you need to have inbound telemarketers available to take the calls. Each agent must know how to process orders efficiently by taking information, putting it into your database, and getting the information to the person who will send out the product. Direct mail and telemarketing are explained in more detail in Chapter 6, *Generating Market Interest* and Chapter 7, *Your Marketing Communications Choices*.

## Featuring Your Product in Catalogs

A number of catalog publishers provide an additional way to market your products. *The Programmer's Shop, UNIX Central, The PC Zone, Tiger Software, Windows Shopper's Guide,* and *Mac's Place* are typical of the catalogs in which your product can be featured. Even large resellers like Egghead Software offer catalog shopping. Most of these catalogs allow you to advertise in their publications for a fee; the catalog passes on to you the orders it receives. In some cases, free listings are available. Some companies, like Tiger Software, mount aggressive direct mail campaigns for products with a lot of potential. However, catalogs aren't without drawbacks. I have heard mixed reactions from companies who have tried to sell through these catalogs. The free catalogs are often discarded with other unsolicited mail, or they sit on shelves and collect dust.

If you plan to use catalogs for your software product, check thoroughly to ensure that the catalog can produce results for you. Make sure their target markets are similar to yours. Ask other vendors about the results they obtained with catalog marketing. Then act.

## The Future: Electronic Distribution

Electronic distribution is dramatically changing the marketing industry. With the proliferation of CD-ROM drives and internetworking, you will be able to reach more users faster by providing your entire product (including full documentation) in electronic format. During the late 80s and early 90s, electronic distribution was unusual. Only progressive companies offered CD-ROM products. Agfa, a division of Miles, distributed an entire catalog of typefaces on CD-ROM. Whenever users wanted a new typeface, they called Agfa, who unlocked the typeface on the CD-ROM so users could load it on a hard drive. Similarly, Sun established its Catalyst CD program which allowed users to view infomercials of applications at their own workstations before buying the applications. O'Reilly & Associates, the publisher of this book, has also distributed free software via CD-ROM. For example, a CD-ROM was packaged with *UNIX Power Tools*, containing compiled software that could be run on the major UNIX workstations.

But that's nothing compared to the electronic distribution options that will be available in a few years. IBM, Apple, two major software distributors, and several independent companies have announced CD-ROM distribution products. These companies differ in the amount that they charge software vendors, how the disks are distributed, and how revenues will be shared. But they have some common traits. Most notably, end users will be able to slip the disks into their own CD-ROM drives, test drive applications, or view "infomercials," then call the organization that is running the distribution program to order the products they want. The users supply their charge card numbers. In turn, the representative on the other end of the phone gives customers an authorization code to unlock the application. The users' name, along with payment of royalty, is sent directly to the software vendor.

This distribution scheme has advantages all around. The advantages to users: they can try before they buy. They don't have to leave the office. The advantages to the company running the CD-ROM distribution program: it gains a captive audience of customers; its distribution costs per application decrease. The advantages to the software vendor: millions of prospects can view your software. You don't have to fulfill each order individually, making it less expensive than direct sales. You get virtually 100% registration because users must give their name to the order taker. Your revenue is provided in monthly or quarterly checks.

Don't stop there, though, if you want to find ways to distribute your software electronically. You can also put it out on the Internet. If you do, you will want to include your own encryption method so your software won't be used without your permission. One way to do this is to disable some essential aspect of the software (e.g., the ability to print, or to save files), and allow users to download and try the disabled version. If they like it, they can call you to get a code to enable the feature you have disabled. In some cases you will be able to base the code on the workstation's serial number or Ethernet address. This would reduce the risk of bootlegging. In short, the world of electronic distribution is just starting. If you are innovative, you can find an electronic distribution method that suits your needs.

## Seeking Out Alternative Channels

Since the main criteria for selling through any channel is to get your products into the hands of the people who can best sell it, you may want to use resellers outside the computer business that sell other types of products to your end user market.

Avery Dennison Corporation sells its LabelPro software through office suppliers. Avery gains direct access to office workers, the people who are most likely to need labels, as well as a way to reach them through the suppliers they deal with on a consistent basis.

This approach can work for software companies with other target markets, too. If your product aids bankers, sell through companies that sell directly to the banking industry. Whether your market is professional athletes, doctors, lawyers, or homemakers, if you can find a unique channel through which to reach your audience, you gain an advantage.

---

### ↪ *Innovative Distribution Methods* ↩

Some say that the future of software distribution is electronic—without the burden of packaging, manuals, or stores. Simply turn on your computer, connect to a resource, choose your software, pay and download. Why wait until tomorrow? On line distribution is available today.

CompuServe, for instance, provides electronic distribution services for all types of products. The simplest is its Electronic Mall, which is essentially a comprehensive electronic catalog. You can order products from many major retailers, including many computer retailers. Your order is shipped to you directly—just like any other catalog order. For software (and graphics, data, documents, etc.), CompuServe provides other services that allow you to receive your order immediately. In most cases, you need only find the proper software in a library and download it. Fulfillment is virtually instantaneous.

You can also distribute software electronically through the Internet. This used to require an expensive network connection and an FTP server; however, if you don't want to set up a server yourself, you can go to someone who has already done the work. O'Reilly & Associates' Global Network Navigator (GNN) is a network navigation center that includes a "marketplace" where you can provide "infomercials" to prospective customers. You can provide information about ordering through traditional channels, allow the customer to order electronically, or allow the customer to download your product directly. Of course, if you put your product on the network (whether on your own node or on somebody else's), you will need to protect it so it won't be bootlegged. You must also provide a way for buyers to purchase it from you (pay for it and have you unlock it for use). Or you can use the "shareware" approach, which is described in the next section.

---

## *Casting Your Fate to the Wind: Shareware*

In 1982, Jim Button, an ex-IBM engineer, looked for a good database program for his IBM PC. He couldn't find anything that satisfied him, so he wrote his own program, called PC-File. PC-File impressed his friends, so he let them copy it. However, the more people that copied PC-File, the more calls Button would receive at home. When Button returned from a short vacation to find a sack full of mail, he decided to ask users to register their copies for $10 (which he did via a screen that came up when the software started). This would entitle

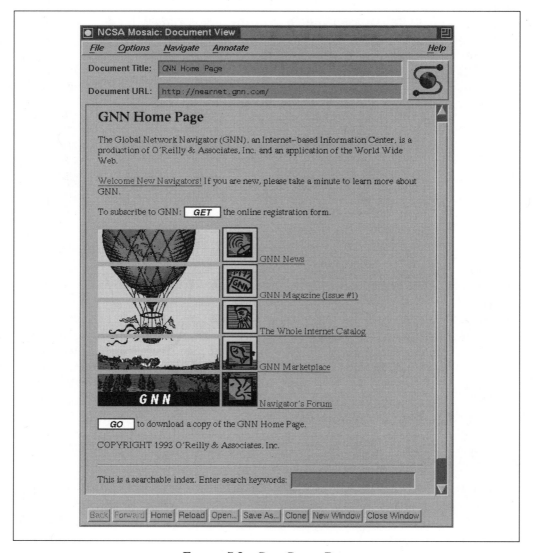

***FIGURE 5-2:*** *GNN COVER PAGE*

them to the next version of PC-File and answers to their questions. Button was on to something. Suddenly, he was making ten times his IBM salary by selling and supporting his new, inexpensive software.

Button invented Shareware. If you use Shareware distribution in its purest form, you allow customers to copy and distribute your software freely, either from floppy or bulletin board. Then, the recipients try it and buy it if they like it. There are no packaging, marketing, or sales costs. You don't even print manuals. Instead, you include them in a file so users can print their own. This is the non-marketer's dream—to let word of mouth about your product sell it for you while you update it and collect royalties.

McAfee Associates used shareware to launch its virus protection products when virus scares started to make headlines. Still predominantly a shareware company today (with only a few OEM accounts), McAfee Associates made $6.4 million on revenues of $13.7 million in 1992—a pretty good return, I'd say. However it's not always that easy. According to Bob Ostrander, founder of Public Brand Software (a company that became the largest vendor of shareware disks) approximately 5% of the 20,000 or so authors who have attempted to use shareware distribution have made enough money to pay back their original investment. He knows of 120 authors making money by working out of their homes; more than half of them are earning $50,000 to $200,000.

Shareware is the least expensive way to distribute your software. You can do it for as little as $500—the cost to copy your disk and send it to Shareware distributors. However, like other channels, the better you support it with marketing communications, the more likely it will be to work. In addition, product quality and support are particularly important when you distribute via shareware because your product is sold by try-and-buy method. If your product doesn't do the job, the prospect will find out quickly and look for a solution elsewhere.

If you want to break into shareware, first talk to the Association of Shareware Professionals. They can send you author's guides and lists of shareware disk vendors and bulletin boards, the primary channels for shareware distribution. Once you send out your software, you generally won't begin to get responses for three to four months. In six to nine months, you will know whether you have a hit. That's about how long it takes until your registrations begin to show up in bulk.

## *Mixing and Matching for the Proper Fit*

After distributing PC-FILE as shareware for a while, Jim Button decided that he wanted to break into the standard distribution channels. It wasn't easy. Large distributors like Merisel and Ingram-Micro didn't understand whether users would be willing to buy from a retailer when they could get same product by downloading a shareware version. This is called *channel conflict*, a situation in which resellers must compete against the same products that they sell because the vendor offers it through several competing channels. To convince the distributors to distribute its next PC-File release, Button delayed the shareware release of PC-FILE. Instead, he waited waited until he could prove to the distributors that PC-File would sell well through their channel. Then he released subsequent versions through channels.

Today, using multiple channels is widely recognized as an acceptable, and sometimes preferred, marketing tactic. This goes for DOS, Mac, or UNIX software. Virtually all of Microsoft's applications are available by mail, through retail outlets, or bundled with OEM systems. Borland International, a company that started by selling exclusively via direct mail, now derives most of its revenue from the retail and OEM channels. Many distributors are even developing special UNIX divisions to meet the special needs of UNIX resellers, end users, and software vendors. In short, you no longer restrict your movements when you choose a channel. You are free to use multiple channels.

Each channel requires its own level of sales, marketing, support and development effort. When you sell directly, you must do everything. With indirect channels, your channel partners will pick up part of your burden; which part depends on the type of channel. Table 5-3 summarizes the most common distribution channels, and what your responsibilities are with each channel.

**TABLE 5-3:** *SOFTWARE VENDOR RESPONSIBILITIES*

| | Product Development | Integration | Support | End User Selling |
|---|---|---|---|---|
| **Reseller** | ■ | | ■ | ■ * |
| **Distributor** | ■ | | ■ | ■ * |
| **Integrator** | ■ | | | |
| **OEM** | ■ | | | |
| **VAR** | ■ | | | |
| **Direct** | ■ | ■ | ■ | ■ |

Often users won't even know who they are buying software from. If you have been invited to a Lotus seminar, it might have been arranged by Software Spectrum (a large software dealer) or by Corporate Software (a distributor). If you replied to one of Lotus' advertisements for a trial license of Freelance Graphics, you may have received an offer from MicroWarehouse. You may even have received a direct mail offer for a Lotus product that was sent by catalog dealer, Tiger Software.

# *Breaking Into the Distribution Channel*

You now know what your distribution options are. You understand the basics of what you need from various channels. But you still can't break into the distribution chain. The remarks you get when you approach distributors are "You don't have enough volume," "You're marketing plan is too sparse," or "Your product is unproven." But after taking all this abuse, you still feel that selling through distributors is the best approach for you.

These people are really saying that you have not proven to them that your product will fly off the shelf instead of sitting in inventory. Your challenge: to prove that your product has pull! The best way to do this: create demand for your product that the distributor wants to be part of.

Here's how:

1.   Start by marketing directly or through catalogs. Sure, it will cost you some money to start your direct mail or telemarketing program, but it may be the only way to prove that your product will sell. If you do it effectively, you will be receiving revenues as you build your case—hopefully enough to break even or make a profit. You will also be building product momentum. End users may call resellers to locate your product; these calls are often passed on to distributors.

2.   Once you feel comfortable enough to convince resellers that they will make money, find several resellers to carry your product. Buy advertising to bring people into their establishments to buy your product. Show them how to sell it. Make sure they have enough in stock to satisfy demands. In short, support them so well that they become success stories that help you achieve broad based distribution.

3.   Put together a marketing support plan. Develop advertisements for your product, and reserve advertising space in the magazines that best target your end users. Put aside money for the distributor to use to sell to resellers.

4.   Go to distributors and larger resellers. Show them how you can help them make money. Share your marketing plan. Tell them about the success of your current resellers. Commit a sufficient amount of dollars to the prospects' marketing programs. Prove to them that your product has the pull to move your software off their shelves.

5.   Support the distributors and resellers so that they want to continue to sell your product because they're making money with you.

6.  Make your end users happy by providing excellent technical support so they want to come back to you for your new products as you develop them. Keep good track of your users so you can sell to them and get them to come to the resellers to buy additional software.

This is the strategy that worked for Intuit. Intuit created demand by marketing Quicken directly to the end user. Then it used its direct marketing success as proof that Quicken will sell. It kept track of its users and sent them product announcements with discount coupons and the names and addresses of local resellers. Now, Intuit has broad distribution and Quicken is one of the best selling software packages in the country. When Intuit comes out with a new release or new product, distributors and resellers quickly embrace it.

Will this method always be successful? No. If the product is a dog, you will not be able to spur demand no matter what you do. But many companies have used this methodology to broaden their distribution channels. Even if you are not successful in breaking into the channel, you may be able to make some money while you are trying to prove your point.

## *Which Channels Are Best for You?*

In making your channel selection decision, consider the following issues:

*   How and where does your target market buy? You must understand where your prospects are most likely to look for the solution that your product provides. They must find your product there when they look. If they need hand-holding and a lot of time to make the decision, you will probably need to get involved in the sale yourself, or train a VAR to do it. If end users want to buy the product on the run, place your product in computer stores. Customers who want an overall system that includes your software as only a small part of their purchase are more likely to buy your product if it is offered through OEM's and integrators.

*   How does your competition sell? If your competitor has a direct sales force, you can either meet it head-on by selling directly yourself, or find an alternative means of getting to prospects that your competitor cannot match. AutoDesk was the first CAD company to use resellers and thus blow away most of the direct selling CAD vendors. It found a better way to sell.

*   How far will your resources carry you? Don't try to do everything at once. Eventually, your resources may allow you to be in several channels, but when you are starting out, you can't afford it. Start with one channel; make it profitable; then grow into additional channels.

Table 5-4 summarizes the properties of different sales channels. Consider it when you're deciding which options are appropriate.

**TABLE 5-4:** CHOOSING YOUR CHANNEL

| Property | Direct sales force | Computer Resellers | Distributors | Manufacturer's Reps | Integrators | OEM | VAR | Direct Marketing | Catalogue | Alternate Channels |
|---|---|---|---|---|---|---|---|---|---|---|
| High dollar value per transaction | ■ | | | ■ | ■ | ■ | | ■ | | ■ |
| Small dollar value per transaction | | ■ | ■ | ■ | ■ | ■ | ■ | ■ | ■ | ■ |
| Large number of potential prospects | | ■ | ■ | ■ | ■ | ■ | ■ | ■ | ■ | ■ |
| Niche Market | ■ | | | ■ | ■ | | ■ | | | ■ |
| Requires sign-off by several levels in the customer's organization | ■ | | | | | | ■ | | | ■ |
| You have resources to broadly provide advertising and marketing support | ■ | ■ | ■ | ■ | ■ | | | | | |
| Complex presentations are required | ■ | | | | | | ■ | | | ■ |
| Can be easily presented in print | | ■ | ■ | | ■ | | | ■ | ■ | |
| Visual product: it demonstrates well | ■ | ■ | ■ | ■ | ■ | | | | | ■ |
| Can be included in other products for resale | | | | | | ■ | ■ | | | ■ |
| External expertise is required | | | | | | | ■ | | | ■ |

New companies are making inroads into the reseller channel daily. Others are using their own sales forces effectively. The key is to match the channel to your product, user, and competitive climate. Then put enough resources (time and money) behind your choice so you will be successful.

# Generating Market Interest

*"In science the credit goes to the man who convinces the world, not to the man to whom the idea first occurs."*

— *Sir Francis Darwin*

Victory or failure for your company may be predicated on how well you get the word out about your software. If you do it well, you will build awareness and generate new customers. To do so, you need a clear message and a convincing manner in which to tell it. You also need to tell it to the right people—those who will buy and use your product. Although it sounds simple, it's not. You will be vying for attention against other companies whose messages conflict with yours. It will be particularly difficult if you are trying to do it on a limited budget or with a small staff.

## *Finally, a Level Playing Field*

Early in this century, companies only had a few ways to tell their customers about their products. For the most part, these ways were slow and expensive. The difficulty and cost of getting information to the market kept most companies from pursuing national and international distribution. When radio became an advertising medium, the situation changed. Companies could describe their products to large audiences without waiting days for the message to reach cross-country. The era of television advertising began in the 50s when Bulova spent $9 for a 15 second commercial. For the first time, advertisers could add visual communications to the aural messages of radio. The added impact affected large markets quickly and at a low per-person cost. However, the total out-of-pocket expenditure quickly became so large that it excluded many companies—a situation that still exists.

As electronic communications and print technology improved, so did the ability of magazines to reach independent markets. Faster communications and transportation coupled with faster, more efficient production methods meant publications could be created to serve niche markets, enabling companies to market their products to targeted, geographically dispersed audiences without large expenditures.

With the invention of the microcomputer in the early 1980s, small companies found a more level playing field. The microcomputer allows small companies to employ direct marketing programs without huge budgets. No longer is a mainframe necessary to handle the transactions required for targeted mailings. Now, small and large companies use sophisticated marketing communications programs based on market segmentation, individualized messages, and even internetwork communications. In fact, it is not unusual for small companies to market successfully in the same market segments as billion dollar corporations. Dell Computer has competed head to head with IBM for personal computer sales since Michael Dell started the company as a college student. Caere Corporation fights Intel in the FAX software market. Computervision must consistently fend off CAD competitors that are a fraction of CV's size. In the network, utility, and groupware markets, competitors of all sizes are facing off to establish market segment supremacy.

The marketing communications (a.k.a. "marcom") challenge encountered by today's small company is to find its target audience with pinpoint accuracy, then convey its message in a compelling way.

# *Getting the Word Out*

When you developed your product and pinpointed your market, you laid the foundation of your marketing plan. Now it's time to reach out to those you targeted, and convince them that they should buy your product. When you direct your effort at one prospect at a time, that's sales. When you use methods that reach multiple prospects at once, that's marketing communications.

Think for a minute about how you last found out about a product that you bought. Perhaps you saw an advertisement in a computer magazine or read an article about the product. In any case, the company somehow found a medium that would reach you, presented a message that would stand out among the other messages, and provided you with enough stimulus to purchase. The challenge you now face is similar to the challenge that was faced by that company.

Building awareness by itself is not sufficient. You must generate sales leads to make spending your money worthwhile. That's not always an easy task. A small software company in Washington used advertising, direct mail, and public relations to market its human resources software. It only sold four copies—barely enough to pay for telephone costs to its advertising agency.

To make your marketing dollars work, you must use them wisely. Each dollar you spend on marketing that reaches a qualified prospect with a message that convinces him to look at your product is a dollar well spent. If it isn't convincing or reaches the wrong person, you have wasted your money.

## *A Recipe for Reaching Your Prospects*

As the company in Washington found out, it's not enough to develop a good product and blindly tell the world about it. You need an organized method—a recipe—to reach the right people. Here's one:

1.  *Choose your audience.* You've already pinpointed the type of person or company that can use your product. Now you must reach him. The problem is that there may be more targets in your target market than you have money to reach. So you must carefully choose the audience that you will attempt to reach first by defining a subset of your target market. The keys to audience selection are (1) the audience should share a common attribute to which you can key your message; and (2) the audience should be reachable via a common method (i.e., the same magazines, the same mail lists, or the same trade shows).

2.  *Determine what matters most to the target audience.* This broad statement will be your product position. (More about positioning later.)

3.  *Figure out how to reach your audience.* Use a common denominator within your audience to choose a method to send your message. Find magazines they are likely to read. Determine which trade shows they attend. The closer you can match your communications method to your audience, the less money you will waste telling your story to people who won't buy your product anyway. By matching your method to your audience, you have greater impact on those who will buy for each dollar you spend. (The most widely used methods of reaching your audience are outlined in Chapter 7, *Your Marketing Communication Choices.*)

4.  *Put your message together.* What exactly do you want to say to your audience that will get them to call you? On the broad level, whatever you say must coincide with (or at least not contradict) your positioning. On a more detailed level, you must determine the facts and images that will support your message so that you can relate them to the audience, thereby prompting responses.

5.  *Get the word out.* Write your copy; develop your graphics; lay out your material; contact your printer, magazines, or list brokers; develop your demos; or do whatever tasks are required to carry out your plan.

6.  *Evaluate how well you have done.* Have you reached the right audience? Did they respond the way you wanted? How many units did you sell? What did you do right? Wrong? What would you change if you were to start again?

7.  *Use feedback from your evaluation to enhance your next try.* Spread your effort to reach the next audience when appropriate or contact the same audience again.

8.  *Repeat the process until you have a marketing communications program that maximizes your sales with a reasonable expense.*

## Choosing Your Audience

The audience you try to reach at any given time is a subset of your target market. As part of your target market, your audience has a high probability of needing your product. But by slicing your market into discrete audiences, you can better appeal to individuals by aiming your message more directly at their specific needs.

For instance, your product may be a Windows utility program that reduces keystrokes for Windows applications. Thus, your target market might be Fortune 1000 class companies that use Windows-based systems. However, your product might appeal differently to users than it does to system managers. If you separate your audiences, you could attempt to send a different message to each group. You can orient your message for users toward ease-of-use or higher productivity, while centering your message for system managers on ease-of-configuration or ability to maintain better control of corporate PC's.

But it's expensive to develop separate campaigns for separate audiences. So you choose the one that you think will best affect your sales. If you need both groups to sign off on decisions, you might decide to do separate campaigns for both groups, but do them on a smaller scale; perhaps by aiming first at a specific geography or industry segment, then rolling your campaign out after your initial thrust brings in sales that supply working capital.

Of course, there must be some way to reach your audience to make audience segmentation feasible. For most small companies, it means using targeted direct mail because mail lists can be split in virtually any way you want to split them. Thus, you can develop one direct mail package for end users and another for system managers. If your budgets and markets allow, you may be able to use magazine advertising to separate your audiences. For instance, the same product might be advertised differently to bankers and real estate agents through separate magazines.

When selecting your audience, select the *highest* common denominator that matches the message you want to send.

# Establishing Your Product's Positioning

Do you associate the terms on the left with the descriptions on the right?

| Product | Position |
| --- | --- |
| UNIX | Open systems |
| Lotus | Spreadsheets |
| Hewlett Packard | Laser printers or computers |
| Easy Working | Inexpensive microcomputer software |
| Macintosh | Easy to use |
| Adobe | Page description standard |
| Disney | Animation |

If so, you have "positioned" each of the products or companies. Positioning is the process by which a product or company becomes synonymous with a concept in the minds of the market. If your positions coincide with the values and needs of the market, they will consider your product. If not, you must reposition or find a new market. The problem is that you do not have final control over the position. The market does that. WordPerfect Corporation sells presentation, spreadsheet, and integrated products, but a large percentage of its revenue comes from its flagship word processor. Many computer users don't even think of WordPerfect when they buy a non-wordprocessing product.

In general, strong positions work in your favor. Once your product occupies a position, competing products are precluded from the same position. For example, many business graphics users consider Freelance Graphics to be the easiest-to-use graphics package, which precludes Microsoft-Powerpoint from occupying the same position. In fact, Microsoft has chosen to position Powerpoint as a high-end, feature-packed package. There is only room for one "easiest," "fastest," or "most powerful" package in any category.

Your planning establishes the position you *want* to convey, both as a product and as a company. Your ensuing planning takes into account the position that you hope to achieve. Although you may be able to achieve most of your positioning goal, you will never achieve 100% because market conditions are dynamic. As soon as you occupy your position, the market changes. So you need a new position. Because of its success with 1-2-3, Lotus' position as a "spreadsheet company" was etched in the minds of computer buyers, causing problems when Lotus introduced other types of programs (like Magellan and Jazz). Computer buyers were reluctant to buy an information navigation program or an integrated application from a spreadsheet vendor. The market had changed while Lotus' position had not. Lotus failed to recognize that its strong tie with its flagship product would become a disadvantage when it tried to market other products. So it also failed when it tried to "push" its new products onto the market. To the market, Lotus was a one-product company. The company finally recognized the issue and, with several years of effort, Lotus gradually positioned itself as a broad-based software company. These efforts facilitated Lotus' introductions of new non-spreadsheet products such as AmiPro and Freelance Graphics, both of which are among the best selling products in their category.

The Lotus situation also points the need to differentiate between your product position and your company position. You need to create separate identities for the two. If your corporation is too tightly linked with your product, you will never be able to break into new areas. Xerox became synonymous with paper copiers, a position that served Xerox Corporation well for many years. But the close link between the company and copiers contributed to Xerox's inability to become a major force in the computer industry—despite major innovations like the graphical user interface and Ethernet. Xerox has been more successful breaking out of copiers in the segments where it does not use the Xerox name. Its Versatec division, for instance, has been a leader in large format plotters.

Be careful not to sabotage your own positioning attempts by sending mixed signals. Deep discounts, for instance, harm efforts to position your product as the top-of-the-category product. Spinnaker sells inexpensive products for the home-office market. It would be very difficult for Spinnaker to market its software based on performance or capability. Users assume that Spinnaker sells inexpensive software, not best of breed.

## Tuning Your Message

Imagine you're trying to sell the prospect a suit. If it doesn't fit, he won't wear it. Similarly, if your message doesn't fit your prospect, it won't persuade him to buy your product. So you must fit (or tune) your message to your prospect.

The more you know, the more closely you can fit your message to your audience. So make sure you learn as much as possible. Don't fabricate your answers in a vacuum. You would be wasting your time, effort, and money by relying on assumptions that were not carefully checked.

*Know your audience*

Physicists get much of their information from technical publications and symposiums. Secretaries rely heavily on their co-workers, newspapers, and television. They read different magazines. They also buy their software based on different criteria.

*Know your product*

A product that provokes interest when demonstrated suggests use of seminars, trade shows, and demo diskettes. If your product is newsworthy, public relations can be a key element of your marcom program. Your message should clearly depict product benefits.

*Know your competition*

Your message will be affected by the messages of your competition. If your competition can complete a task in 20 minutes and you can do it in 19, don't make a big deal about it. If you do it three times faster, though, you may want to crow about it. If you stack up well against the competition in many categories, you might even decide to provide a comparison matrix. Be careful, though. I have seen some companies compare their products to old versions of the competitor's product. This rarely works because there is always somebody smart enough to set the prospect straight.

*Know your limitations*

If you have a small budget, concentrate your efforts on a small segment of your target market. Distributing your budget too far will not increase sales, but will increase costs. Use highly selective programs such as direct mail and telemarketing. Forego high circulation advertising in favor of more targeted methods such as seminars and highly targeted publications.

Rather than guessing which tactics to use, do some research. Get on the telephone and talk to potential users; go to computer stores to watch people make buying decisions; ask your associates what they think; use the "net" to gain important insights.

## *Putting the Recipe to Use*

Let's look at two different companies to see how they might use marketing communications. Furst Software Corporation has developed manufacturing software that runs on IBM RS/6000 and HP/Apollo UNIX workstations. The product's single copy license sells for $25,000. Sekond Software Associates has developed a backup utility for Windows and DOS. Its street price through the computer channel is $50.

Furst Software sells its product to companies that manufacture parts on an assembly line. Its software helps manufacturers produce parts within tight tolerances. So it positions its product as a cost-effective solution to reduce returns due to defective parts. For its product introduction, it targets manufacturing directors at companies with sales greater than $100 million who have IBM or HP workstations on the shop floor already. (It's worth noting that many other companies can make good use of the product too. It's just that Furst Software is operating with a limited marketing budget. So its initial audience is only a small subset.) Since the product requires a direct sales call and Furst Software only has two salespeople so far, it decides to initially go after an audience in the New York and Southern California areas. (That's where its salespeople are.)

Furst Software's first task is to develop good sales collateral that its two sales-people can use to get into the door of prospects and leave behind as a reminder of what the product will do for the buyer. Then it purchases lists of manufacturing directors at companies that have IBM or HP workstations. It uses these lists for a targeted direct mail campaign. Since many people from its target audience attend AutoFact (an annual trade show in Detroit), Furst Soft-ware obtains a spot on the show's seminar agenda and demonstrates its soft-ware in the IBM and HP booths. To instigate press coverage, it also sends out press kits to magazines targeted at certain types of manufacturers, introducing the product and showing how it can be used in production environments.

Sekond Software's potential market is much broader, and its software is sold indirectly. Therefore, its marketing communications challenge is different. Not only must it get its message to the end user buyers, it must also reach resellers. It puts together collateral too. But it uses the collateral, along with demo disks, to embark on a public relations campaign to get product reviews in the major personal computer magazines. Sekond Software then puts together a direct mail campaign to reach the resellers who need to stock the product. The mes-sage: "You can make money by selling our software. Here's why ... " This is Sekond Software's second product in the channel, so it reminds the resellers how successful they have been with the first product from Sekond. To create demand for the resellers, Sekond Software selects one or two key personal computer magazines in which to advertise.

Furst Software can execute its campaign inexpensively because its audience is narrow. It uses marketing to supplement its direct sales force. The campaign I outlined for Sekond Software, though, is not for the meek. It will probably cost hundreds of thousands of dollars just to gain initial exposure. The marketing communications stakes get large when you deal with the reseller channel. That's because marketing communications is the major expense for companies that sell inexpensive software.

## It's Never Too Early To Start

If you want to start making sales as soon as your product is ready to ship, don't wait until then to start attracting customers. It will be too late. If you want to get off to a quick start, begin early.

It takes time to produce your marcom programs. Bulk mail can take several weeks to process and several more to go through postal channels. Prime trade show booths are often selected a full year in advance. Advertisement insertion deadlines for trade magazines can be 60 to 90 days before publication. Some magazines fill their editorial needs months before their deadlines. So you must start early enough to complete your tasks on time.

Sure you can rush some things. Printing, for instance, can be accelerated. But you will pay extra for rush service and might even have to redo a shoddy print job. Not having to reprint a sloppy 25-cent mailer will save you $5,000 on a run of 20,000.

For many companies with long sales cycles, sales collateral is given out months before the sale is made. Therefore, you should highlight your next release instead of the one that is already on the street. Have it ready so your salespeople can use it early in the sales cycle. That's when you need it most—when your salesperson doesn't yet have a product to demonstrate. If your sales cycle is six months, your salesperson needs some printed information six months before release.

A side benefit of starting early: You will have plenty of time to think about how to make the most effective program. After all, the cost is important, but an increase in revenue is probably more important.

## A Marketing Communications Checklist

Here are some questions to guide your marcom planning:

### Defining Your Audience

- Who is your audience? Are you aiming at engineers, doctors, office managers, programmers, or some other group?

- What are the characteristics of your marketplace? Do your intended customers buy for convenience, to look good for the boss, to save money for their stockholders, or some other reason?

- How do they form their opinions? Do they read magazines?

- To whom do they turn for advise about software? Do they ask tech support, consultants, magazine reviews, or competitors?

### Understanding Your Product

- What problem is your market trying to solve? Getting the job done more quickly? Getting the product to market sooner? Reducing costs?

- How does your product solve their problem? Does it decrease raw material usage? Increase throughput? Increase quality?

- Are there other products that solve the same problem? Which ones? How does yours differ from theirs?

- Why would somebody buy your product? Because it runs on the platform they use? Because it's better than competitor X, Y, or Z in a specific way?

- Why would somebody decide not to buy your product? Is it missing features that are important? Does it run on the wrong platform?

### *Communications Methods and Media*
- What communication methods are available to you? Are there trade magazines, newsletters, mailing lists, and trade shows you should be part of?

- Are there any trade publications the prospect is likely to read? Does she read UNIX World, NASA Tech Briefs, CFO Magazine, or others?

- Are there specific events that your market attends? Do they attend shows like Comdex, Autofact, or Power Selling?

- How do your prospects get their information? Do they get it from magazines, local business paper, or associates?

### *Figuring Out Your Resources*
- How much money do you have to spend? How far will it go for design and execution, using various methods?

- Who in your organization has the time and background to develop and orchestrate your marketing communications plan? Is the president doing it part time? Is there a full-time marketing person? Are you using an external marketing company or agency?

## Evaluating Your Marcom Program

A startup company in Atlanta made the mistake of entering a 12-month contract with a computer magazine at a monthly cost of $5000. The president of the company (a three-person firm) figured that the increase in sales of their $300 product would easily offset the cost of the advertising. It did not. Approximately 10% of 30 to 40 monthly respondents bought the product, yielding an incremental monthly revenue stream of only $1000. Their problem was so bad that they quickly realized their marketing communications program was poorly designed. In many cases, though, the problems are not as easily seen. Wishful thinking on the part of executives and the need to look competent on the part of marcom personnel often lead to repeats of ineffective programs. It doesn't have to be that way. With a few simple additions to your program, you can incorporate an evaluation procedure.

1. Code your materials so that you can find out which parts of your program have been the most successful. For example, you can put a differentiating code on business reply cards and advertisements that indicates the content

of the mailing or ad, the specifics of the market that was targeted, and the date.

2.  Tabulate the codes so you can figure out which materials have been most productive. If customers respond by mailing in a coupon, this is simple. If they respond by telephone, make sure to ask for the code printed on the literature that caused them to call.

3.  Whenever possible, link your actual sales to the method and message that attracted the initial request. Compare the total responses generated by each marcom activity, and if possible, compare the quality of the responses. (See Chapter 8 for a discussion of "qualification.")

4.  Keep track of the money spent on each activity. By comparing the revenues to the direct cost, you can understand whether it is a worthwhile method of reaching your market.

5.  Evaluate and adjust your activities based on money, medium, and message. If you're reaching the wrong audience, figure out who the right audience is, and redesign the program to reach them. If you find that seminars work better than advertising, broaden your seminar marketing while reducing advertising expenditures. If you find out that certain messages work better than others, use the successful messages. Don't underestimate the value of a customer. If the typical new customer purchases three items every five years, factor it in.

If you have approached your communications program strategically, you probably won't have to worry about hit-and-miss marketing. Instead you have fashioned a well-conceived program that can be executed precisely. And you will stretch your marketing dollars. But if your evaluation shows that your marcom program isn't working, don't try to fix a poorly conceived program by throwing money at it. Additional money doesn't mean better results. Time and time again, I see companies throw away marketing communications dollars. In many cases, the management recognizes that its marketing program has not performed properly. But instead of fixing the problem, they spend more money on the same poorly conceived program hoping to make it succeed. A more appropriate response would be to "re-engineer" the program.

The overall measure of your program's success is how much revenue it generates. Therefore, you might be tempted to evaluate your marketing communications by linking it to total revenue. The problem with this approach is that your communications might be doing its part, while your sales force (or some other part of the mix) falls short. The real correlations are: communication generates inquiries; inquiries become leads; leads become sales; sales generate revenue. Insufficient revenue can reveal that a problem exists. But it doesn't tell you whether it is a communications problem or not. (Remember that there are several items that are necessary but not sufficient to assure success, including the right product, the right channels, the right price and the right communications. Make sure that you examine all parts of the cycle.) The way to pinpoint problems in marketing communication is to determine whether it is generating enough inquiries, whether there are qualified prospects in the inquiries, and whether your sales team finds it easier to open doors or close deals.

To evaluate their programs, some companies separate a market into two discrete segments. They send out different mail pieces at the same time and try to compare the results. The same type of test marketing can be used for all types of marcom activities, including advertising. This split market testing is a reliable way to obtain performance data quickly; however, it is more costly because it requires multiple designs.

If your marketing communications programs do not attract enough revenue to make a profit, re-evaluate other aspects of your business plan including your distribution channel, pricing strategies, and product capabilities. You might have to make major adjustments to make money.

Let's see how this might work in practice, using a direct mail example. You send 10,000 mailers on January 30 and 10,000 different mailers on February 15. You use two lists for each mailing, 5000 bankers and 5000 accountants, assigning the following codes:

Mailing to Bankers, Jan 30    JB
Mailing to Accountants, Jan 30    JA
Mailing to Bankers, Feb 15    FB
Mailing to Accountants, Feb 15    FA

When you get the responses back, you see the following results:

JB    250 responses
JA    50 responses
FB    255 responses
FA    55 responses

You've received a 5% response rate from bankers to both mailings, but only a 1% response from accountants. This indicates that either bankers are more likely to want your product, or the message in both mailers is more suited toward bankers than accountants. You can do further testing by designing a new piece specifically for accountants, then mailing it to one of the two accountant lists. If your response rate rises dramatically, say to 4%, you know your initial design or message wasn't working. If you get similar response to the third mailing, you should probably target your efforts on bankers instead.

When analyzing your response rates, judge your program on percentage reply rates, not raw numbers.

## When Do We Start Seeing Results?

The effects of your marcom program are seen in two ways: the short-term response from real prospects and the long-term effect on your company's (and product's) image.

My experience is that most prospects respond to marketing within a few days after they receive your message or within a few days of the expiration date of your offer. I have received responses to monthly magazine advertisements up to three months after publication, but the majority of the responses happen during the first month. Trade show attendees rarely call you. You must follow-up with them. Prospects unearthed by seminars tend to call within a few weeks after the seminar.

The long-term image-building effect is a result of consistent exposure to your message. After frequent exposure, your prospect is more likely to think of your company when he is ready to buy. This long-term effect is the reason that so many consumer products companies advertise on television. Consumer product companies are looking to maximize the number of exposures to their products because the decisions to buy soda or soap are made often and with very little thought. In the computer industry, decisions are typically made only once and the amount of thought put into the individual decision is high. Therefore, image-building advertising should only be used by companies who can well afford it—the big guys. With your small budget, you will never be able to break through the clutter to make image advertising worthwhile.

Small company executives tend to dismiss their inability to evoke short-term response because they are building an image. Don't get caught in this trap. Small companies do not have sufficient resources to spend on image-building programs. To be effective, your program must draw responses that turn into real customers. To increase your odds:

* Be decisive in targeting your key markets instead of trying to be all things to all people. You will put your arrow in the bull's eye instead of in the outer circle. Universal Analytics aims its UAI/NASTRAN product, a mechanical analysis package, at users of other NASTRAN products instead of at the general mechanical analysis marketplace, a focus that they have found to be profitable.

* Get the details done right. If you have a seminar, make sure your date doesn't conflict with a major trade show in your market. Don't forget to

put your phone number on your mail pieces. Use qualified mail lists or the right publications that reach your real target audience.

- Marketing communications doesn't work by itself. You still need a product that performs, a way to get the product to the customer, and a procedure to fulfill orders. If any of them are missing, you won't get your revenue.

- Immediately contact people who respond to your marketing to continue the sales process. If you wait, you increase the risk that the prospect will forget your product or buy from a competitor.

# Your Marketing Communications Choices

There are many ways to reach your audience. Choose the way that best suits your market segment and how they make their buying decisions. Here is a comparison of those that are used most often by computer and software companies. Read the entire section, or refer to a specific method when you need to know more about it. A summary chart is at the end.

## *Sales Collateral*

Sales collateral refers to any information (printed or otherwise) that can be used by the sales force to generate revenue. Collateral can take many forms depending on specific use. Here are a few of the common types:

*Product Descriptions*

These are usually one or two page sheets that describe your product so the prospect can understand when and where the product can be used, what the system requirements are, and most importantly, the benefits of the product for the user.

*Customer Testimonials*

Customer testimonials help the prospect see how happy other users are with your product. Testimonials are more credible than your own literature because they are based on an unbiased viewpoint. They can take several forms:

a.  Thank-you letters from your users.

b.  Article reprints that show your product being used by a real customer.

c.  Your own piece in which you quote a satisfied customer.

*Article Reprints*

Reprints of magazine reviews and articles. You can include an advertisement on the reprint.

*Ad Reprints*

Reprinting advertisements lets your design serve double duty.

*White Papers*

White papers are in-depth technical papers involving your product and its applications. They can be written by your staff or a credible third party, and are used to show how your product is useful to your market. Sample white paper subjects: "Using FEA to Optimize Jet Engine Design" or "How OCR Software Is Changing the Way Offices Receive Faxes."

*Company Descriptions*

These are used when the previous experience of your executives or company history aid your selling effort. Often included in press kits.

*Application Briefs*

Descriptions of specific uses of your product can be used to target markets more narrowly than product descriptions. Applications briefs help when your product can be used for many applications or in many industries.

*Demo Diskettes*

Demo software can provide a self-demonstration for the prospect. This type of demo should not be used for products that require a lot of training.

*Videotapes*

Videotapes let the prospect see your sales presentation and product capabilities without you being present. They also help you show canned presentations as part of your normal presentations.

*Overhead Transparencies and Slides*

Visual aids are a strong stimulus for reinforcing the presenter's words. These visual aids are still among the most widely used presentation aids.

# Advantages

- Collateral is flexible. It can be used in many sales and marketing situations, including sales support, training, direct mail, and public relations.

- The information can be designed to suit the specific needs of one market or for use in multiple markets.

- Collateral can be used individually or in sets. For instance, a salesperson can combine a product description and an application brief so the prospect can see the details of the product she is considering as well as how it is used for *her* application.

- Collateral is inexpensive. It can be created in many forms ranging from single-page, black and white sheets to full color-brochures, video tapes, or demo diskettes. The black and white sheets can be designed and produced in-house for pennies apiece.

- It can be delivered directly to the prospect's desk by a salesperson or by mail.

# Disadvantages

- Collateral requires a delivery mechanism (i.e., a salesperson or direct mail) to get into a prospect's hands.

- This information is usually ignored if it is delivered to the prospect when he is away from his office.

# Relative Costs

- Collateral is generally inexpensive, but price varies. Inexpensive data sheets can be laser printed on precast forms. Prices depend on number of pages, number of printing colors, quantity, special papers, and unique requirements (i.e., die cuts or appliques).

# When To Use

Always! Sales collateral should be prepared at the onset of marcom or sales activities. Pieces should be kept up-to-date. When new products are introduced, your sales collateral should be available by the time your sales effort begins. Specific uses include:

- Sending to new prospects who have contacted you for information or who have responded to your marketing efforts.

- Supplementing information given to existing prospects during sales calls.

- Use as a reference when a representative of your company is not available.

In essence, a piece of sales collateral is your representative when you are not there.

## The Universal Element in Any Marketing Program

Virtually every software company needs sales collateral of some type, although your actual needs depend on your product and market. Most companies should have product descriptions. Beyond that, figure out how you will be selling your product. If you sell to prospects with specific applications for your products, use application briefs to target them. Multiple applications briefs can be produced to target your efforts when your product has a broad range of applications. Customer testimonials never hurt. If customers are willing to say good things about you, commit them to paper, and use them to sell.

The level of technical detail that you must put into your literature depends on the product's price and level of risk. An inexpensive product that is purchased on the spur-of-the-moment may not need an end-user piece at all. Instead, you may need to put together literature to help sell the resellers. That typically means product descriptions and ad reprints. If your product is expensive and takes a lot of deliberation on the part of the buyer, a white paper explaining technical details may help you persuade him to buy your product.

If in doubt, start with those pieces that you know make sense, then add the other pieces. But don't let your sales people walk into a prospect's door empty-handed.

Figures 7-1 through 7-4 show several well-designed examples of the collateral material.

*(courtesy of Logictech)*

**FIGURE 7-1:** SCANMAN-LOGITECH

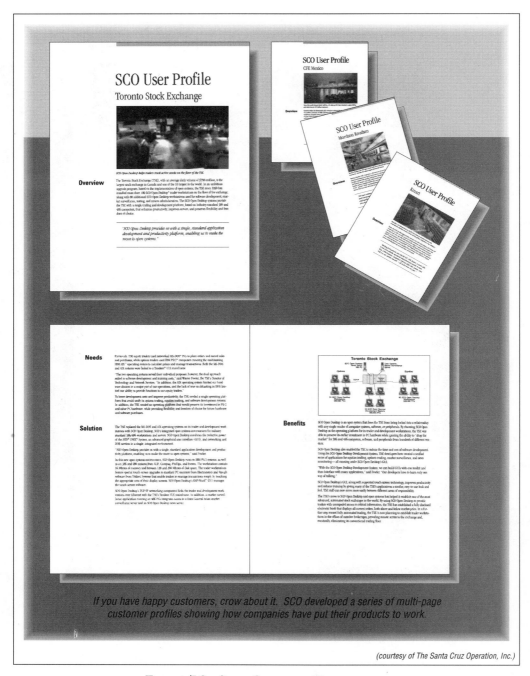

If you have happy customers, crow about it. SCO developed a series of multi-page customer profiles showing how companies have put their products to work.

*(courtesy of The Santa Cruz Operation, Inc.)*

**FIGURE 7-2:** *SCO'S CUSTOMER TESTIMONIALS*

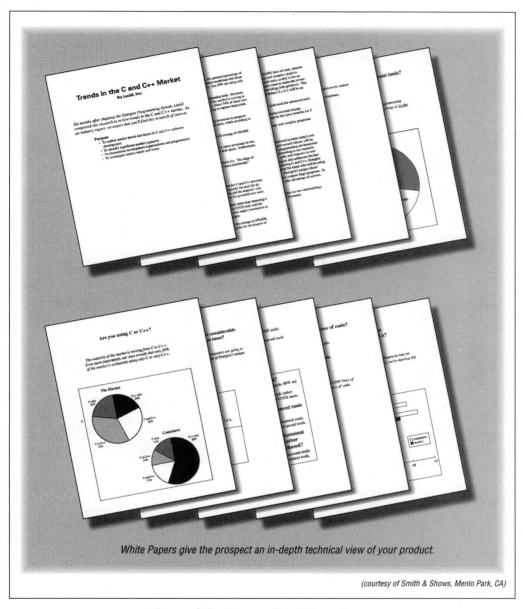

*White Papers give the prospect an in-depth technical view of your product.*

*(courtesy of Smith & Shows, Menlo Park, CA)*

***FIGURE 7-3:*** *LUCID'S C++ WHITE PAPER*

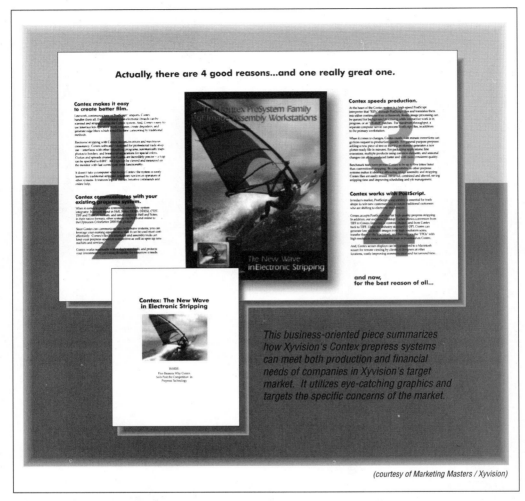

*This business-oriented piece summarizes how Xyvision's Contex prepress systems can meet both production and financial needs of companies in Xyvision's target market. It utilizes eye-catching graphics and targets the specific concerns of the market.*

*(courtesy of Marketing Masters / Xyvision)*

**FIGURE 7-4:** XYVISION'S CONTEX APPLICATION BRIEF

# *Direct Mail*

Direct mail is good for delivering your message to a core audience that you select by demographic distinctions such as geography, company type, what platform they use, or title.

## Advantages

- Direct mail can be tailored to any budget.

- You maintain a high level of control over who receives it. You select the list based on your needs.

- Direct mail can accommodate large amounts of printed information. It's easy and inexpensive to add more information to a mailing.

- You choose the schedule for mailing.

- Your message stands apart because you determine the entire content of the packet.

- Direct mail easily accommodates a reply card.

- It easily accommodates a "call to action": an offer that entices the recipient to pick up the phone, fill in the card, or purchase the product.

## Disadvantages

- Direct mail has a high cost per exposure: 40 cents to several dollars per piece.

- It requires a large staff.

## To Use

- To raise awareness of your product within a narrowly defined market.

- As a direct sales program in which respondents can actually purchase your product by return mail or telephone.

- To gain exposure and generate leads from a limited budget.

- To introduce new products or upgrades to existing customers.

- To attract attendees to your seminars, trade show booth, or speaking engagements.

# Focusing Your Marcom Efforts

Direct mail is a natural method to use for your initial marketing communications tasks. It can be highly targeted; it can cost under a dollar per piece; and you can track it easily. As with other alternatives, the content and the presentation are important. After all, you have less than ten seconds to get a recipient's attention to keep him from throwing away your mailer. Your mailer must stand out from the clutter in the mailbox and it must be easy to skim so the reader can find the key reasons to read on with only a cursory look.

Of all marcom programs, direct mail is probably the best at reaching a large number of users and getting them to buy. Advertising, for instance, does not have as large a response rate. Telemarketing cannot reach as many people as quickly. If you think your product can be sold without direct personal contact of a salesperson, direct mail is probably for you. It's a particularly effective technique for selling microcomputer software.

If you want recipients to buy your product based solely on the mailing, be prepared to accept credit cards or checks and make sure your price is clearly stated. You must include enough information to persuade the recipient to buy as well as the information she needs to do it (how to contact you, price, how to get delivery, etc.). If you are able to incorporate a special dated offer, you will increase purchase rates. Your response rate will go up with the value and quality of your offer. Your offer might be a free additional software product or a special rate if the purchase is made by a certain date. The key is that the person who receives the mailer must recognize the value to her, and be able to act upon it.

If you are concerned about channel conflict, your direct mail piece can include information about how your recipient can contact your resellers. In its direct mail campaigns, Intuit gives its own 800 number plus the addresses of several local resellers of its products. The recipient buys from whomever he wants. You may even be able to get one or more resellers to do a joint mail program with you. For example, Tiger Software and SoftLogic split the cost of a one-million-piece direct mail campaign for Winsense.

If you have a high-priced product, you may have difficulty getting the prospect to purchase sight-unseen. You can still use direct mail to get her to contact your sales office, invite her to a seminar, or simply to make her aware of your product so your salesperson's impending phone call will be welcome. Some companies with moderately priced products are now including protected demo disks in their mailers. With a single call, the user can obtain a full working version of the software in the demo. That's a powerful call to action.

# Your Cost Varies With Your Response Rate

Although direct mail has a high cost per exposure, it's actually one of the most cost-effective marketing communications programs you can use. That's because of its ability to focus directly on your best prospects. Since you're not spending money on people outside your target segment, you're spending your money wisely. An advertisement in a trade magazine, by comparison, reaches a much broader range of readers than you want to reach. Even though your cost per exposure is low, you're paying for exposures you don't want. An ad in a magazine like BYTE may reach millions of readers—but only a small percentage will be interested in the kind of product you offer. If your cost per exposure for direct mail is ten times your cost per advertising exposure, but you only need to reach ten percent of the readers of the magazine, you have broken even in cost. Factor in the amount of information you can put into a direct mail piece and you're far ahead.

More important than cost per exposure or cost per exposure to your best prospects are cost per response and cost per sale. That's what determines whether it's worthwhile. To simplify the discussion, let's assume that everybody who responds buys your product. (The assumption may or may not be accurate, but it's simple.) A 1% response rate to a $1.00 mail piece means that your cost per response is $100. If your product sells for $99, that's unacceptable. (It's probably okay if it sells for $199.) Therefore, you need to work on bringing up the response rate or bringing down the price of the piece. If your piece costs only 50 cents and still gets a 1% response, your cost per response is $50 and will probably work for a $99 product. Similarly, if you raise your response rate to 2%, you will get a similar decrease in cost per response to $50.

If the percentages seem low to you, surprise. These are pretty good numbers. Companies who mail to prospects who already know and use their products may be able to get 5% to 10% response, but the typical direct mail campaign to new prospects often yields 1% or less. If you can get 2%, you have done very well. Many companies receive responses from 1/10% of the recipients of their mailers.

Like other marcom methods, the success of your direct mail program depends on your product, message, and audience. That means you must put together a piece that sells and get it to the right prospects. It's also important to note that direct mail has a built-in call to action, whereas advertising does not. That call to action can induce the recipient to contact you, thereby raising your response rate dramatically.

The Shiva mailer shown in Figure 7-5 was part of a successful joint campaign with Novell. The offer on the envelope motivates the recipient to look inside where he finds a poster summarizing the product's features and business reply

<![CDATA[

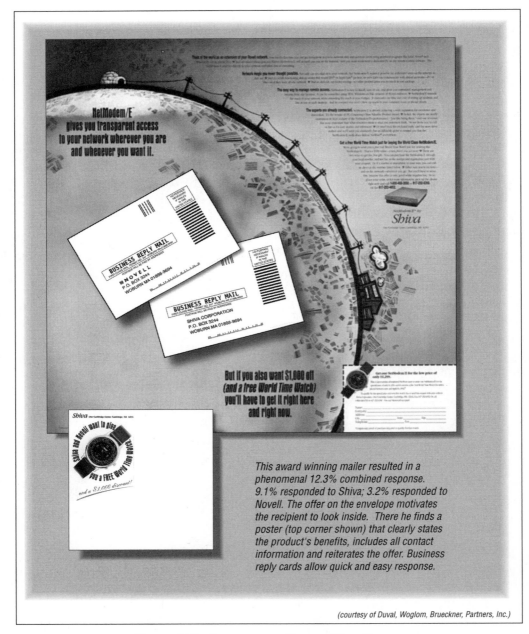

This award winning mailer resulted in a phenomenal 12.3% combined response. 9.1% responded to Shiva; 3.2% responded to Novell. The offer on the envelope motivates the recipient to look inside. There he finds a poster (top corner shown) that clearly states the product's benefits, includes all contact information and reiterates the offer. Business reply cards allow quick and easy response.

*(courtesy of Duval, Woglom, Brueckner, Partners, Inc.)*

**FIGURE 7-5:** *SHIVA-NOVELL DIRECT MAIL PACKET*

]]>

cards to facilitate response. The rest is history: this mailer yielded a phenomenal 12.3% combined response (9.1% to Shiva; 3.2% to Novell).

## The All-important Mailing List

There is nothing more important to a direct mail campaign than the list you use. When you combine a well-targeted list with a mailing that suits the audience, your results are always better. A poor list can doom the campaign to failure.

There are many sources of lists. Your own internal customer list, for instance, provides a known market that already likes your products. You may even keep extra information that helps you individualize the mailing to suit the recipient. For instance, you might segregate your list by industry, then include a separate, personalized cover letter for each industry.

Externally, you can rent lists from list brokers or publications. You can also obtain rights to use the lists of companies with whom you do business, for example, computers, peripherals, or other software companies. To send out invitations to Marketing Masters' Word Processing Showcase tour, we purchased lists from trade magazines such as *Computerworld* and *WordPerfect Magazine* to supplement a mailing directly from WordPerfect Corporation.

Many magazines rent their subscriber lists. Renting such a list allows you to target specific types of people within the subscriber base such as electronic engineers or people in a specific geographic area. For one of our mailings, we rented a list consisting only of Vice Presidents of MIS, Chief Information Officers, Data Center Managers, and a few other similar titles. By being selective, we defined a small, precisely targeted list. Any time the list contains demographics, you can use them to define your own special subset.

Not every list allows segmenting by demographics, only those that collect the data, otherwise known as "qualified circulation lists." *PC Magazine*'s list is unqualified. Subscribers pay for their subscriptions and don't have to supply much more than their name and address with their payment. If you want to reach certain geographies, you can obtain a subset, but not if you want to segment by job title. *SunExpert*'s list is qualified. The publisher sends questionnaires to subscribers. If the questionnaire is completed, the subscription is renewed. If not, the name is taken off the list. Qualified circulation magazines typically collect a subscriber's job title, industry, spending habits, product interest, company size, and buying plans. The publication or broker will tell you what criteria are available for the list you want to rent.

Be prepared to pay 10 to 20 cents per name because list rental prices usually include a base list cost of $85 to $150 per thousand names plus $5 to $10 per 1000 names for each selection criteria ($5 to choose titles, $5 to choose industry, etc.). So if you rent only the presidents of real estate companies in the southwestern U.S. from a list that costs $100 plus $10 per selection, you will pay $130 to rent 1000 names, or 13 cents ($100+($10×3))/1000) per name. There are often minimum rental charges ranging around $400 per rental. For this price, you get peel-and-stick or Cheshire-style labels (labels that are automatically applied to your mailer by a so-called Cheshire machine).

Lists are normally rented for one-time use. Otherwise, you will have to pay a larger fee. Don't expect to use the list more than six months after you get it. They change so quickly that your cost of mailing to non-existent people will go up dramatically.

If you plan to use multiple lists, you should take into account duplicate names. For example, assume that you purchase lists of subscribers to *UNIX World* and *UNIX Review*. These magazines share many readers. Consider getting a mailing house to merge and purge your lists. This will eliminate much of the cost of duplicate mailings. Mailing houses can also help you with all of your mailing chores. For a few cents per operation (stuffing, sealing, applying postage), they will do your mailing without distracting your operation. Some list providers require you to use a bonded mailing house that they approve. By doing so, the provider protects its list (you never see it) and ensures that your mailing conforms to its requirements.

## Taking Advantage of Bulk Mail

When creating direct mail materials for domestic use, keep in mind that you can pack a lot of information into a mailer at a relatively small cost. The United States bulk mail rates are almost identical whether you mail one ounce or eight ounces, giving you the flexibility to include a cover letter, a reply card, and several descriptive pieces very inexpensively. To earn the discount, you do some of the postal service's work. You sort your pieces by zip code (easy to do because you can print the labels in zip code order) and bundle them by destination, making sure you mark the sacks according to USPS specifications. Be forewarned: the regulations are strict on what you must do to receive the discount. If you don't do it according to the USPS specifications, you will pay more. Contact your local post office to get instructions and current rate information and to buy your bulk mail permit. When you use bulk mail, allow two to three weeks for delivery. If you need faster delivery, use first class.

---

### ☞ *Direct Mail Tips* ☜

1.  Make it easy to respond. Include a preposted reply card, and prominently display your telephone number on each piece. If you take orders by mail, make it easy to order by including enough space for his credit card or purchase order number.

2.  Incorporate an offer that expires. Make the offer worthwhile to the buyer.

3.  State the benefits clearly. If the recipient does not see how he benefits, he will not reply.

4.  Focus your mailings on your key audience. If your audience consists of distinct groups, send separate cover letters with your product information to cover the different needs of each group.

5.  Leverage your other marcom activities. If your product has received a rave review from a magazine (or even if you advertise in it), mail to its subscriber list.

6.  Take advantage of bulk mail rates. They can save you thousands of dollars in postage costs.

7.  Code your reply cards so you can understand which mailings gave you the best reply rates.

8.  Direct mail easily accommodates multiple pieces. Don't skimp to save a few cents. Include whatever it takes to make your mailer work.

Use direct mail early and use it often. It is one of your best marketing investments.

---

# Telemarketing

Telemarketing is a form of direct sales. "Outbound" is when you contact the prospect; "inbound" is when your prospect contacts you. This section discusses outbound telemarketing, except where noted.

# Advantages

- Telemarketing is personal. Prospects feel comfortable buying from a real person.

- The method is interactive. Your telemarketer can answer prospect questions and field objections.

- It's flexible. Your telemarketer can set up a follow-up sales call, send literature, process an order, or register the prospect for a seminar.

- It's thorough. Your telemarketer can take as long as required to reach his objective with the prospect.

- Telemarketing can be used to find new prospects, qualify existing prospects, or sell.

# Disadvantages

- Telemarketing is staff intensive. Depending on the objectives of the campaign, a telemarketer can contact two to ten prospects per hour.

- It can be tiring. Most people find it difficult to call prospects more than a few hours per day.

- Obtaining lists is difficult. Many of the lists that are available for direct mail do not allow phone calls.

- Telemarketing is slow. A single caller can only reach a few dozen to a few hundred people in one day. Contrast that with thousands per mailer or advertisement.

# When To Use

- To follow up quickly after trade shows and seminars.

- To find information about your market. One of my telemarketing projects at Multiflow, for instance, found signal processor users in government contractor installations. Because the government does not readily give out this type of information, telemarketing allowed us to reach users that we could not easily reach by direct mail.

- To register attendees for your seminars (inbound telemarketing).

# The Right Way To Telemarket

Telemarketing is cost-effective when used correctly. It is also easy to throw away money. Unless you have the budget to hire a large telemarketing staff, you can usually make your project more effective by subcontracting to an outside telemarketing company. They will help you develop the script, train one or more callers on your behalf, and execute your campaign. Your cost will be $40 to $80 per hour including long distance charges.

If you decide to do your own telemarketing, select a telemarketer as if you are selecting a salesperson. I have seen companies attempt to do telemarketing by grabbing staff without any sales experience (often from software development or support), putting scripts and a phone in front of them, and expecting them to telemarket. While these people are often willing, they do not have the training. The net result is a program that does not work.

The key to successful execution of an internal program is preparation. Teach your telemarketers about your product so they can answer questions easily and confidently. Practice with them so their technique becomes automatic. Provide them with a script or written guidelines so they have information at hand during telephone discussions.

## Cold-calls by Telephone

Many companies try to drum up new business with cold-call telemarketing, a method that often wastes time and money. Cold-call telemarketing should only be used if (1) you can target your prospects very tightly; (2) you can obtain fairly qualified lists with telephone numbers; and (3) the dollar value of each customer is high. If all three conditions do not exist, telemarketing should only be used as a companion to other methods (i.e., follow up after trade shows or seminars).

These conditions are important because telemarketing is cost-effective only when you quickly reach the decision influencers. One well-known department/appliance store wastes a lot of money attempting to contact home owners by cold-call telemarketing to sell them aluminum siding. Their lists are not well targeted. I know of many occasions in which the personnel would contact dozens of condo owners in a single evening, extolling the virtues of their siding. Of course, condominium owners are not interested in siding because exterior maintenance is covered by condominium associations.

Cold-call telemarketing makes sense for:

- Manufacturing software that sells for tens of thousands of dollars
- PC security software that usually sells as a site license
- Software that spurs continuous add-on or supplies business

Cold-call telemarketing doesn't make sense for:

- Game software
- Home-office software

# *Public Relations*

Public relations focuses your message on a small number of industry liaisons (editors, writers, analysts, and consultants) who assimilate your message and convey it to their markets as articles, reports, or suggestions. The primary goal of public relations is to increase awareness of your company and product among the people who influence your market. Over time, and through repeated exposure, this awareness will develop understanding. The secondary effect is that your product or company may be mentioned positively in key periodicals and included in multi-vendor evaluations by key media sources, consultants, and potential purchasers.

## Advantages

- Your message is presented to the market by credible sources.
- You enjoy high exposure with low cost.

## Disadvantages

- Public relations tends to lessen your control. Once you place your message into the hands of the editor, he decides how much to use and how to convey it. In some cases, the outcome may even be detrimental to your sales efforts. You can't stop someone from giving you "bad press."
- Hiring public relations personnel is expensive—especially at the executive level.

## When To Use

- As a new company—to add credibility to your message.
- Almost anytime. Whenever you have news about your company, product, industry, or application.

## Hidden Costs/Hidden Value

For startup businesses, public relations can be among the most effective communications available. But it's never free. In addition to the cost of the PR staff or consultants, your key executives need to spend time helping the PR process: attending meetings with consultants and press, giving interviews, writing articles, etc. According to Smith and Shows, a high tech PR firm, a PR budget typically runs about 20% of the established advertising budget. If you hire a PR agency, expect the cost to be between $8000 and $40,000 to introduce your new product.

If your new product is really unique, or if there are unique ways to use your product that are newsworthy, then public relations can provide a strong communications channel into your market. The key to public relations is that the market receives the information about your product from an unbiased third party. This adds an enormous amount of credibility to the message that you present.

## How Public Relations Works

Public relations should not begin when you send press releases to industry publications. Build your foundation before contacting the press. To begin your public relations process, familiarize your executives and PR person (whether internal or external) with your product and all the information they need to support the PR process. The next step is to line up several beta test sites as references. Then contact key consultants. Make sure they understand your product concept and disclose the success that your reference customers have achieved. By laying this groundwork first, you have cultivated a set of individuals who will corroborate your story when the press asks for opinions. Now you are ready to contact the press.

Target the publications most likely to feel that your product is news. Contact your top few publications by phone or send them personalized letters with ideas for stories that fall in line with their editorial preference. Then send concisely written news releases to your secondary list of press contacts. In some cases, publications may allow you to submit articles that highlight your product, company, or concept.

Here is the tough part—accepting the fact that you will not be covered by every publication that you target and that you may get some publicity that is less than flattering. You do not control the final product. If you have a vigorous public relations campaign, though, you will increase the good press and decrease the possibility of bad press.

It sounds simple. But when you get on the telephone with editors, you will find it is not always simple. It is often difficult to reach editors. When you do get through, they may not think your story idea is as important as you do. That is where the public relations firm comes in. Even if you have an internal PR person, you can benefit from an external firm's contacts and suggestions. Outsiders can also supplement your internal PR capability.

The pitch letter shown in Figure 7-6 had the desired result: it got Combinet mentioned prominently in an article in the *New York Times*. It works because it is brief and emphasizes the issues that are important to *Times'* readers—and hence, to its editorial staff.

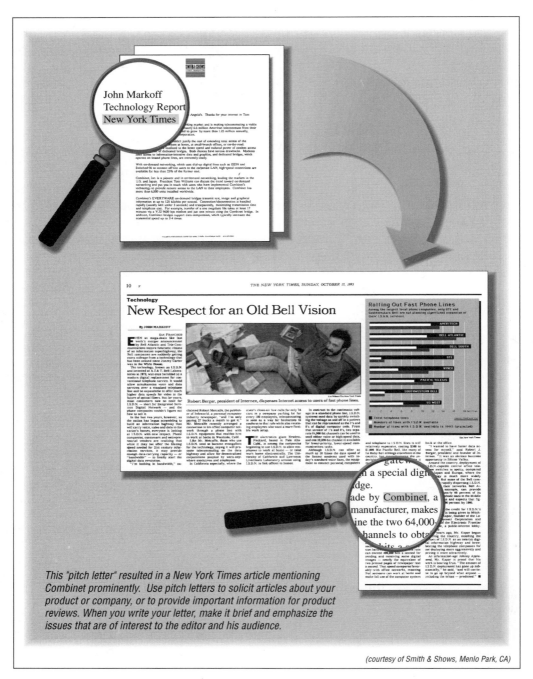

This "pitch letter" resulted in a New York Times article mentioning Combinet prominently. Use pitch letters to solicit articles about your product or company, or to provide important information for product reviews. When you write your letter, make it brief and emphasize the issues that are of interest to the editor and his audience.

*(courtesy of Smith & Shows, Menlo Park, CA)*

**FIGURE 7-6:** COMBINET'S PRESS RELEASE

## ☞ *Public Relations Tips* ☜

- Work with a public relations specialist or agency to develop a comprehensive plan. If you can't afford a specialist, use Bacon's Publicity Checkers to find editor names, or call publications directly to find out who is in charge. Most publications have an editor-in-chief; many also have specialty editors (new products, events, industry news, etc.).

- Before calling, read the publication to learn about its market and editorial inclinations. Editors get dozens of calls every week. If you understand the editor's needs, you will increase your chances of getting space.

- Keep editors informed. If you have lots of news, lay it on heavy. If you don't, repackage news that relates to your market to feature your product.

- Get editorial calendars so you can pitch articles and plan advertising for specific issues. Editorial calendars are usually published once or twice per year; they show which subjects will be highlighted in upcoming issues. *Windows Magazine* lists a main feature (e.g., multimedia), a group review (printers), and a comparative review (tax software) for each monthly issue.

- Offer evaluation copies of your product to feature writers. If the writer is doing a review, it's essential. If not, he might try it anyway, and like it enough to write about.

- Offer to write an article. Have an idea together before you call, so you can sell the editor on the details. Such articles usually can't be "hard sales," but they can highlight your product, and tell about your successful users.

- Get reprints of articles that feature your product. These can be used as sales collateral and featured in advertising, direct mail, and seminars.

- Be available for editors and writers. Return their calls promptly. Help them do their job and they will give you the press you deserve.

- Do not dispute an editor's judgment. Editorial judgment is hers, not yours.

# *Advertising*

The vast majority of computer industry advertising is placed in magazines—either computer magazines or trade magazines aimed at target markets.

## Advantages

- Advertising reaches large numbers of people at a low cost per exposure. Typical computer magazines have circulations in the 100,000's.

- It provides a backdrop for your message. You can coordinate your advertisement with the editorial content of the publication.

- Advertising has low staffing requirements. Simply design the ad, buy the spot, and send the design. Administration is simple.

- Appearing in print adds credibility to your mailings, phone calls, and sales calls. People are often more willing to consider your product if they've seen it in a magazine.

- Advertising adds visibility. When you advertise, you convey the image of a large, stable company. The more you advertise (assuming you use high-quality ad designs), the more important your product looks.

## Disadvantages

- The response rate is low. Most readers will miss your ad. If they do see it, a small percentage will respond.

- Control over placement is limited (unless you pay for guaranteed placement).

- When you advertise in a heavily used medium, your ad may get lost among the other advertisements.

- Total cost is high. You are paying to expose your product to people who are not part of your target market.

- Advertising doesn't sell your product. It only builds awareness. You still have to close the sale.

## Relative Costs

- Although cost per exposure is low, total cost is high. Generally, the larger the circulation of the magazine, the higher the cost.

# When To Use

- To satisfy the requirement of your distributor. (Many distributors require an advertising plan to be in place before they will commit to carry your product.)

- To lend credibility to other programs.

- To communicate with a large distribution channel. (There are specialized publications to do this.)

Advertising is appropriate when the product appeals to a wide audience (i.e., a software package that appeals to virtually every business computer user) or when the target market correlates strongly with the medium (i.e., software that predicts horse race outcomes can be advertised effectively in racing publications).

# Use Advertising Selectively

Advertising may not be appropriate for you because other targeted communications strategies (direct mail, public relations) can expose your most qualified prospects to your product, more often, at the same cost as advertising. This is particularly important if you have a young company with limited marketing budget. Use the other techniques first, to get some revenues flowing. Then, if you can find publications that target your audience, advertise. Unfortunately, many new managers don't realize that most of the people who read a magazine are not interested in their product. So they blow their initial marketing budget on a series of advertisements. Once they realize it, it's too late. They have spent the money that they could have put into a highly targeted direct mail program that would have reached their best prospects. The irony is that they probably would have used a list that was culled from the readers of the magazine anyway. But the program would have cost less money and might have been more effective. (Remember the company in Atlanta that only got a few sales from a $5000 monthly advertising investment. See Chapter 6.)

When advertising is appropriate, choose the publication that best fits your target market. If you already subscribe to an appropriate magazine, you can get the contact name and address in the magazine itself, usually located a page or two behind the table of contents. If not, you can find publications in *Standard Rate and Data Service* (SRDS), a multi-volume reference set that lists national periodicals that accept advertising. Write to or call the publications to get media kits—packets of information that explain the publication's audience, rates, and requirements. Compare their rates and demographics. Don't choose the wrong magazine just because it's cheaper. It's still the wrong magazine at any price.

Instead of wasting your money on image advertising, produce an ad that will draw responses. Small companies need to make every dollar produce revenue. If you get low response, call it a failure. Don't excuse yourself by saying you're trying to enhance your image. Even though Borland can certainly afford image advertising, their ad for Quattro Pro in Figure 7-7 is to the point. It highlights the product's benefits and the aggressive introductory price, shows the product package so the prospect can find it on the retail shelf, and includes a phone number so the reader can buy it now. Borland sold 500,000 copies within the first 60 days of introduction. Here's a tip: if you're going to run advertising, you're better off running a small ad repeatedly rather than a large ad once or twice—as long as the ad is not so small that it won't be seen by your audience. If you can't produce an ad that will stand out, don't run it. Many a software company has purchased ineffective advertising because they ran the smallest ad in the lowest visibility section of the publication.

To be effective, advertising must provide share of mind. Share of mind is determined by the amount of time the audience thinks about your product compared to the amount of time the audience thinks about the other products in the market. In order to maintain your own market share, you must maintain share of mind equal to your market share. In order to increase your market share, you must increase your exposures by a factor several times larger that the amount of increase in market share you hope to attain. Of course, since a new company starts off with no market share, the advertising expenditures needed to create a significant market share are enormous. While your company is small, it's best to limit your advertising and investigate other marketing communications strategies.

## Placing Your Advertisement

Magazine advertising rates are based on the size of your ad, the number of colors (black and white, black with second color, four color), placement, and the number of times you run it. A recent rate card for *LAN Magazine*, for instance, listed a full page ad at $3925. If you run the same size ad 12 times, each ad costs $3190. Adding color adds $485 to $965. If you want a special position, you pay a premium of 15%. Since LAN Magazine's subscriber base is about 46,000, the cost of a one-page full-color ad is around $4800, or ten cents per reader, not including design or production of the ad. A quarter-page black and white ad would cost $1425, or three cents per reader.

When the magazine sends you its media kit, it will include rates, mechanical requirements (dimensions of each ad size), printing specifications (what you have to supply), an editorial calendar, and closing dates for each issue (when subscribers receive, when it goes on sale at the newsstand, last date to buy your ad, when your materials are due). Make sure that you use the magazine's

This advertisement was used to introduce Quatro Pro 5.0 for Windows. It highlights the product's benefits and the aggressive introductory price, shows the product package so the prospect can find it on the retail shelf, and includes a phone number so the reader can buy it now. Borland sold 500,000 copies within the first 60 days of introduction.

*(courtesy of Borland International, Inc.)*

**FIGURE 7-7:** BORLAND INTERNATIONAL'S QUATTRO PRO ADVERTISEMENT

specifications when designing your advertisement. If you don't, you may pay a surcharge for editing or miss the issue you want. Materials are often due several months in advance of publication.

# *Trade Shows*

Trade shows are events in which industry groups come together to discuss topics of mutual interest and see products from vendors of general use to the industry group. Software companies can display their products in shows aimed at end users (Uniforum, PCExpo, Interop, AutoFact), the computer channel (Comdex, High Tech Direct), or other industry groups (American Bankers Association, Power Selling).

## Advantages

- Prospects with similar interests are in one place at the same time.

- You can demonstrate your product to many people in a few days.

- Prospects can compare your product with that of your competitors.

- Trade shows are a good place to make industry contacts (analysts, press, potential recruits).

- If your product or message is compelling enough, you can turn the exposure into large amounts of press.

## Disadvantages

- Preparation time is extensive. You need to coordinate logistics and prepare your exhibit and demonstrations.

- Attendance is expensive. Major national shows can cost $10,000 to $1,000,000.

- You often get the attention of the prospect for only a few minutes. Because there is so much to see, people cannot spend significant time at each booth and can retain only a small portion of the information they receive.

- Your sales team is taken out of their territories for several days.

## When To Use

- Use trade shows if your total trade show expenses would be only a small fraction of your total marketing and sales budget. You need other marketing and sales activities, too.

- Use trade shows if the market is closely aligned with your product and you can meet major purchasers there.

- Use them if you can increase the value of your trade show investment by jointly participating in a booth of a partner company (a computer manufacturer or a complementary software product).

- Use them if the show is small and closely targeted to your market and a member of your company is on the seminar agenda.

- You can always go to trade shows to collect information, to give a presentation, or to conduct meetings with industry associates. You do not have to exhibit.

## Be Wary of False Trade Show Expectations

It seems that after virtually every trade show, I hear several vendors say something like: "There weren't a lot of real prospects—only tire kickers," or "I wish we could drop out of the show, but my competitor did and the rumors were flying that he was going out of business. We can't afford that image." It seems that most vendors go to shows expecting every attendee to be interested in buying their product. When they find only a handful of near-term prospects, they become very disappointed. If you have a small booth at a trade show, you only have the capacity to speak with a few hundred people over a three- or four-day period. Many of them have never heard of you before, but just happened to walk by your booth. Don't expect them all to be "real prospects."

Instead, use trade shows to enhance your credibility. Have your best prospects and customers meet you there. Show them your commitment to the market. Ask members of the press to stop by your booth to see a demo and just chat. Meet industry associates or competitors. Trade shows are your opportunity to keep in touch with the nerve center of your industry or market.

There are some shows that attract lots of real buyers. For instance, vendors consistently tell me that COMDEX has helped them build their distribution channels because they meet many serious prospects looking for new technology and products to resell or integrate.

## Making Your Investment Pay

Join forces with your partners to stretch your trade show dollars. Instead of getting your own booth, be part of a booth from a large organization. If your software runs on SCO UNIX, ask SCO to let you demonstrate it in the SCO booth. Whether you run on OS/2, DOS, HP-UX, Cray UNICOS, or some other platform, get close to your platform vendor. Chances are that the larger company will have a better placed booth and will draw more traffic than you will. It also costs less. Many hardware and operating system companies want their software partners in their booths because software shows off their products. Most of them give you the space for free. Your only expenses are demo, prep, and travel. In 1989, Multiflow had its own booth at Autofact plus a display in the HP booth. Even though the booths were less than 100 feet apart, we received ten times the exposure in the HP booth, and at a fraction of the cost of our own exhibit. Similarly, if your software runs with a complementary package (i.e., your mapping software with someone else's lead management software), cooperate with the other vendor to share an exhibit and the associated costs.

The position of your booth is an important factor in your success. If you can get a spot near an entrance or on a heavily traveled corridor, you win. Keep in mind, though, that most of the prime positions are saved for larger booths and there is usually a lottery at each show to choose the best available booths for the next year's show.

Close proximity to directly competing products can work for or against you. The closer your booth is to your competitor's, the easier it is for your prospect to visit you after visiting your rival. If your product is better and your demo highlights its advantages well, you will benefit. Although, if your competitor outperforms you with her product or presentation, the proximity may hurt you.

Trade shows are long and tiring. Send enough staff to give sufficient breaks and to allow time for your team to look at other exhibits.

# Seminars

In seminars, a company meets with multiple prospects (usually in a hotel conference room) to present its product, company, and opinions.

## Advantages

- Seminars offer almost all the benefits of face-to-face selling at a relatively low cost per client.

- Seminars allow your sales force to leverage their time by speaking with multiple prospects concurrently.

- Seminars can be highly interactive; prospect questions can be answered and objections discussed.

- You can include presentations, product demonstrations, and show video-tape screenings about your agenda.

- You have a high degree of control. Seminars combine the best aspects of direct sales with the best aspects of broadly based marcom activities.

## Disadvantages

- Seminars are more difficult to use for low-priced products (unless the product is often sold "in bulk" to customers who buy many licenses).

- Seminars are manpower intensive. Many logistical and marketing tasks must be coordinated to successfully complete a program.

## Relative Costs

- A typical 12-city program in first-class facilities could cost $50,000 to $100,000, whether conducted by in-house or external personnel.

- The cost per sale usually ranges between $50 and $200.

## When To Use

- To reach high-value customers. A high-value customer is one to whom you can sell (1) a high-priced software package, (2) many copies of a low-priced software package, or (3) a seed copy of a low-priced package with possibilities for many repeat purchases.

- To generate additional quality leads. (A prospect who takes the time and effort to attend a seminar is immediately considered more qualified than one who fills out a business reply card or calls an 800 number to have you send him information.)

- To build your market. Seminars offer a way to give your sales presentations to a large number of qualified prospects in a short time frame.

## When Seeing Your Product Is Believing

A seminar combines the best features of a marketing program with the best features of direct sales. Like other marketing communications tactics, seminars can reach many prospects concurrently, and thus costs less (per prospect) than would personal sales calls to each prospect. Like a personal sales call, a seminar provides a high degree of personal contact, the ability to qualify prospects, opportunities to demonstrate your product, and enough time to tell the essence of your story.

Seminars can be used to generate leads, qualify prospects, and close deals. However, you have to find a way to get the prospects into your presentation room. To fill up your room, combine the seminar with a direct mail or telemarketing campaign to raise interest and invite potential attendees. Instead of trying to sell the recipients your product, invite them to see a free presentation on some relevant topic. For example, rather than pitching your general accounting package, plan your seminar around a concept like "Recent Improvements in Accounting Technology." A prospect qualifies herself just by attending. If she is willing to spend a half day discussing accounting techniques and software, she probably considers the subject important. You can further qualify the prospect with on-site questionnaires. When you have your captive audience, educate them about your subject, then make your case for your product. Some prospects may want to buy on the spot.

You get a lot for your money with seminars because they generate and qualify leads. Let's say your $5000 full-page advertisement exposes your product to 50,000 people (around 10 cents each). If your response rate is .1%, your cost per response is $100. Marketing Masters recently ran a client seminar program that cost just a bit less—let's say they were equal. Both programs gained lots of exposure. (The seminar program's exposure was via targeted direct mail.) But the seminar qualifies the prospect and provides a captive audience that sees your demonstration and hears your sales presentation. Now, who's the better prospect: the person who came to hear your half-day presentation or the one who circled a number on a magazine reader service card?

---

### ☞ *Getting the Most Out of Your Seminars* ☜

1. Aim your seminars at your target market. If you define your agenda narrowly you will get highly qualified prospects. If you define the agenda broadly, you will get more attendees, but they will be less qualified.

2. Conduct multiple seminars over a short period of time, using a central coordinator. This will minimize the effort that must be exerted for each seminar.

3. Reserve your facilities six months in advance to get the best accommodations.

4. Send your invitations four to eight weeks before each seminar. Request a reply by phone, fax, or card.

5. Get further qualification information from attendees—when they plan to buy, what their buying criteria are, who makes buying decisions, what other products they are considering, etc.

6. Follow up swiftly with the attendees after each seminar to convert them to customers.

---

## User Group Meetings

User group meetings are forums designed for users of a specific type of product to discuss how they can improve their use of the product, and to explore new products or improvements available from sponsoring vendors. These meetings can be conducted on a national or regional level.

This section is about conducting your own user group. Sometimes, you can speak or show your product at meetings of users of other products. See the next section about external societies or organizations for details.

## Advantages

- User group meetings are aimed at likely candidates for additional sales—your current user base.

- You have a high degree of control over the agenda.

- You can "pre-announce" products to your users, thereby arranging beta test sites and producing good initial references.

- You can resolve support, product, or training problems.

- You can learn about your product from the people who use it every day.

- User group meetings can be held regionally, nationally, or internationally.

- They can build an almost religious fervor for your product and company.

## Disadvantages

- User group meetings are costly. Although the users pick up their travel expenses, you often are expected to buy a lunch or provide a special function. Your staff may also incur large travel costs.

- User group meetings require manpower, and demand preparation of presentations, logistics, and demonstrations.

## When To Use

- If your product attracts enough attention from your users to make it worthwhile for them to attend a user group

- When you have solutions to customer satisfaction issues

- When you are announcing a major new product of interest to your user base

## A Short, Happy Story

When I was a salesperson at Auto-trol, I found gold in gathering my customers together for meetings. My company provided the inspiration by taking part in an annual international user group meeting in Denver. While the meeting actually belonged to the organization of users, Auto-trol had plenty of influence. It provided speakers, helped with facilities, and kicked in money to put together a first class meeting. It was usually several days long, allowing users plenty of time for informal discussions and formal training. It also gave Autotrol the opportunity to present new products and help customers who were having problems. In short, everybody benefited.

But not everybody could attend a multi-day meeting in Colorado. That's where I got lucky. You see, I had inherited dozens of unhappy users from the salesperson before me. In fact, when I entered the territory (Ohio and Pennsylvania) in 1981, my territory had the lowest satisfaction rating of any in the company. So I held a five-hour user meeting in Akron, the city with the highest concentration of users. We didn't spend our time selling. We were too busy handling complaints and fixing problems. But we did let the users know that they come first, that their problems would be fixed, and that there were more new products coming down the road. And somehow, I got $250,000 worth of business as a result. I scheduled one of these meetings in my territory every six months. Each consecutive meeting had a smaller percentage dedicated to fixing user problems and a greater percentage to showcasing new products. The users became the most satisfied users in the country; and I got lots of business. Everyone was happy.

## Can You Use User Meetings?

Not everybody can put together a user group. Some products don't allow it. I can't imagine a mouse user's group, for instance. But some products are vital to a company after they have been installed and have become part of the fabric of daily operation. The products become so important that users will go to great lengths to keep up-to-date on the latest upgrades and ways to use it. Companies with products in areas like CAD/CAM, FEA, and databases as well as many others can benefit from user meetings.

If you want to make your user group particularly effective, let your users run it themselves. It will require less of your time and provide an excellent conduit to your customers. You will probably need to start the group for them, then turn over the reins; as a minimum, help your users get the group started by doing mailings and providing funding. Then become their resource. Do what you can to help your user group accomplish its mission. You will benefit with more add-in sales and more referrals.

# *External Speaking Engagements*

There are many computer societies and trade organizations that invite vendors to speak to their members.

## Advantages

- Speaking engagements are inexpensive; generally they cost only a few hundred dollars for contribution to refreshments. Travel costs can be shared by doing other business while in town.

- Your sponsor provides added credibility. When he mails invitations, he often mentions the benefits of your product and why the members should come to see you.

## Disadvantages

- You have little control over the attendance or meeting facility.

- In some cases, your presentation happens only after other business has been completed.

## When To Use

- When your sales team is attempting to penetrate a specific geographic territory

- When the user group demographics coincide with your target market

- When your presentation or demonstration is key to attracting new customers

## Additional Information

Presenting to trade groups is an excellent way to get your message to a targeted audience. Every company should do it, from startups to billion dollar companies. You will be exposed to the market in a highly interactive way. You get great product ideas from prospects who have a real-world perspective. In turn, they hear your pitch and may buy your product. Startup companies should actively look for organizations to whom key personnel can speak. New salespeople should open their territories by looking for these situations. Do it now; do it always.

# *A Comparison of Your Marcom Choices*

**TABLE 7-1:** *VARIOUS MARCOM OPTIONS*

| Program | Control | Cost | Manpower | Cost per prospect | Exposure |
|---|---|---|---|---|---|
| Collateral | n.a. | Low | Low | n.a. | n.a. |
| Direct Mail | High | Medium | Medium | Medium | Medium |
| Telemarketing | High | Medium | High | Medium | High |
| Advertising | Medium | High | Low | Low | Low |
| Public Relations | Low | Medium | High | Low | Low |
| Trade Shows | Medium | High | High | High | Medium |
| Seminars | High | Medium | Medium | Medium | High |
| User Groups | Low | Low | High | Medium | High |

You can choose between many different methods for generating inquiries and awareness about your company or product. They all have different strengths and weaknesses. By using a combination that suits your product, market, and budget, you will optimize your results. The marketing term for this is "synergy." Synergy can be quantified as $1 + 1 = 3$. Although the equation may seem inaccurate, it means that the combination is greater than the sum of its components. A coordinated attack using direct mail, telemarketing, and trade show appearances will benefit you more than any of the three components used separately. This suggests that planning your marketing communications strategically will give you the most effective exposure. If the potential customer sees your name in multiple contexts, she is more likely to remember you when she's evaluating products.

# *Preparing Your Marketing Literature*

Virtually all of these marcom techniques rely on printed materials. You obviously need to print specification sheets and write advertising copy. You need to take equal care in crafting your press releases, seminar or user group invitations, and trade show handouts.

The cost-effectiveness of your materials depends on how well they are designed and how they are used. You should be personally involved in the decisions about which pieces to print and how to use them, but leave the actual design to a trained designer, who will do them faster and make them look more professional. But, of course, you should evaluate the final product.

Make your materials work hard. Each piece should be able to stand alone and tell the reader important points about your product and how it will benefit him. In some cases, a combination of pieces can play well together. For instance, giving the prospect a product description and an application brief shows him what your product does as well as how it fits his specific need. (I'll describe the individual pieces in the next chapter.)

Design your materials so they don't become obsolete quickly. Offers with expiration dates, for instance, should be placed on pieces that are made for short-term promotions, not on your generic literature. Of course, new versions of your product will outdate old versions of your literature. Have the new literature ready for distribution before the product is released. Distributing obsolete literature will cost you more in lost sales than you can save by using up old materials.

Information gets separated easily in the prospect's hands. Coupons get clipped and saved. Pages get thrown out, lost, or passed to associates. Include your most important information (your company name, address, telephone, product name, and price) on each piece, including coupons, business reply cards, and cover letters. Assume that the prospect will lose every piece except the one in his hand. Does he have enough information to buy your product—or at least to contact you for more information?

As time progresses, the number of pieces that you need to track will expand. Confusion is likely if you fail to develop a tracking mechanism. A code number on each piece usually suffices. Many companies put a code in small print at the bottom of each piece. For example, Marketing Masters uses MM10-9401 to signify piece number ten revised January 1994. In addition to aiding internal tracking, this allows you to find out whether the prospect has your most recent information.

When you create materials for magazine use, submit camera-ready art work or film. You will decrease the probability that your ad will have mistakes.

When designing the individual pieces, keep in mind that you are trying to deliver a specific message that will help the reader buy. Even if you develop a piece that attracts enormous attention, it is worthless if it does not convey your message. Therefore, all other design activities should follow from the overriding goal of delivering your key message.

# Graphic Design Tips

The design of your piece is crucial in getting your message across. If it does not attract attention, no one will read it. The following design tips will help you deliver your message.

- Attract attention with your headline and graphics. According to David Ogilvy, founder of the advertising agency, Ogilvy and Mather, five people will read your headline for every person who reads your body text.[*] Compelling headlines and appealing graphics will draw the reader into your text. Make sure these attention grabbers relate to the proper audience. Lotus' magazine advertisement for Freelance Graphics uses the headline "When you have the right presentation software, you don't have to say a word," accompanied by a photograph of an audience watching a screen that shows the symbols of five awards presented to Freelance Graphics.

- Use common design elements to create recognition. By using similar layouts, typefaces, and design elements on all of your printed material, you will create a link in the reader's mind between what they are reading and what they have seen before. IBM's materials are very conservative. Corel uses lots of glitzy graphics. Microsoft uses common layouts and typefaces. Volvo, the automobile maker, does it particularly well with their unique layouts and headline type styles. Their ads are recognizable with a brief glance from several feet away. Your common elements can be extended to your product package and your trade show displays.

- Convey the image of high-quality software with high-quality printed materials. The reader will associate the quality of your product with the quality of your marketing communications. Don't rely on laser-printed letterhead or low-quality dot matrix text. Your letter, collateral, mailer, demo, and advertisements are your envoys.

- Use design dollars to decrease printing costs by making your efforts do double duty. A well-designed direct mail piece can be used as sales collateral, alleviating a second design cost and allowing you to produce the piece in larger quantity (meaning lower cost per piece). This concept can be extended dramatically. Design a single template to be used as the basis for several of your multi-color printed pieces. You can add black and white text to the preprinted color template to create separate pieces, thus decreasing your printing costs substantially. (Black and white printing is less expensive than color printing.)

---

[*] David Ogilvy, *Ogilvy on Advertising* (Vintage Books, 1983), page 71.

# Copywriting Tips

When you write your marketing text, you are said to be "writing copy." This is your chance to persuade the reader to call you, send in a reply card, or buy your product.

- Speak the reader's language. If the reader can identify with what you are saying, he is more likely to believe it and act upon your suggestions. If you aim at accountants, use accounting terminology. If your target is architects, talk in architectural terms.

  Examples: "We slash interface development time across DOS, UNIX, POSIX, VMS" (Ad for *Vermont Views*)

  "Your HP workstation users can share files between HP-UX and PC environments on HP Series 9000 workstations." (Ad for SoftPC by Insignia Solutions, run in *HP Professional*)

- Be benefits oriented. People buy products to receive benefits. Tell the reader the benefits he will receive if he buys your product.

  Examples: "The ultimate weapon against programming errors" (Ad for Sentinel Debugger by Virtual Technologies)

  "With other tools you still have to code to do graphics. We do it the other way." (Ad for VAPS, by Virtual Prototypes)

- Make it easy to pick out the key points. Make your point quickly. Write your copy so the reader can skim your information and get the most important points. Use bullets, bold copy, or larger headlines.

- Don't leave out important details that may be obvious to you, but not obvious to the reader. Include product benefits, important awards, and your company address, phone, and fax number.

  Example: "Receives Faxes in the background" (Ad for WinFax Pro by Delrina Technology)

- If you are in the fax software business, receiving faxes in the background might not seem like much; most of your competitors have this feature. But to a prospect who has never purchased fax software before, it may make a difference.

- Be succinct. You are working with limited space. Make every word count.

- Increase your reply rate by making it easy for the reader to reply. Include your telephone and fax numbers, your e-mail ordering address, and a reply card. The reader will choose the method that is easiest for him. The key is to make sure that you can handle the replies in a timely fashion.

Copywriting is not easy. You will find yourself writing your copy, then editing it several times before it is ready for use. When you're done with it, look at it from the view of the person at whom it is aimed. Then approve it only if you think it would make him buy your product. Otherwise, get back to the drawing board.

# Turning Prospects Into Buyers

The adage "build a better mousetrap and the world will beat a path to your door" (Emerson) just isn't true. Even with the best product, you still have to find potential buyers and convince each one that he should buy your product by appealing to his primary motivation—his need to fulfill a specific requirement or reach a certain goal. The art (or science) of arousing desire for your product is called salesmanship, and it is practiced by most successful entrepreneurs including Scott McNeally (Sun), Steven Jobs (Apple), and John Swanson (SASI). In essence, each of these men has become a missionary, inspiring others to buy into the idea that his product provides benefits that make it worthy of purchase. Their willingness to become missionaries strongly contributes to their success.

This chapter covers issues related to direct sales. Most people typically think of "direct sales" as one salesperson trying to convince one customer to buy one item—a kind of sales that is most appropriate when the item you're selling is expensive. However, direct sales is really much broader. It occurs whenever there is a one-to-one conversation between your representatives and your prospect—whether your prospect is a single user buying a $50,000 product or a reseller who will buy 10,000 copies of a $50 product. The key is the value of the account as a whole, not the individual sale. You can't afford putting people on the street to sell individual copies of an inexpensive product. But you can put people on the street to sell your product in quantity to retailers. If your product can justify direct contact with your prospects, this chapter is for you.

## *People Will Buy If You Consult*

How many times have you purchased a product because the salesperson or company representative provided advice about solving your problem? If you say "often," you wouldn't be alone. Most successful computer industry salespeople adhere to a methodology called *consultive* selling, in which the salesperson locates a prospect, determines his needs, and provides the product that can meet those needs. Consultive salespeople know when their solutions fit a customer and when they should walk away. In a consultive selling situation, the salesperson educates as he sells. In fact, few companies use the title "Salesperson" anymore. The title has been replaced by Account Representative and Regional Manager, among other titles.

# What Qualifies Prospects as Prospects

When you identify an individual who might buy your product he becomes your "sales prospect." There are several levels of prospects: qualified prospect, lead, and suspect. Each of these levels has certain qualities.

*Qualified Prospect*

A qualified prospect is someone who has a need for your product and the wherewithal to purchase it—the money, the reason, and the authority.

*Lead*

A lead is a person who has a base level of interest in your product. She may have responded to your ad, been referred by one of your current customers, visited your trade show booth, or registered for one of your seminars. A lead is not necessarily qualified—because she does not meet one or more of the criteria that define your qualified prospects.

*Suspect*

As the name suggests, a suspect is somebody who you think can be a future customer, but for whom you have incomplete information. For instance, a list of corporate controllers to whom you send mailers is a list of suspects for your spreadsheet product. Finding the leads in a list of suspects is called lead generation.

A prospect is not qualified if he does not recognize his own need or does not care if he satisfies it. Until he does both, he will not purchase your product. An associate of mine, because he is a frequent presenter, needs a presentation graphics package. Although he has requested information about several packages, he has not purchased one. For two years he delayed his purchase, not due to a lack of need, but a lack of desire. Until he decides that he wants to purchase, he is not a qualified prospect for any presentation software company.

Prospects are often willing (and even eager) to buy your product if your salesperson shows that your product satisfies several key areas of concern:

1. Your product meets the prospect's needs. It solves his problem, allows him to achieve new goals, or enhances his current capabilities.
2. The risk of implementing your solution is small.

3. You offer enough support for his situation.

4. Obtaining your product makes him the hero of his department, division, or company.

5. He has the resources to purchase your product and install it successfully.

My friend, the presenter, delayed his purchase because he was afraid that presentation software would lengthen the time it takes to change his presentation. Therefore, he felt that the software posed too great a risk on his livelihood. Recently, somebody showed him that the latest presentation products will allow him to remain flexible. Now he is truly in the market and becomes a qualified prospect.

When selling to corporations, you will often encounter situations in which multiple people are part of the decision process. Often, a purchase requires every person to say yes, but only one to veto the purchase. Expenditures over $100,000 are almost always like this. Smaller purchases can have similar traits too, especially when two departments are involved, when one person makes the technical decision while another holds the budget, or when the purchase is made by committee. I remember the first time Marketing Masters attempted to convince a major computer company to participate in one of our marketing programs. The prospect's product marketing manager wanted to participate, but did not control the budget. The marcom manager who controlled the budget turned us down because she had already committed her budget to another program. In hindsight, this company was not a qualified prospect: the person we were talking to didn't have the authority to spend the money.

## How To Identify Prospects

One of the keys to sales success is recognizing the qualifications of a prospect. Proper qualifying allows sales people to spend their time with the most qualified accounts and drop the least qualified accounts from their prospect lists. Prospects don't always make it easy. Some tell you they will buy even when they don't plan to. Others conceal budget constraints that are lower than the price of your software or refuse to reveal the real decision makers. Here are some tips to help you qualify your prospects.

1. Ask tough questions, like "Who is the decision maker?" "Have you allocated sufficient funds to cover the purchase?" "When will you buy?" and "Is there anything about my product that you do not like?" These questions are tough for both you and the prospect. They're tough for you because they can yield disappointing answers. Likewise, they're tough for the prospect because many people avoid giving disappointing answers; they don't like saying "no."

2. Repeat your questions as time progresses because sales situations are dynamic; they change and evolve with the sales process. It is critically important to be attuned to the ebbs and flows of the process. If a competitor has sneaked in after you, or if the customer finds something about your product that he doesn't like, you may not find out unless you ask. If you only ask once, you may miss important changes.

3. Don't be afraid to walk away. In most well-selected markets, there are plenty of good prospects. If you spend your time with the wrong ones, you will not have time to meet those who will buy.

4. Compare the profile of the prospect to that of your ideal customer. How closely do they match? The fewer things that fit, the better the reason to walk away.

5. Don't try to force fit a product on a prospect who doesn't need it. I'll never understand why the phrase "He can sell air conditioners to Eskimos" is often used as a compliment. Force fitting products is bad for the user and often leads to a bad reputation (therefore reduced long-term sales) for the vendor.

6. Don't leave just because your competition is trying to woo your prospect. Find ways to beat him. (For hints, see Chapter 10, *Defeating the Competition.*) At the same time, don't fight battles you can't win. If you have assessed the situation properly by asking good qualifying questions, you will understand whether you should stay and battle it out.

7. Removing a prospect from your funnel does not mean that you must say goodbye forever. Just don't waste time with him now. He may be a long-term candidate for purchase of your product. Sometimes putting him on a tickler or mailing list is all that is necessary to optimize your own time and his until he becomes a real prospect.

8. Even if you have no other good prospects, don't keep an unqualified prospect in your sales funnel. You would be wasting your time with him when you could be finding new prospects.

---

### ☞ *Sample Qualifying Questions* ☜

Does he have a need for my product?

Does he want the features that my product offers?

Does he have purchase authority?

Are there other members of his organization that I must reach?

How much revenue will be associated with his order?

Is there significant potential for follow-on business?

Does he have sufficient money in his budget?

When will he purchase?

When will he install?

Why does he need the product?

Why might he decide not to buy my product?

Is he examining my competition? Which competitors?
  Who is winning? Why?

What will it take to win his business?

Is it a strategic win? (Will it influence other companies?)

Do I have sufficient resources to win?

---

# The Five Rules of Selling

The five rules of selling coined by Percy Whiting[*] have been productively used by sales professionals for decades. Their appeal is so universal that the Dale Carnegie sales course uses them as a foundation. They can easily be applied to any software selling situation. The five rules really describe phases through which each prospect passes before purchasing a product. They are (in the order in which they most commonly occur):

*Attention*

A salesperson must attract the attention of his prospect. For example, direct mail and advertising attempt to get a customer's attention with a catchy headline or graphic. People who make cold telephone calls use a catchy opening phrase. (That's catchy, not necessarily clever. Find something that will be of interest to the prospect.) In one way or another, before you can tell somebody why you have the best solution for them, you must get them to notice what you have.

---

[*] Percy H. Whiting, *The Five Great Rules of Selling*, McGraw-Hill, 1947.

### Interest

Now that you have gained their attention, you must make your prospects interested in what you have to say. Perhaps you can ask questions that pertain to their situation, or raise issues that concern them. Here, the objective is to make sure that your prospects are actively listening to your product presentation in such a way that relevant information passes through.

### Conviction

At some point, your prospects must be convinced that what you say is true. They must believe that your product does what you say. And they must see the correlation between your product and their situation.

### Desire

Even though he recognizes the need and is convinced your case is true, he may still prefer not to purchase your product. His needs may differ from his wants. In the desire stage, you satisfy his wants, a critical step in making the sale. If he has other alternatives or feels that the risk of using your product is too high, he will not want to buy the product and you cannot sell it to him.

### Close

This is when you get the order. It is nirvana for the salesperson, and uplifting for everybody in your organization, especially when the deal is big or when it is a competitive win.

Every person who buys any product goes through all five phases, although not necessarily in the same way. Depending on your product, the prospect might pass through the five phases in a few minutes—maybe even concurrently—on the phone, or take several years and dozens of meetings. Generally, if your products are mission-critical, the time frame will be relatively long. The decision is so important to the buyer that everything must be checked and double checked. Similarly, the more digits in the price, the longer it will take. Additionally, if you are trying to unseat an incumbent product, or must deal with several decision influencers, the sales cycle will expand. In a complex selling situation, you may even go through a few of the phases several times. For instance, you may have to produce desire for your product, then inspire the prospect to want to become a hero. You may not notice the five stages as they occur, but upon reflection, you can usually pinpoint when they have occurred. After you gain experience in selling, you will be able to actively move your prospects through each of these important phases of the sales cycle.

# *Timing Is Crucial*

In the market, you are constantly fighting against the clock. If you are not available when a customer needs your product, he will find another product to meet his need. Alternately, time also makes products obsolete. A software package that sold well in 1990 won't sell well as you read this—at least not without modification. It will have changed form dramatically or will have been pushed out of business by superior products.

When it comes to making the sale, timing can be more important than superior product functionality. If your product is so advanced that you have to educate everybody in sight, you will spend your time educating instead of selling. Your sales cycles will be long; you will have fewer prospects because you cannot handle as many; and your competition will let you educate the market before swooping in to steal your business. Conversely, if you get to your prospect too late in his decision process, you may not have enough time to win the deal, even if you have a better product. Either way, timing proves to be the most important determinant of the sale.

Time can help you too. One of your most powerful sales tools is the "impending event"—an event or deadline before which the prospect must solve his problem or purchase a product. You can use impending events to sell virtually any product: If your product is tax software, your prospects must buy and use it before April 15. If your software is to fly on the space shuttle, the buyer must purchase it with sufficient time to learn, integrate, test, and deploy it. Sometimes the prospect simply must purchase the software before he loses his budget at the end of his company's fiscal year. In any case, find out which impending event encourages a purchase for your prospect. If none exist, make one, perhaps by offering a time-restricted discount or by limiting the available quantities of your product.

By the way, the sales cycle is not over when the purchase order is issued. Taking care of your customer after he buys leads to repeat business and referrals. Therefore, it is in your best interest to make sure that shipment, installation, and support are provided in a timely, effective manner.

# *Your Sales Funnel*

Sales is not an event; it's a process. It can be monitored, accelerated, guided, and managed. Every prospect with whom a salesperson is working is a "work in process," and can affect whether he attains his sales goals during the quarter or in subsequent quarters. A shortfall in revenue this quarter is often a direct result of what was not done last quarter.

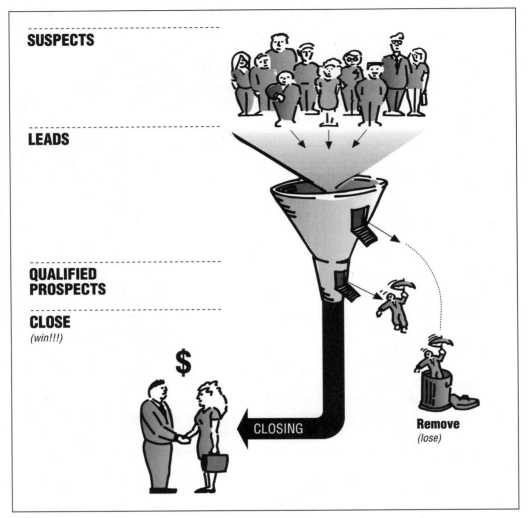

**SUSPECTS**

**LEADS**

**QUALIFIED PROSPECTS**

**CLOSE**
*(win!!!)*

$

CLOSING

**Remove**
*(lose)*

*FIGURE 8-1:* THE SALES FUNNEL

The worst thing a salesperson can do is spend valuable time chasing the wrong prospects. He needs to make the most of his time by spending it with those who are qualified to buy. This is particularly important because salespeople have an overwhelming impact on the top line of your finances. Therefore, the effects of an unproductive salesperson can devastate an otherwise outstanding company. The fewer salespeople you have, the greater will be the impact of each one.

By using a "sales funnel" paradigm, you can track your sales efforts to make sure you are spending your time wisely. Leads go into the wide-end of the funnel and a small portion of them come out the narrow end as customers. Sales is, at least in part, a numbers game. If you speak with more prospects, you close more sales. For most software products the bulk of your sales time should be spent in two ways: closing sales with your few hottest prospects and filling the funnel with new leads. It's common sense that you will be in trouble if you don't close deals. But the sales funnel shows that you're also in trouble if no new leads enter the funnel. The sales funnel paradigm helps you avoid the problems that result from not enough prospecting by showing your lack of leads in your empty funnel.

When creating your funnel, estimate the percentage of leads that should become hot prospects and the percentage of hot prospects that should actually buy your product. (Be realistic please! Not everybody will actually buy it.) The shape of your funnel is based on these percentages. The narrow end of the funnel correlates with your revenue goals.

Using your funnel as a guideline helps you spend your time in the right place, makes sure you have enough prospects to meet your goals, and provides a communications vehicle between the salesperson and management. For most software products, each salesperson should have a mix of short-term, easy-to-close deals and one or two large, long-term development accounts. This helps create a steady stream of revenue to use as a base while reserving some large potential revenue deals to produce big wins. It also serves to keep spirit high because sales can happen frequently.

## Picking Your Sales Team

Choosing your sales team is difficult. Even the most experienced sales recruiters make their share of unsuccessful hires. The most common mistake is hiring a good salesperson who does not match your sales requirements. Both your company and the salesperson will be unsuccessful. Even the best salespeople will not be successful in all situations. It takes a balance of the person's sales skills and market knowledge, and your ability to provide the support and infrastructure that person needs. Following are eight criteria that you should consider when building your sales team.

1. *Locate somebody who exhibits the characteristics of a successful salesperson.* There are many people whose natural sales skill is clearly visible. They are eager to help others. They feel comfortable with new people in one-on-one or group situations and they speak well. Most importantly, they have a sense of how to find solutions to problems by using their product, and they are

highly motivated to meet their goals. These people are more likely to sell well for you.

2.  *Find individuals who know your market.* A person who knows your market has a distinct advantage. If you sell to bankers, find somebody who has already sold to bankers or has relevant experience with them. For sales through computer resellers, look for somebody who has sold computer products to the channel or who has worked for a major computer products distributor. If you are targeting a specific geography (i.e., New England), find someone familiar with the region.

3.  *Match your sales team to your product type.* Sales people perform better when they sell products they are comfortable with. When selling products purchased on technical merit, your salesperson should be comfortable dealing with prospects on a technical level. If the main benefits are financial, she should understand the monetary implications and benefits of your product. If your product is typically sold over the phone, the salesperson should be comfortable telemarketing and closing sales quickly. Products with large price tags, on the other hand, often require team selling, and always require salespeople who are used to long sales cycles that involve many visits and discussions.

4.  *Determine that your salesperson's work ethic corresponds to your expectations.* There are two types of good salespeople: those who make 101% of their quotas consistently, and those who make 250% one year followed by 90% the next, followed by 250% again. Sales people in the first group often make sure they reach their goal. After meeting their goals, they concentrate on their avocations. People from the second group are more driven and are more likely to spend extra hours becoming the top salesperson or reaching their own internal goals. They will spend more time on high-risk, big-payoff deals that might occasionally cost them their annual quota, but will make them big heros if they win. Even if they don't quite make it during a year, they're usually close; and they make up for it the next year with interest. The type of salesperson that you choose should match your expectation level for drive and extra work. Both types can be successful. Large sales forces should have a mix of the two types: one group provides revenue stability while the other provides the extra tenacity that breaks records.

5.  *Look for somebody with contacts, but don't make it your overriding criterion.* A salesperson with established contacts in his sales territory can ramp up to achieve sales quickly. By approaching the people he already knows, he gains easy access to prospects for his new product. If you want to find salespeople with a lot of relevant contacts, look for people who currently sell a

complementary or competing product. But don't overemphasize the importance of hiring somebody with contacts. The long-term value of a large initial contact base is minor; any good salesperson will establish additional contacts as he sells, thereby acquiring an equally good contact base over time.

6. *Find someone whose personality matches your current team.* Good salespeople fail if they do not get along with their managers. Make sure you have a reasonable match between you and your salespeople to reduce this risk. A good rule of thumb: if you are not sure you like the way he does business or whether he will fit in with your company, pass him over and continue your search.

7. *Match his abilities to the expected working situation.* When you hire a salesperson, you are actually providing him with a complete working environment. Make sure his sales skills match that environment. If he will be located in a remote office, make sure that he has successfully worked in one in the past. When you cannot provide technical support, be certain he can support himself technically, at least to the level required to sell successfully. If your management team has little marketing or sales experience, make sure that he is comfortable working with managers and support personnel that may not understand all of his needs. In addition, less experienced salespeople usually need more supervision than seasoned professionals. In short, if you cannot provide him with the tools and support he needs to be successful, he won't be.

8. *Don't accept an inadequate experience level.* Let somebody else teach him how to sell so all you have to do is teach him how to apply his sales skills to your product. Don't try to save a few dollars by hiring an inexperienced salesperson who may not be successful. Hire an experienced sales professional who meets your full criteria. Your risk is much more than the cost of the salary—you're risking revenue. For most software companies, each salesperson is expected to bring in anywhere from a quarter million dollars per year to several million. Are you willing to risk that sum on inexperience?

## Helping Your Sales Team Be Productive

Sales fuel your company. Therefore, once you have chosen your sales team, you have got to set up an environment that helps them work effectively. You can't just shove them out into the street and expect them to work magic. They need your help. Here are a few tips to help you make them more productive:

- *Give your salespeople the support they need to close business.* If they need a presentation, demonstration, or technical support, make sure they can get it from you or somebody else on your staff. Don't prevent them from selling by withholding resources they need.

- *Provide your sales team with full information.* Inform your salespeople before you inform your customers. Avoid the embarrassment of customers mentioning information your sales people don't have—this makes your entire company look foolish. Make sure that you communicate important issues—both positive and negative—to your sales force so they can guide their prospects in the direction that makes the best sense.

- *Deliver on your promises.* When salespeople make promises, they commit your entire company to delivering. Hire only those that try to come through on promises. Tell them which ones they can make. Then help them fulfill their promises to prospects, customers, or other important outsiders.

- *Set reasonable expectation levels.* Don't expect salespeople to win every sale, but expect them to use resources to maximize their total revenue. Give them a quota based on the needs of your company and a reasonable, attainable goal.

- *Provide incentives to go beyond the call of duty.* Increase commission percentages for sales beyond quota or provide a bonus when they reach prespecified levels such as 100%, 125%, and 150% of quota.

- *Listen.* Sales people are your closest link to your customers.

## Anatomy of a Salesperson

- Sales people like to use leverage to make lots of money. They are willing to base a substantial portion of their compensation on their own personal success (i.e., commissions). Because of commissions, it is not unusual for the best salesperson to make more money than the president of a company. Because of their high leverage, salespeople will fight hard to command the resources they need to close important sales.

- Successful salespeople find the deals that are most likely to be won and they put their efforts into making those deals happen. They tend to drop other activities that keep them from devoting attention to their hot prospects. They resume the other deals when the hot prospect is won.

- The best salespeople are good listeners. They constantly search for information that will help satisfy the needs of the prospect.

- Good salespeople are usually in control. If they sense that events are being controlled by others, they'll often attempt to take control themselves. This characteristic helps them increase the odds of reaching their own sales goals, which are typically similar to the goals you have for them.

• Sales people learn to look past "no." They have to do this to survive because they usually hear ten "nos" for every "yes." Successful salespeople learn how to turn "no" into "yes."

Just because you have hired a sales team, you are not off the hook. You are still an integral part of the sales process as are all members of your organization. The next chapter outlines some of the most important acts you (and your staff) can perform to support your sales effort.

# Supporting Your Sales Effort

For many types of software, the sales cycle can involve multiple sales calls (either telephone, in-person, or both) involving various people from your company including executives, technical people, financial coordinators and, of course, your sales and marketing people. For others, a sale may consist of a single phone call or a mailed response to a direct mail piece. If you are in the first group, your support is instrumental in helping your salespeople complete their sales. You might make presentations or demonstrations to key accounts, help generate leads, provide logistical support, or help your salespeople manage their time better by off-loading them. In short, sales support consists of everything that anyone in the company can do to help make the sale.

## *Information Your Sales Staff Needs*

Without accurate information, your salespeople cannot sell. They need to know what they're selling, to whom they're selling it, and what will make it sell better. And you must tell them. Sales people need both technical information and general background information, including:

- Strengths and weaknesses of your product

- Strengths and weaknesses of your competition

- Typical questions asked by the prospect

- Significant wins and losses and the main reasons for winning or losing

- Disposition of development projects (including release dates and projected features, benefits and advantages)

- Information you are sending to your user base

- Marketing programs you will be using in the near future

- Best types of prospects for current and future products

- Any changes that may affect their ability to sell your product
- What not to do or say when presenting or demonstrating the product
- Names of customers (including beta testers) willing to provide references

Each salesperson will use this information to form his own personal sales presentation (probably consisting 90% of presentation material you provide). While he may have his own list of prospective presentees, you should also furnish him with the names of leads that contact you to find out about your product.

# Managing Prospect Data

To foster efficient use of sales talent, collect and manage prospect data on a company-wide basis. Instead of having islands of data in the hands of individuals, you will have an effective tool to help penetrate your market and provide your sales team with important contact information. Every time a new prospect contacts you for information, put it into a database that can be used continuously.

- Separate your lists. There is no reason to keep customers in the same database as prospects. The lists are normally used at different times for different purposes. In fact, the customer and prospect databases usually have different configurations because they contain different types of information.

- Collect the information you need. Your customer database should include name, address, phone, fax, revision level installed, platform type (if multiple), and name of the actual buyer. Include a code that tells how each prospect heard about you. While this may seem like common sense to you, I have actually seen a company that was not able to contact their existing customers when they launched a new product. Their only database had no listings for people involved in the purchasing process—only contacts for maintenance purposes.

- Purge expired data and update records frequently. A list that has not been updated for six months is 15% to 20% incorrect (wrong address, telephone, person left company, etc.). If you use first class mail for your targeted mailings, your returned envelopes indicate which pieces did not reach your target. You can also request address correction on second- and third-class mail.

- Rent lists where possible. The only lists that you should maintain internally are (1) your own customers and (2) prospects who contacted you (i.e., telephone inquiries, reply cards, seminar attendees, and trade show booth visitors). Lists can be rented from publications, trade show management companies, and list brokers, at a cost of 10 to 15 cents per name, with better accuracy and lower cost than you can possibly achieve by maintaining the list yourself.

- Give your sales force easy access to your data so they can keep in contact with customers and prospects. Either provide updates on an ongoing basis (for each individual territory), or have them send you letters that they want distributed to your mailing list so you can do the work for them.

# *Managing Administrative Details*

Selling requires a lot of administrative overhead: travel reservations, scheduling, etc. The less time your salespeople spend on these details, the more time they can spend selling. By providing administrative help, you can make your sales staff much more efficient. Your goal should be to free them to do what they do best. Skimping on the proper support is usually a false economy. If your top salesperson spends a half-day a week making reservations and arranging meetings, that's 25 days a year that he's not selling. Here are a few ways that you can minimize a salesperson's administrative burden.

## Client or Prospect Visits

Have somebody at your office make all the necessary arrangements for hotels, company participants, demonstrations, presentations, facility tours, lunch, and any other administrative items. The salesperson should be able to make one call to your office (if he is remote) and get "turnkey" support.

## Seminars

Seminars offer an effective method to increase the amount of face-to-face time that salespeople can spend with clients. In a half-day seminar, one salesperson can easily present your product to 40 to 50 prospects. It would take weeks to present the same information in one-on-one meetings.

- Assign a central coordinator for all seminars. Seminars take large amounts of time to coordinate. Your central coordinator can perform the administrative chores for many seminars concurrently, thus supporting your entire sales force. If you do not have an available person, contract with an external agency to do the seminar coordination.

- Have an on-site manager. A company who has its presenters manage its seminars looks like a one-man band, not like a viable, long-term business partner (the type of company most people want to buy from). Send some-body to take care of all the logistics so your sales person and presenter can give their full attention to the attendees. More sales will result.

- Ask for advance registrations; confirm with letters and follow up calls. By getting information about attendees before the seminar, you can better plan your seminar (hotel rooms, presentation substance). In addition, sending registrants directions to the seminar site and reminding them a few days prior to the event makes it easy to attend. Advance information may also help your sales person target particularly attractive prospects.

## Trade Shows

Even though trade shows are often expensive and resource intensive, they allow you to collect leads and expose your company to hundreds of interested people. There are ways to make them more effective and less resource intensive:

- Before the show, develop your trade show strategy and share it with your team to make sure everybody knows her or his part. Determine your message, methodology, who is responsible for what, preparation time line, and how your booth will be staffed.

- Don't make your sales team run your national shows. Do it for them. Have them help you staff the booth to speak with visitors. At the show, give them plenty of free time to use the telephone and to watch the presentations at competitors' booths.

- Create a structured demo that will be effective in a two-minute period. That is all the time you will have with most visitors to your booth. Be ready to expand your story or demonstration when the prospects visit.

- Announce new products. Announcing new products gives your salespeople an excuse to invite their prospects to the booth. In addition, many members of the trade press attend large industry events to see new products. Leverage this opportunity into nationwide industry exposure.

- Allocate free time so your salespeople can have you (or other company executives) meet key prospects.

- Schedule yourself and other key employees (executives, developers, support managers) for booth duty. During the lulls in booth traffic, take the opportunity to exchange information with your salespeople. You would be surprised at how much information changes hands when you work side by side with your sales force. You'll learn more about how to help your field. Your salesperson will learn more about how the product satisfies market needs.

- Pass trade show leads to the salespeople quickly. The faster you get the information to them, the better they can react to entice real prospects to buy your product.

- After the show, qualify the leads by phone before passing them to your sales force. A qualified lead gets more attention. In addition, your salespeople need not waste time with "tire-kickers."

- Review your performance after the meeting to understand how you could improve your next trade show. Strive to make each show better than the last.

## *Making Presentations Sell*

Most of your salespeople will already know how to give good presentations. But you or other key employees may also need to give presentations or demonstrations as part of your sales effort. Your presentations are as important, if not more important, than your salesperson's. When you need to present to prospects or demonstrate your product, consider the following:

- Preparation is the largest part of the time commitment. It takes five to six hours to prepare for each hour of presentation. For demonstrations, it takes ten hours. Your preparation consists of:

  — Identifying your key points

  — Designing the flow of your demonstration

  — Developing graphics that fit your story and illustrate your points

  — Putting the pieces together

  — Testing your demonstration

  — Practicing your demonstration until you can consistently present it without any problems

- Find out about your audience in advance so you can speak directly with them. Don't use jargon they do not understand, but do not speak down to them, either. If you cannot learn about your audience in advance, try to ask a few questions at the beginning of your presentation to help you gauge their interests and knowledge levels.

- Focus on benefits to the listener. Don't dwell on the *features* of the product. Use the features to illustrate the benefits that the listener will gain.

- Present sizzle with the steak. Don't just present dry facts. If you present your information in interesting ways, your audience will visualize how they can become involved with your company and product.

- Act as a consultant to increase your credibility and rapport with your listener and increase the probability that he will do business with you.

- Prepare for (and be willing to accept) questions. Your confidence level will increase and you will help your audience discover important information that you may inadvertently leave out. If appropriate, bring along additional technical support.

- Don't be afraid to say "I don't know, but I will find out and get back to you." Being honest about your knowledge is better than trying to fool the listener. Make sure, though, that you can deliver the answer as promised.

- Get off to a strong start. The first few minutes of your presentation sets the tone for your entire presentation, establishes rapport with the audience, and gives you the confidence level you need to make the entire presentation effective.

- Support your presentation with visual aids, hand-outs, and literature. People retain 70% of what they see and hear compared with 20% of what they hear alone.

- Dress professionally, be prepared, and be on time. Doing the opposite would be like telling your audience that they are not important. In addition to communicating important information about your product, presentations convey an image of your company. Displays of professionalism communicate quality.

- If you are not a seasoned speaker, take a presentation class or public speaking course to build your confidence and learn how to increase the effectiveness of your presentations. Practice your presentations by yourself and with associates. The more often you present, the better you become.

## *Balance Critical Time Allocation Trade-Offs*

With multiple salespeople vying for your time, you need to prioritize how to support every one. Since your sales people are compensated according to what they sell, conflicts arise. Yet if your remain cognizant that your goal is to maximize revenue, you will be able to deal with the conflict. Here are a few tips.

- Send in your heavy hitter based on sales requirements. Just as a baseball manager would send in a left-handed or right-handed pinch hitter to increase his odds of winning a tight ball game, you should evaluate each individual sales situation so you can supply the support person most likely to help the salesperson score. If you anticipate technical questions, send in a key developer or technical support person; to tackle important business issues, send in a company officer.

- Ride your fastest horse to the finish line. Sometimes you are simply going to have to choose between helping one salesperson or another. Bet on the salesperson who you have more confidence in to win the account. Let's say Jack, the salesperson who consistently attains 150% of his quota, needs you to make a presentation to a $100,000 account. Jim, who never has exceeded 80%, needs you on the same date to present to another $100,000 account. Jack should get priority, because his account is more likely to come in. (In reality, you will try to satisfy both sales people whenever possible. But it's not always possible.)

- Use feedback from your sales team to prioritize your general support activities by asking them to give you their top five or six support requirements.

- Be flexible with your product and support plans, but do not change them consistently. If you deviate too often, you will lose your direction, thereby decreasing revenue and missing development target dates. The key is to be responsive to the market without basing all your plans on one or two accounts.

## Everybody Participates in Sales Support

Your entire company should become a sales support machine in which everybody takes part. If this idea is unappealing, then you should rethink whether you really want to be in business for yourself. If you are not willing to make sales support a top priority, you are likely to fail. "Is it good for the field?" should be your company battle cry.

- Each of your executives should play her or his own roles. Don't let your financial manager play the role of a marketing person, or your sales manager a software developer. They will not do it well, thereby jeopardizing your business. A salesperson asks for specific resources to help with an account because he wants to illustrate specific points to his prospect. He calls in the VP of Finance because he wants to show financial stability, VP of Development to show product direction . . . etc.

- If necessary, go out of your way to get the sale. Don't be averse to flying to important meetings, working late to hammer out legal agreements or spending hours on the phone to support a trial installation. If it helps the sale, do it.

- Help your salespeople fill their funnels with good quality leads. The more quality leads you can present, the more time they can spend closing deals.

- Customer support after the sale is just as important to your sales success as presales support. It means happy customers, repeat business, and good references. To support your sales efforts after the sale, make it easy for the user to install your software and get it running. Make sure you can answer customers' questions on a timely basis. Let the customer know about additional capabilities or products that can help him.

- Vary your sales support to meet your market needs. If you sell PC- or Mac-based software, you probably can provide good support by providing reseller sales tools such as canned demonstrations, videotapes, and reseller training. If you sell higher-priced software directly to end user organizations (i.e., based on UNIX systems, mainframes or supercomputers, or if you normally sell site licenses), you probably need to provide technical presentations or live interactive demonstrations.

- Even if you only have only one salesperson, he needs to spend as much time as possible with his prospects. Anything that you can do to help him increase his direct selling time will pay off handsomely.

- Make sure every member of your staff exhibits "problem ownership" with every customer, prospect, or sales situation. Whenever a problem or situation comes up, the salesperson should simply take care of it instead of assuming that "someone else will do it."

One of my favorite stories about problem ownership in a sales cycle involved Larry Belcastro and Rich Wright, two support engineers at Auto-trol. On a snowy 1982 day, they braved a blizzard and emergency conditions to drive 120 miles from Pittsburgh, Pennsylvania to Akron, Ohio with 300 pounds of demonstration equipment for a series of seminars. (It took them over eight hours!) This followed two weeks of 12-hour days to prepare their demonstrations. Their efforts won an extra $250,000 in business. Any salesperson would be pleased to have support like that.

# Defeating the Competition

Let's face it. There is a lot of competition out there. You and dozens of companies just like yours are fighting over the same customers. They may be better armed than you—with more money, more people, or more technology. They may even have a better product. But don't hang up your sword and go home. You can still win if you take the time to understand the competitive issues and act accordingly. Let's look at the nature of competition and what you can do to counteract it.

## *Don't Discount Competition*

No matter how unique your product is, competition exists. Instead of trying to convince yourself and your employees that you have no competition, identify as many of your competitors as you can and keep up to date files on them. The information will help you battle them whenever you meet them. In the following sections, I have described several types of competitors you will encounter.

### Competitors With Similar Products

Directly competing products have similar capabilities to yours, but each has its own strengths and weaknesses, and may even be aimed at different niches within the market. In some product categories, there are dozens of competitors.

Products similar to yours that run on the same platform are the most likely to compete with you on a broad scale. Articles will be written that compare the products; they will be featured side by side in retail outlets or catalogs; prospects looking to purchase new software will be calling these competitors for information when they call you. After all, the prospect has probably already chosen his platform and only wants to examine products that run on it. This type of competitor will probably be your toughest, and should receive the majority of your competitive attention.

## Products Based on Other Platforms

Even though they run on different systems, products with similar capabilities compete. If you have a UNIX software package, you may find competition from DOS packages or mainframe software; and vice versa. Competing cross platform is unique because it usually happens when (a) the customer has several types of systems at his disposal; (b) he has no system and will buy one specifically to run the software; or (c) he wants a totally integrated solution from a single vendor that includes software, system, training, and service. If you are competing with a vendor whose software is based on a different platform, either somebody is in the wrong account (either you or your competitor is pursuing a prospect that is not qualified to buy from you), or one of you has a distinct advantage. For instance, if you are selling a spreadsheet package to a large corporation, you have an edge if you run on a PC instead of a Mac—unless of course, the prospect has standardized on the Mac, in which case, *you* are chasing the wrong customer. Similarly, a UNIX-based compute intensive scientific package has an advantage if the customer has a Convex or Cray at his disposal.

## Non-computer Products

Not everybody migrates to computerized methods from manual methods (i.e., carrying a paper calendar, using a wallet checkbook, or hand coding NC paper tapes). Some staunch conservatives even prefer typewriters (or pen and paper) to word processors.

There are a number of reasons that companies and individuals are using older methods. First is the human factor: not everybody migrates to computerized methods at the same pace. Some are early adopters, eager to try out the latest technology; others are laggards, perhaps unaware that something better is even available.[*] Then there's the cost. Even an inexpensive PC costs several thousand dollars. That's out of the reach of many homes and out of the budget of many businesses.

One of the toughest issues to beat is the lack of perceived or actual need. If the prospect doesn't perceive the need that is actually there, you may be able to convince him. However, if he really doesn't need the software because his old method works fine, you will have trouble winning. The adage, "If it ain't broke, don't fix it" has beaten salespeople time and time again. I once tried to sell a large drug store chain a $300,000 CAD system. I didn't get the sale because the

---

[*] David L. Loudon and Albert J. Della Bitta, *Consumer Behavior* (McGraw Hill, 1979), p. 275.

company had found a manual method of cut-and-paste that got almost as much productivity as I could offer—at "a buck-and-a-half per day."

These factors explain why certain types of software have penetrated 90% of their market, while others, only 10%. There will be further penetration for the latter group; but it will take time.

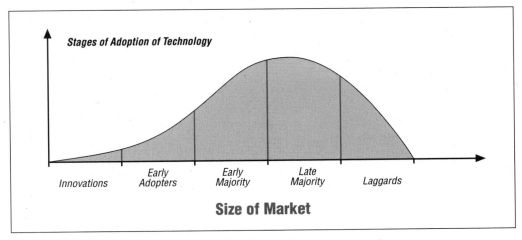

*FIGURE 10-1: HOW THE MARKET RESPONDS TO A PRODUCT*

## Your Prospects

Some prospects are also your competitors. Many companies have internal development people who prefer to invent their own software than to use off-the-shelf software. This problem is particularly acute in corporations with large MIS staffs. MIS management often feels threatened if it cannot provide home-grown solutions.

Competing against an internal development group is one of the most perplexing sales situations, because politics often determines the winner. There are two strategies to win one of these battles. The first is to find an end user prospect willing to fight against an internal foe to purchase your software. The second way is to sell your product to the end user without the internal group knowing. This is actually pretty easy to do when the prospect's organization has decentralized purchasing powers. Then, once you have proven the value of your software in that division or department, try to sell it in other departments using your first installation as a reference. If enough departments purchase your product, the development group will become your friend instead of your foe.

In many cases, you have some other advantages. It's very expensive to develop and maintain in-house software. This argument works very well when the development department is busy, but use it carefully. If workers in the department become idle, you become a threat to their job security. And it costs nothing additional to utilize staff members that are being paid anyway.

You will gain an advantage with the end user if you can promise him swift updates that keep up with his needs. In most corporations, updates to internally developed codes happen slowly because internal development and support staff have so many applications and users to support. It's rarely fast enough for each user. Conversely, when a product is developed specifically for the user, it is theoretically "perfectly adapted" for his needs. So, you will have to convince him that your "generic" solution will fit his needs just as well as the in-house solution. Your greatest advantage at many companies is one that should not even exist, the incompatibility between corporate information services departments and end user departments. Don't ask me why, but in the majority of the large companies that I have done business with, the MIS department head does not get along with the head of the end user departments.

A personal note: Competing against internal development groups is a task I dislike immensely. I'd much rather be on their side. In most cases, I have been—and you will be. In fact, you will probably be selling directly to them much more often than selling against them. To do so, help your prospect become a hero by installing your product. From the start, make it clear how she will benefit by installing your product rather than making her own. If she sees that you will help her win, you will win too.

## Budgetary Competitors

Totally unrelated purchases can be powerful competitors if they deplete your prospect's budget. Imagine walking into an end user's office, presenting your software, getting rave reviews, and having him tell you he can't purchase your software because he has to purchase similarly priced test equipment. It happens; in fact, it's one reason that many large-ticket software sales take 9 to 12 months. Part of the cycle is for submitting budgets and getting them approved.

To avoid budgetary competitors, work with your prospect at budget time to help him justify and submit a request for enough money to include purchase of your software during his next budget period. Then keep in touch so he doesn't divert the funds. Alternately, you can show him a financial case that catapults your software to a higher priority. I did that at the Goodyear Tire and Rubber Company. They purchased a $500,000 CAD system because one of their engineers showed his management how the system would pay for itself in two years. (He is now a high-level manager.) If your proposal has a higher payback than any other budgeted alternative, the prospect will find a way to buy from you. Additionally, you can work out creative financing or licensing terms so the customer can fit your product into his budget and subsequent budget periods.

# *The Myth of the Level Playing Field*

The level playing field only exists in sports. In the computer industry, some vendor always has more monetary resources, better distribution, more aggressive salespeople, or a better product. A level field does not endure because a company always comes along to tip it. It is your job to tip the field in your favor. You can do it by using several key tactics:

- Know yourself and use your knowledge as a weapon

- Understand your competition

- Fight the battles in which you have an edge

- Garner your forces

- Emphasize your unique advantages

- Go into battle with your allies

- Beat their best, not their most unlikely, efforts

- Avoid price competition

- Have backup plans

## Know Yourself

Examine your product, company, financial resources, and marketing/sales team to determine your strengths and weaknesses. Your prospects and competitors will. Your prospect will be assessing whether your product meets his needs, whether your company is moving in the same direction as he is, and whether you have the staying power to provide support into the future. He will not buy unless you have convinced him that all these areas are covered.

Your competitors will be searching for problems—and they will find them. Some competitors may even make up problems just to make it tougher for you. If you miss a key trade show, they may spread a rumor that you are going out of business. If your product is slower than theirs, they will publish comparative performance results. If they find a customer who is unhappy, they will spread the word.

In 1986, Floating Point Systems dominated the minisupercomputer market. Their attached processors performed high-speed calculations when connected to a minicomputer like a VAX. However, it was not a complete system. It had no compilers. Users would use libraries to call functions from the VAX. In 1987, Convex and Alliant came on the scene with real minisupercomputers, complete systems on which users could write, compile, link, and run their software. In competitive situations against FPS, they would exploit FPS' position by getting the prospect to make a compiler a requirement of sale. If they got the prospect to agree, they automatically ruled out FPS. In response FPS marketeers instructed their sales people to "tell the prospect he doesn't need a FORTRAN compiler," but this response was often insufficient to turn the prospects around. In the end, FPS lost their market to these two aggressive companies.

Take a good hard look at yourself. Find your weak points and try to fix them. Find your strong points and reinforce them. Understand how to react to pressure when competitors make accusations. Only then will you be carrying your sharpest sword into battle. The following issues are among those you should examine:

*Product Issues:*
> Performance, accuracy, ease-of-use, platform, cost, applicability to the prospect's mission

*Company Issues:*
> Expertise in the customer's field, ability to support users, willingness to handle unusual user requests

*Financial Issues:*
> Available capital to fund market penetration, long term viability

*Marketing and Sales Issues:*
> Product positioning, products and requirements of potential customers, distance from potential customers

## Understand Your Competition

How much do you know about the competition? It's not enough! You should learn everything you can—how they advertise, where their salespeople are located, their channels of distribution, how well they are funded, the strengths and weaknesses of their products, and any other information you can imagine.

If possible, test competing products. This is the best way for you to find holes (i.e., performance problems, bugs, inconsistencies, or missing features), and is particularly easy to do if the product is Mac- or PC-based. One of Marketing Masters' clients recently purchased the top four competing packages and had three people (one technical, one marketing, and one sales) use and compare them for a month. They formulated a product launch to exploit the competitive advantages. Before release, their own product was modified to be faster and easier to use. They created marketing literature that stressed their advantages, without directly referring to the competing products. And as a result of the test, the salespeople knew precisely where the competitors fell short, and where they could be attacked.

In addition to testing, talk to users of the competing products. It is relatively easy for you, as a competing vendor, to believe bad things about the competition, but their user base may see things differently. Users always provide interesting new information or a new way to look at existing knowledge. Additionally, you may find unexpected weaknesses and strengths.

Whenever you find out about another product that may compete with yours, do a literature search. To find articles and reviews, search through computer databases such as Computer Select or those that you access via USENET newsgroups, America On-Line, or CompuServe. These will give you input regarding how the market is accepting the product. You can also send away for literature. Start a file with information to which you can refer whenever you have questions.

Don't underestimate products that only compete with yours peripherally because companies are always looking to expand their market. A few changes to their product and they may end up trying to take you on directly. Companies with structural analysis codes end up adding capabilities to compete with modeling software; optical character recognition leads to document management; operating systems yield network software; CAD becomes technical documentation software. Microsoft, for instance, introduced True Type when it launched Windows 3.1. Suddenly font companies like Adobe and Agfa had a new, powerful competitor.

## Fight the Battles in Which You Have an Edge

I cannot state strongly enough how important it is for you to fight the battles that you can win. From a technical standpoint, this means developing a technical advantage. From a marketing standpoint, this means picking the right market and highlighting your competitive advantage. From a sales standpoint, this means selecting the right prospects to whom your advantages are important. If you have a software/hardware bundle that increases resolution on a laser printer, your technical advantage is the higher resolution. When your marketing case embellishes the resolution issue, you have put together a stronger case against a lower resolution solution. However, your salesperson must bring that case to the right battlefield. He must approach people who have applications that require high resolution, such as desktop publishing. If he approaches

## ⌒ *Collecting Competitive Information* ⌒

Cloak and dagger espionage always makes a good story. However, spying is not the easiest way to get competitive information, and the penalties for getting caught are large. Borland is suing Symantec because it alleges that Symantec stole trade secrets when it recruited one of Borland's managers.

There is plenty of public information that will give you a clear picture of your competition. You only have to keep your eyes open and ask lots of questions. Here are some effective data collection methods:

- If you see an ad for a competing product, send in the reader service card, or call and ask for their literature.

- Visit competitors' trade show booths; sit in on their presentations.

- Speak with competitor's customers.

- Read magazine reviews about competing products.

- Subscribe to a database service such as *Computer Select*, a subscription service that has a database of articles and information from many computer magazines. Similar information can be found on CompuServe, America On-Line, and Prodigy in services such as "PCWorld On-Line" and "Byte Information Exchange" (BIX).

- Buy or borrow competing products. Get users to give you in-depth demonstrations.

- Talk to competing salespeople at industry events. Who knows what someone might say at a cocktail party? People like to boast.

- Talk to the competitor's distributors—particularly if you share distributors.

- If your competitors are public corporations, use Value Line, Dow Jones News Retrieval, or other financial information services. Obtain their annual and quarterly reports. Buy a share of stock so you get put on their mailing list.

somebody who only prints checks, he will lose to a product that prints faster at standard resolution.

You have already unearthed the strengths and weaknesses of your competitors as well as your own. Now, use your knowledge to pick your battles. Don't try to beat the competition where they have all the advantages. It's like handing them your armor before you draw your sword.

## Garner Your Forces

In 1815, Napoleon was defeated at Waterloo. He lost, not because the British forces were strong, but because his military machine had become weak. Prior to his defeat, he had spread his forces for a romp around Europe in which his armies lost men along the entire campaign. By the time he got to Waterloo, his war machine was in a shambles. Similarly, the European Allies may have won World War II because Germany had spread its forces thin by fighting campaigns in eastern Europe, western Europe, and northern Africa. Had Germany united its troops, the map might look different today.

In both war and business, if you spread your resources too thin, you die. There are too many markets to penetrate every one. You don't have the resources or the money. Therefore, you must garner your resources. Silicon Graphics aims at compute intensive scientific and engineering applications that require graphics; The Santa Cruz Operation specializes in commercial UNIX applications for Intel processors. Even large companies have limited resources. Yours is no different. Whether there are two or 200 potential markets eagerly waiting for your product, concentrate your efforts on the top few. You will win more, and the effort to win each sale will be a lot less.

Companies that spread their development resources over too many projects don't complete any; as a result, their products are inferior and late to market. If they try to reach too many markets, they stretch their financial resources too thin and cannot effectively reach any of them. Those that have small marketing staffs cannot cover every industry show. Even salespeople can only cover a certain number of accounts concurrently. (For large multi-call sales, the number of top priority accounts is probably only three to 15.)

## Emphasize Your Unique Advantages

Don't be subtle when it comes to showing your most important advantages. Emphasize them. Find reasons to make them important to your prospects. Make it easy for your prospective customers to understand your products by telling them what you think is important.

In the early eighties, Apollo Computer was the leader in standalone workstations. Its proprietary Aegis operating system was considered advanced and its workstation concept was unique—until Sun Microsystems came along. Since I was selling an Apollo-based software package at the time, I ran into Sun in competitive battles. Sun didn't try to win by comparing operating systems feature by feature. It emphasized the plain vanilla nature of its UNIX operating system. It was a compelling story that won many battles for Sun. Interestingly enough, Sun was actually selling the concept of "open systems" (if not the term) as its own unique advantage, even though it was several years before open systems became widely accepted. Today, Sun is a leader in workstation computing.

Make your differences substantial; most prospects will ignore a minor, inconsequential difference in product features or capabilities. For example, a 2% performance difference, or even a 10% difference, will not sway a purchase decision. Other factors, such as ease of use and compatibility with the customer's existing installation, will be more important. However, a 200% performance increase is a substantial advantage, and can swing a decision in your favor.

## Go Into Battle Alongside Your Allies

You don't have to do battle alone. Find companies with products that accentuate yours and put together joint marketing and sales programs. You will provide your customers with a more complete solution and have more money and personnel with which to beat your competition. Hold joint seminars; show your product in their trade show booth (or vice versa); or even package your products together for joint sales.

In 1992, several of the large DOS applications vendors introduced suites of products—Lotus introduced Smart Suite consisting of 1-2-3, Freelance Graphics, and AmiPro; Microsoft introduced Microsoft Office featuring Word, Excel, and Powerpoint. WordPerfect and Borland were at a disadvantage because their product lines didn't have all three components, until 1993, when Borland Office was announced, consisting of Borland's Quattro Pro and Paradox for Windows, together with WordPerfect for Windows.

Getting the industry powers to help you market can give you a competitive edge, thereby catapulting your sales to new heights. A handful of vendors, including IBM, HP, Apple, and Sun have such large clout that getting them to introduce you to their users greatly increases the salability of your product. There are several ways to work with an industry power:

- Be part of its formal third-party program (e.g., Sun's *Catalyst* program).

- Informally work with its headquarters marketing.

- Work directly with its sales offices.

Working with the major players is a competitive weapon, no matter how you do it. Your partner's large sales and marketing organization helps you find new opportunities. You leverage the time of your own sales team so that you can spend more time in fiercely competitive situations. Best of all, by bringing you into the sales situation, your partner provides an implied endorsement, an extremely effective competitive weapon.

Most small companies opt for the formal third-party program. In most cases, this means your company must satisfy certain criteria (i.e., run on certain platforms, leverage the sales of a certain number of their brand workstations, or pass certain financial stability requirements). The vendor usually lists you in its third-party catalog and sends notices to its sales force about your product. The vendor often assigns a third-party liaison and provides discounts if you buy its products.

If you have a product that is particularly appealing to a marketing person at one of these companies, he may be willing to work with you, whether or not you are part of their formal program. To do so, your product must fill a specific void. For instance, if the workstation company is attempting to show an integrated manufacturing solution at a key trade show, he looks for a suite of products that make his product look good when shown on the trade show floor. If you catch him at the opportune moment with the right product, you may have the chance of being one of the products he demonstrates. A few years ago, I was able to place a client's product in Sun's AutoFact booth because it showed a unique visualization capability that enhanced the appeal of Sun's workstations.

The way to win big is to identify salespeople within your targeted vendor who are trying to sell to prospects that require your type of product. Then use your product to help them sell theirs. After they win their deals, make sure that your sales contact trumpets your success to other salespeople and marketers within their organizations. By helping them win three or four major deals, you will become a favored partner who is brought into many deals, not just another approved vendor in their thick catalog. Working with the vendor's sales force is not easy. It takes lots of time, patience, and the willingness to seek out the proper salespeople in the vendor's many field offices. But it is effective. Palette Systems, an almost unknown graphics vendor, follows DEC salespeople into manufacturing accounts that need shop floor graphics. They win most of their deals because of DEC's recommendation.

## Beat Their Best Efforts, Not Their Most Likely

Don't misjudge the intentions and actions of the competition. Many companies base their entire action plan on their expectation that the segment leader will act a certain way. Unless they have inside information, their guess will probably be wrong.

It makes better sense to base your plans on what your competition is *capable* of doing if they do everything right with their full resources. Replace "I expect (company name) to . . ." with "If they do it right, they can come up with this capability in X months, will exceed our performance by Y times, and can spend Z dollars in marketing the new product." If you have researched the competition thoroughly, you should be able to estimate what their capabilities really are.

If you can beat them at their best, you can win virtually all battles. On the other hand, if you aim only at their *expected* (average) capability, you're as likely to lose as you are to win.

## Avoid Price Competition

Occasionally you will find yourself competing against a product that has a lower price or for a prospect who has a budgetary constraint. Some salespeople would be inclined to lower the price to win the deal. However, discounting is generally an ineffective tool. It is rare that a buyer makes a decision to purchase from a specific vendor solely on price. In most cases, discounts are given to prospects who would have purchased anyway, even if the price was higher. The only thing discounting accomplishes is reducing your profit margin. There are better ways to compete:

1.  Compare values. Instead of lowering your price to match that of another product, show the prospect how much more value you can provide. This requires discipline and tenacity: the ability to hear "NO!", but come back with more selling

2.  Stay with your price, but add additional value. For large purchases, you might add a week or two of on-site support, installation, and consulting. For smaller deals, you might extend the length of your warranty or throw in a free upgrade. You might even enhance your package by including the prospect's favorite feature in your next release. The idea is to find out what you can include that will make the prospect buy from you.

3.  If the issue is budgetary, allow the buyer to delay a portion of his purchase until his next fiscal year even though you install your product now. This helps him meet his budget constraints, but does not decrease your selling price.

4.  Provide a payment schedule or lease. Most of your competitors will not be able or willing to loan the money. If you cannot extend the credit, arrange for credit with an independent computer leasing company. (If you extend the credit yourself, make sure the prospect is credit worthy.)

## Have Backup Plans

Except in bleeding edge situations (where the market is not yet ready for the technology), the first one to the market has a distinct advantage. If you can complete your product quicker, you increase your competitive strength. Your product will become synonymous with the product category; you will gain editorial exposure; and you will rouse a loyal user base. If you are late to market, don't expect the market to wait for you. Loyalty will be built around a competitor's product.

There's a strong chance that a competitor will beat you to your market or offer a new or improved product that is a serious threat to yours. Have backup plans ready so you can react quickly to major changes in the competitive environment.

Enhance your total offering with non-technical benefits important to the buyer—better support, lower price, higher margins for resellers, better marketing, or an upgrade path to your next version. In the real world, you won't always have the best product; you will be playing technological leapfrog. But since decisions are not made strictly on product capabilities you will still be able to sell. Besides, you can't just wait for the competition to roll over. As Will Rogers once said, "Even if you're on the right track, you will get run over if you just sit there."

If a competitor has started shipping a new product that is better than yours, you can try to ship an interim release that decreases their advantage. WordPerfect, for instance, staved off Microsoft Word by shipping an interim release of WordPerfect for Windows with drag-and-drop text, a Microsoft Word feature that was missing from WordPerfect's initial Windows product.

Be careful. Announcing a new version of your product too early kills your revenue stream. Prospects tend to wait for new products if the choice is between two versions of the same product. Therefore, wait until your product is ready to ship (or nearly ready) before announcing it. Or, as in the drag-and-drop case, include the new capabilities in the current version without any formal announcement.

# *Weathering the Storm*

There are a number of other market factors that affect your viability and success. While each one of these factors merits a long discussion, we will simply note their importance here.

## Keep a War Chest

Have a cash buffer available that will carry you through the tough competitive times. You are not IBM and cannot afford to lose $4 billion while you become more competitive. Your cash buffer will provide working capital so you can finish your development and market your revised product. The longer your development time and the more people on your staff, the more cash you need.

If you have another source of revenue (i.e., another product or consulting contracts), you can use the revenue to displace the cash buffer.

## Protect Your Installed Base

During product transition times, you can count on the support of your installed user base. They often purchase additional licenses, find additional prospects, and provide excellent references for large potential prospects. Take care of them and keep them loyal.

At least one of your competitors will undoubtedly try to steal your customers. Perhaps he will offer features that you don't support, provide competitive upgrade pricing, or include a special incentive. If a competitor goes after your user base, meet him head on. You have the advantage. It is difficult to get users to change the way they work; therefore, it is difficult to get users to change software. If you lose them, it is more difficult to win them back. Protect your user base.

## Keep Your Competition in Your Sights

Since your competition is improving daily, you must be vigilant in following the competitive environment. Your strategies, tactics, and direct sales approach must change to reflect this changing environment. Otherwise, your company and your product will become a memory.

# External Market Forces

No matter how hard you try to control your company's destiny, there are external factors you cannot control. They can create opportunity (both short term and long term) or cause problems. This chapter outlines the most common external, uncontrollable factors. First I will identify the factors; then I will suggest a few courses of action to help you deal with them.

## *Existing in a Virtual Marketplace*

You would be surprised at how seemingly distant events can impact your software marketing efforts. A decrease in airline traffic, for instance, ripples through the economy to harm your revenue stream. The airlines, with less revenue coming in, purchase less software. The aircraft manufacturers get less business from the airlines and decrease their software purchases. The entire air transportation industry lays off workers, who purchase less software for home use. Even the small companies that cater to the airlines and aircraft manufacturers (parts manufacturers, advertising agencies, engineering firms, secretarial agencies, office supply stores . . . ) buy less software. Sales decline in all parts of the software industry including spreadsheets, word processors, CAD, FEA, electronic design, numerical control software, PC utilities, project management packages, and e-mail. If the situation reverses itself so that demand rises for airplane seats, the airlines and aircraft manufacturers may accelerate their software purchases, resulting in increased sales for the entire industry.

This example shows just one way that external markets are linked to yours. Extend the example to all industries and you have a virtual marketplace—a marketplace in which your ability to sell your product is affected by the entire worldwide economy. The condition and direction of the computer industry, your channel, your suppliers, and your end user markets all influence your ability to sell your software at a profit. Other industries and markets can indirectly influence your profitability. While you are keenly interested in your own bottom line, you must take external factors into account when making marketing and product development decisions.

The computer industry directly impacts your profitability. When computer shipments increase, your revenue will probably increase. More computers means more total software licenses, and your company should receive its share. Conversely, when computer sales shrink, you can expect to sell less software.

Other industry vendors also impact your profitability. The number of competitors and their aggressiveness, the state of technology (i.e., introduction of a new generation of microprocessors), the way systems are being bundled, and current pricing policies all affect your ability to sell your product. Here are some examples showing how computer industry vendors have affected the companies around them.

- Lotus Development purchased Samna, thereby owning AmiPro which it pitted against WordPerfect and all Windows word processors. Lotus has more cash with which to develop and market AmiPro, thereby making AmiPro a more viable competitor than it was under Samna. The net effect for other vendors was smaller market share.

- MacNeal-Schwendler developed a relationship with Aries Technology allowing MSC to market Aries' modeling software with MSC's analysis software. Since Aries' product is a much stronger modeler than MSC's modeling software, all FEA vendors faced tougher competition.

- Borland introduced competitive upgrade pricing to attract users of competing PC software products. The new pricing strategy gave significant discounts to people who wanted to switch to Borland's products. Competing vendors had to choose between two alternatives: (1) lower prices to meet Borland, thereby lowering margins; or (2) keep prices at historical levels and risk losing users to the competition. A longer lasting impact has been that competitive upgrade strategy is now an accepted marketing tactic. Many users wait for competitive upgrades to switch or try new software.

- Microsoft created Windows. When Windows 3.0 came out, many new software opportunities opened, leading to the creation of hundreds of new companies and products. It also forced many companies with existing DOS products to jump on the Windows bandwagon, or lose part of their market to new Windows-based competitors.

- Microsoft added new functions to DOS. The new functions deprived software vendors of sales opportunities because many DOS products became redundant with the operating system capabilities.

- Frame Technologies ported its publishing software from UNIX to DOS. Quark ported its publishing software from Macintosh to DOS. Companies that produced supplemental products for users of Frame or Quark gained new opportunities in the large DOS market. Companies with DOS-based publishing packages suddenly faced two new aggressive competitors.

Although there are many actions that other vendors can take, their actions generally affect you in one or more ways. They can (1) increase or decrease the number of units you can sell; (2) lengthen the time it takes to sell your product; or (3) decrease your profit margin—either by decreasing your prices or increasing the costs of competing.

Distributors and resellers affect your sales by stocking up or cutting back on inventory to meet market demands and cash flow requirements. To increase your sales (or sometimes to retain current levels) you may have to decrease prices, provide special payment terms for your customers, or use a more liberal return policy.

Similarly, you are linked with your suppliers. To obtain goods from your suppliers that are in short supply, you may have to pay higher prices or commit to long-term purchase agreements. You may also have to live with long lead times on deliveries. If your suppliers have an overabundance of product or capacity, they may cut prices or provide liberal payment or return policies. You may depend on a certain print shop to produce your documentation. If your printer goes out of business, you will have to find another printer. The new printer might not be able to meet your delivery schedules, or he may have to charge higher prices.

The industries that exert the strongest influence on your fortunes are those that you sell to. Whether you sell to bankers, manufacturers, energy producers, or some other group, your fortunes are tied to theirs. If they cannot buy, you cannot sell.

## *To Everything There Is a Season*

You can expect your revenue to fluctuate with seasonal changes. During summer, many individuals take vacations making it tougher to move large purchases through the approval cycle. A similar slowdown takes place in December as many employees take holiday vacations. Many corporations formally shut down for a week to ten days over Christmas and the New Year.

If you sell to corporations, your revenue is also influenced by budget cycles. In many corporations, budgeting is a lengthy process that may last from October to February. Orders at the end and beginning of the year are often delayed or accelerated as managers fight for unused year-end funds and wait for new budget approvals. Even when you remove the seasonal effects, most corporate budgets are based on quarterly goals. If a corporate customer overspends in a particular quarter, you may have to wait until the following cycle to receive your order.

External events can also change buying patterns, thereby affecting your revenue stream. Many resellers and end users delay their purchases until after major shows like Comdex so they can examine competing products before choosing which to order. This can dampen your revenue until after the event. Some vendors take advantage of the events by introducing new products. These introductions can dampen your revenue once more. Of course, you can use these shows too.

Additionally, end user markets have their own seasonal idiosyncrasies that can cause your revenue to fluctuate. For example, Intuit (publisher of Quicken personal finance programs) reports that its highest revenue quarter ends in December while the months of May through October are below average. This coincides with the tax season, which starts with end of year planning and goes through the April 15th filing deadline.

# *The Permanence of Structural Change*

Not every acceleration or dip in revenue is caused by a cycle. Some are caused by structural changes: permanent changes in the way the marketplace works, such as movements to open systems, graphical user interfaces, or microprocessors. Structural changes can be caused by introduction of new technology, government direction, or simply changes in consumer or corporate tastes.

If you have a unique technology and a lot of funding, you may be able to cause a structural change by introducing a new type of product that changes the way your market works. But be aware that markets resist change. Unless you have a compelling application, have signed up influential companies to embrace your technology, and have plenty of money to spread the word, you probably won't be successful. For every Apple Computer Company that actually does influence the market, there are twenty others that can't even survive. Even the big guys fail. IBM introduced the Micro Channel Architecture for the PC, but couldn't battle market momentum (or resistance by other vendors to IBM's proprietary licensing scheme). Today MCA is not the leading bus technology for personal computers.

In most cases, you need to identify structural changes and take actions in accordance with the change. This is one of the toughest challenges you face. Wang did not recognize the move to word processing software from dedicated word processing systems. Apollo, DEC, and IBM fought the movement to open systems. Each company had the information it needed to react to the changes. They either failed to react, reacted too slowly, or resisted it.

If, for instance, you are creating word processing software, you might want to ask whether pen-based computing or multimedia might not significantly change the market, and adjust your future plans accordingly. If you see a trend, you should analyze what opportunities it presents. For example, the move from mainframes to workstations and PC's created tremendous opportunities for networking companies.

Although "corporate religion" often works to solidify your company, it can adversely affect your ability to analyze structural market trends and adjust accordingly. Whether it's similar to IBM's "protect current businesses" philosophy, Apple's "change the world" ethic or some other model, corporate religion can make you resist a market trend that you cannot possibly buck. Auto-trol Technology, a leader in CAD systems in the early eighties, resisted the mid-eighties trend to personal systems while AutoDesk, Computervision, and Intergraph, among others, found ways to offer PC-based products. AutoDesk and Intergraph are now leading vendors, while Auto-trol has seen little or no growth and has lost money during many periods.

Don't get blindsided by your own views. React to a structurally changing market by following it.

## *The Effects of Government Practices*

When the government spends money or begins a new practice, opportunities arise:

- The space program provided a launching pad for many technical products including supercomputers, software, and energy sources. The federal government, through spending programs, funded innovations in areas of importance. NASTRAN is one of many software packages that grew from space program funds.

- National defense has created markets by spurring innovations in computer technology. Hardware and software for signal and image processing are among the product categories that were cultivated to aid defense.

- The CALS (Computer Aided Logistics Support) initiative provides specifications about technical documentation with which companies must comply to sell technical products to the U.S. government. Hundreds of companies produce software that complies with the CALS spec so they can sell their products to the government and government contractors.

- The federal government sometimes provides aid to industries to bolster the domestic economy as well as to developing countries to create stable markets for U.S. made products. These developing nations often become aggressive buyers of technology, generating new markets for you.

- By lowering interest rates, the government increases the amount of money available to make purchases. When interest rates rise, spending decreases. When tax rates decrease, spending from the private sector rises. The converse is true, too.

# Tricks of the Trade

You cannot control the factors that I just outlined, but you can control how you react. Here are some ways that you can take advantage of the external forces and alleviate the risks that they pose to your company.

### Strategic Tricks:

- If you cannot control a specific factor that affects your company, live with it. Put your efforts into factors that you *can* control: your product, marketing, and cost containment.

- Diversify away from shrinking markets. If your market is shrinking, you need a new market to support continued sales. In 1990, banks were going out of business by the score while accounting firms were much more stable. The logical strategy was to decrease dependency on the banking market, perhaps by moving into the accounting market.

- Find a high-priority technology project. If the Clinton presidency is indeed "the high tech presidency," as it has been called, there should be lots of opportunities for entrepreneurs. The administration has earmarked funds to spur innovation in applications that utilize high bandwidth digital networks. In addition, with defense budgets being cut, the armed forces must find new ways to maintain defense programs at lower cost. The armed services will probably attempt to use high technology to reach their cost containment goals.

- Find the next market that the government will embrace. As of this writing, health care, education, and insurance are all high-priority projects for President Clinton. Each one represents software opportunities.

- Time your product introductions and sales thrust to coincide with the cycles of the market. Many companies introduce new products at Comdex or at end user trade shows. Some, such as Silicon Graphics, put many marketing activities on the back burner during the last few months of the fiscal year, so marketing people can fully support short term sales situations.

- Become active in industry groups, consortiums, and third-party programs that influence your technology and markets. Join Sparc International, Software Publishers Association, COSE, X/Open, or other groups that embrace your philosophies. Work with IBM, HP, DEC, SGI, Sun, Microsoft, SCO, or other influential companies that have third party liaisons or formal third party programs. You'll gain a better understanding of the dynamics of your market, get access to information earlier than the general public, and receive help from the companies who are trying to make the market move in similar directions. You may even be able to influence the market's direction.

- Embrace government and industry standards. If your product supports the standard, more prospects will include it on their "approved vendor" lists. CALS, SGML, STEP, IGES, and EISA are a few of the standards important in particular industry segments. Embrace *de facto* standards too. Although *de facto* standards are tougher to pinpoint than regulated standards, they are just as powerful. If you meet them, you'll prosper. If you don't meet them, many prospects just won't consider you.

### *Tactical Tricks:*
- Find end-of-year budget money at key accounts. In most corporations, shrewd managers find ways to hide extra budget money in a slush fund. If you can identify which manager has the slush fund, you can often find additional sales even when company budgets are frozen.

- Provide an impending event that forces your market to buy early. Offer a discount or free upgrade until December 31. Bundle on-site support or training. Provide something that your prospects want so they will buy now, instead of waiting until the next fiscal year.

## *Keeping Up With a Moving Market*

The computer market is a moving target. Every eighteen months, new generation microprocessor chips are introduced, forcing software vendors to port existing applications to the new machines and even creating totally new markets and applications opportunities. To capitalize, you must understand what is happening in your market and in the computer industry. Determine which changes are cyclical and which are permanent; tweak your product to fit the new market dynamics; keep enough cash available to withstand inaccurate projections. Most of all, aim where the market will be, not where it is now. Don't hesitate to anticipate where it will be, and venture in that direction. But also be willing to change direction if the market is not headed where you anticipated. After all, no matter how you try to control your destiny, a large part of it is in the hands of outsiders. Don't be surprised if you must move in their direction instead of your own.

# PART 2

# Customer Fulfillment, Training, and Support

# Cultivating Customer Satisfaction

Take a solid product. Add functional documentation, ample training, and a proficient support staff that uses suitable problem-solving techniques. Deliver it all to your customer. You have a satisfied customer.

## *Great Companies Need Great Customers*

Great companies are built by developing lasting relationships with a stable customer base. The importance of these close relationships can be seen in several ways:

1. *Repeat purchases.* In a competitive market, repeat purchases from a satisfied user base are less costly to obtain than purchases from many new customers. You have already established a working relationship and rapport with your existing customers. Satisfied existing users should be a consistent source of revenue that you can depend on year in and year out.

2. *Customer references.* New customers are always more willing to purchase from a vendor if existing customers say positive things.

3. *Valuable market feedback.* Your customers find problems that can limit your ability to sell your product, show you new uses, and illuminate differences between your product and the competitor's.

It's no longer good enough to simply satisfy the customer. You must delight him! The best way is to build a business partnership with him to help him get the most out of your product.

One of the most successful companies in the history of the computer industry is IBM. For more than forty years, corporate computer purchasers bought IBM products because "nobody ever got fired for buying from IBM." IBM rarely had leading-edge products and they usually weren't the first to the market, but IBM did have excellent support. Even though IBM has shrunk from its peak of 400,000 employees in 1991, their skill at maintaining customer relationships gives IBM an ongoing competitive advantage as well as a continuous revenue stream.

When you build a quality product, you increase your customer's satisfaction and decrease your cost of serving her. Your customer is pleased when the program doesn't crash or give erroneous results. If she can install it easily, she is thrilled. And if it does virtually everything she wants it to do, she is ecstatic. You should be ecstatic too, because her ability to do-it-herself decreases your costs. Every support call that you eliminate saves $21, according to the estimates of Claris Corporation. By saving ten calls per day, you add over $50,000 to your bottom line—while making the customer happier!

## Teach Him To Fish . . .

You share the responsibility of increasing customer satisfaction with the customer himself, but only if you empower the customer to help himself by giving him the tools and showing him how to use them.

If your customer has to call you every time he has a question about your software, he'll become pretty annoyed. So put tools at his disposal that make it unnecessary to contact you. Provide online help, detailed documentation, and explicit, easy-to-comprehend error messages so he can help himself without calling you.

Educating your customer is one of the most important practices you can undertake to increase his satisfaction. By setting your customer's expectation prior to his purchase, you provide him with a mark against which he can judge his own success. His satisfaction rises as it becomes evident that your product and company are on the mark.

But don't stop there. Continue the education process after he installs your software. Educating your user after the sale leads to extra productivity and better understanding of your product. It also prevents him from becoming exasperated as he attempts to incorporate your product into his routine. An educated customer is an excellent ally. He spreads the word about the quality and usability of your product in a convincing manner, which a poorly informed customer cannot do.

# *The Basics of Training and Support*

Let's assume that you have developed a quality product and have sold it to people who need it. Now, your challenges are to teach your customer how to use your product and to support him whenever he calls. Although there are a variety of methods from which you can choose, not all will be appropriate for you. We'll look at the most common, as well as outline some approaches to choose among them. Finally I'll suggest a few ways that you can measure your satisfaction and support levels.

There are trade-offs among the methods that you use to train and support your customers. For instance, telephone support is more expensive than fax support, but the instant gratification of telephone support yields higher customer satisfaction. Additionally, the software industry is currently undergoing a major transition, especially regarding PC software. While most companies used to provide telephone support for free (sometimes using toll-free numbers), there is a movement toward unbundling support. It has not yet caught on, but by the time you read this, several large vendors may have made the move. With software prices going down, the unbundling is inevitable. It's still too early to know whether the shift will be toward pay per call, pay per month, unlimited call or some other method. Check out your competitors before planning your strategy.

## Documentation and Structured Learning

Let's imagine that you are a software user who has just run into a problem. What do you do? If you are a Windows user, you pull down the help menu or press F1 for context-sensitive help; if you use UNIX, you might use manual pages. In any case, you use whatever online help is available to you, or you reach for the manual. "Oh no! The manual doesn't have an index!"

As a minimum, documentation should have explanations of features and procedures, configuration requirements, how to get support, and an index. It is amazing how many companies put together otherwise good documentation, but forget the index, making the documentation difficult to use. Don't forget yours! The easier you make your documentation to use, the more often the user will use it. If your software is Mac- or Windows-based, you should also include hypertext links in your online help.

Technical and non-technical users interpret information differently, so make your documentation and support reflect the technical level of your user. A non-technical user wants to find out how to get his job done without having to know how the product works. The technical user often looks for explanations about how to get more performance from the product or how to customize it for efficient use.

If your product is easy enough to learn without a live instructor, consider providing a "structured learning" tool like a videotape or a tutorial (either computer-based or on an audio cassette). These tools allow your customer to learn the product at his own pace in his own office. You can include it in your basic software or sell it as an add-on. Computer-based tutorials can be placed right on the program disks. If you decide to sell your structured learning separately, make sure to include information with your product about how to buy your add-on tutorials.

---

### ☞ *Three Common Documentation Mistakes* ☜

- *Writing manuals as if the user is a software designer.* Users think differently than software designers. While software designers often want to find out about the syntax of commands, menu structures, and data structure, the user typically does not. He usually wants to find out how to start quickly, make it work for his specific task, and minimize the amount of time needed to learn the software. Write your documentation with the user's needs as the documentation design criteria, not your needs.

- *Making the user read everything in the manual.* The user wants to get enough information to do his task, and no more. Don't make him read everything. Give him a "quick start" guide, a tear-out quick reference card, graphical icons in the margins that point to key issues, and other devices that will help him get started quickly and easily.

- *Designing the documentation in a vacuum.* Let's face it. You know your own software intimately. Therefore you can't really understand the problems in your documentation. So test it by having a few customers use and review it before making it part of your product. Beta-testing your documentation is as important as beta-testing your software.

---

## Telephone Support: Time Is Money

Let's face it. Today we live in a world where instant gratification is important. Telephone support is the quintessential instant gratifier. Time is money to corporate users; by allowing you to resolve problems immediately, telephone support saves your customer money. The problem is that you cannot provide adequate telephone support to a large customer base if you only have a few knowledgeable people to answer support calls. Nevertheless, telephone support is practically a requirement.

To do an effective job, you usually must provide a dedicated telephone number that will be answered rapidly twelve hours per day (8 a.m. Eastern to 5 p.m. Pacific) by technically knowledgeable people. That costs money. Besides, most of your technically knowledgeable people are already busy on development projects. So you have three alternatives:

1. Put together a structured telephone procedure using current staff.

2. Hire a dedicated telephone support staff.

3. Create a combination of the two—the hybrid staff.

If you decide to use your current staff, you must pull your qualified people from their development projects to share telephone duties throughout the day. You must ensure that, when they are in the customer support role, they give full attention to the task at hand. When they are answering support calls, they must make sure the customer understands that he or she is the most important person, and not a burden that's preventing the developer from doing "important work." Sure, customer problems complicate software development. But without the customer, there would be no development staff.

Consider the following questions before you set up a system:

- How quickly will you handle the call? If you decide all callers must reach a technician within five minutes, you will need more people than if you allow 20 minutes.

- What type of person handles the call? If you allow a receptionist to take down a problem description and then pass it to a technician, your total technical support team can be smaller. However, having trained technicians handle the call immediately promotes higher customer satisfaction.

- Where will calls be handled? If technicians can handle calls in their own offices, they can sometimes handle their regular tasks between calls. However, their other tasks can suffer from lack of dedication.

- How are calls documented? If you require documentation or database entry for each call, you must factor in enough time.

- Is domain knowledge (that is, knowledge of a specific industry or discipline) required? If you sell a CADD product, you may need some people who are trained drafters or designers to understand the work that the customer is doing with the system. On the other hand, if you sell a spreadsheet product, virtually any technically competent person can be trained in the basic uses of the software to be able to trouble-shoot.

With a few exceptions, using a dedicated support staff raises similar issues. The biggest advantage of a dedicated support group, though, is that your support staff doesn't need to be drawn away from other projects, and thus doesn't jeopardize development. In addition, your total staffing requirements may decrease because your support personnel will become very adept at assisting customers, particularly those with the most common problems.

Your best solution may be the hybrid staff: dedicated support staff backed by the developers. The rationale for this is the 80/20 rule: 20% of the problems cause 80% of the calls. This means that you are going to be answering the same small group of questions repeatedly. There is no reason to ask your software developers to do this. They have better ways to spend their time. However, there *will* be calls that only they can answer, so the dedicated support staff needs access to them. This hybrid solution makes sure the tough problems can be dealt with adequately, but doesn't bog down research and development.

## Electronic Support: High Value, Low Cost

E-mail, fax, and bulletin board support lets you address customer issues without the primary staffing concerns of telephone support, because your staff can handle customer calls sequentially while the customer turns his attention elsewhere. The customer sends you a written description of his problem. You devise a solution and send it back. For answers to common questions, you can send prewritten answers by calling them up on screen, adding some personalization, and dropping it in the customer's e-mail box or in your fax queue.

There are several key considerations involved with electronic support:

- Make your electronic support vehicle accessible for your users. For example, if your product is a UNIX-based scientific application, obtain an e-mail address on the Internet. If you have a PC product, consider renting a mailbox on CompuServe or Prodigy. You might even set up your own BBS.

- Make sure that the user knows how to contact you. Publish your fax number, BBS number, or e-mail address and make it easy to find (i.e., in help files; prominently in your documentation; or on stickers that the customer can put on his system or fax machine). In your documentation, list any items that should be submitted to help your support effort. (See Figure 12-1.)

- Devise a procedure for handling support messages, including how often there are picked up, and by whom. Even though you do not need momentary response as you would with telephone support, you are still judged by how quickly you respond. Any user who has requested electronic support can tell you how nice it is to get a response the same day.

Here's a sample form that you might give customers for submitting questions through e-mail or fax: In some cases, you can set up dial-in support procedures where you connect directly to your customer's system to diagnose problems. To make this option viable, the problem must lend itself to remote diagnosis, the user must have a modem, and the user must be willing to let outsiders access his system. Many companies won't allow outside access because it might breach their security or expose them to viruses.

---

### *Sample Support Form*

```
        In order to help us respond quickly, please use the
        following format when requesting support:

1. Your name, company, phone, and fax (or e-mail address).
2. The best time to reach you by telephone (if required).
3. Software name and model and version number.
4. Configuration of your system:
      include brand/model, memory, available disk space, network
      related information, and any memory resident software.
5. Description of the problem.  Please be as specific as
   possible.

   (Helpful information includes what happened, what you did
   prior to problem (sequence of keystrokes or programs),
   whether you have made any system changes recently, when you
   last changed or added software or hardware, and the steps
   that are required for us to reproduce the problem).

When we receive a request by fax or electronic mail, we attempt to
reply within XX hours.  If we have not reached a satisfactory solution
within XX hours, we will send you a confirmation with a time frame for
expected resolution.  Please retransmit your request if you have not
received a reply within XX hours.  State that it is a duplicate request.
```

*FIGURE 12-1: A TYPICAL CUSTOMER SUPPORT FORM*

## Live Support

Even though it is the most costly method, face-to-face support provides the closest link to your customer, and often heightened satisfaction. It can be furnished in the form of on-site fixes of customer software problems, training classes, or update seminars. By connecting your personnel to your customer, you create an atmosphere in which "bonding" can take place. Both parties tend to learn more about the other, which results in better solutions for him, and a stronger ally for you. (He understands better what you must go through to give him service.)

If you sell inexpensive software (anything less than a few thousand dollars), it is impossible to justify on-site repairs of software problems. The financial return is just not there. Consequently, on-site service is generally reserved for customers who spend a lot of money on your software, either by purchasing a large single license, a site license or many individual licenses. In most cases, it has been contracted in advance, or is used as part of an effort to sell additional software to the customer. If you can provide the support without spending the time and money to visit the site, do it.

Some products don't lend themselves to fixes off-site, though. For its first version of DPAM (Distributed Parallel Application Manager), HR Systems provided on-site service because it could not duplicate its customers' computing environments in its lab. A live visit was necessary. In this case, live visits were appropriate because DPAM license fees exceed $100,000. If your pricing structure doesn't support on-site maintenance but customers want it, charge them for it—either by call, by hour, or by monthly support fee.

For most software companies, face-to-face support is more appropriate for training classes or customer seminars (taking place at your own training facility or at the customer's location). If you plan to include a workshop, make sure there are enough stations for each participant. You can use one of several compensation techniques:

- Include training credits with each software license (these credits are actually bundled into the price).

- Charge tuition for each student as a separate item.

- Charge a set amount for the teacher's time.

Whichever technique you use, account for travel cost, facility cost, and equipment cost that you may incur.

### EXAMPLE

AAA Software sells a $150,000 manufacturing software package. Training is typically done at the AAA Corporate Training Center in classes of ten people (often from separate corporations) at a cost of $500 per day per person for the five day class ($2500 per person for the week). AAA Software includes one five day credit with each software package sold. Thus, their revenue is $25,000 per week if their class is full. (We consider the training credits to be training revenue collected in advance.)

### EXAMPLE

BBB Manufacturing Company wants to have their seven people trained at their own site instead of at AAA's Software Training Center. The quote they receive from AAA is $26,000, which represents the amount of revenue that the trainer would have commanded for a one week standard session plus $1000 for his travel expenses. Although the customer pays $8500 more than if they simply sent their seven people to AAA's training center, they save $7000 in travel expenses and their people do not have to leave town. In addition, they may be able to train a few extra people for the same price.

Customer seminars are merely occasional training classes or update meetings for multiple users. The main advantage for you is face-to-face education without the cost of visits to customer sites. Your customers benefit because they can attend your regional seminars without large travel expenditures. All you need to do is hold your meetings in a convenient location (i.e., local customer site, hotel, or field office).

My experience with update seminars has been particularly satisfying. When I first took over a sales territory at Auto-trol, I inherited an angry set of customers who felt they had been receiving inadequate support. By immediately instituting a regional biannual seminar series, we uncovered customer problems and resolved them quickly. Our agenda typically included a software discrepancy discussion, usage tips, details of new releases, and a "gripe session". Our director of customer service, vice president of sales, and other influential Auto-trol officers participated, giving our users direct access to decision makers. Satisfaction levels rose dramatically (as did revenue).

There are many productive ways to use seminars. MacNeal-Schwendler, for instance, holds seminars in Germany, Italy, Japan, Israel, and several U.S. locations to train users in MSC/NASTRAN basics, advanced techniques, and application of MSC products to user problems (i.e., thermal or aeroelastic analysis). Users pay fees to attend.

Another cost-effective use of live personnel time is the "train-the-trainer" class, at which one representative from each customer site learns about the product and receives tips on how to conduct his own corporate classes. Your customers are adequately trained without the expense of sending many people out for training. In addition, the local trainer can conduct more classes to train new hires.

## Providing Support Through Affiliates

If you sell through VAR's or OEM's, you may be able to shift some or all of the support burden to them. While your VAR or OEM furnishes direct service to your end user, you provide backup support and training for the VAR or OEM. This is actually a common practice.

- Microsoft Windows is commonly supported by computer companies that package Windows with their systems.

- Swanson Analysis Systems, Inc. works with a network of Ansys Support Distributors (independent companies) that sell and support Swanson's Ansys product.

- Sun Microsystems contracts to Bell Atlantic to do much of their support.

- Novell users are often supported by the VAR from whom they purchased the Novell product.

- In addition to telephone, fax, bulletin board, and field support, WordPerfect has an accrediting process for independent instructors.

To make this arrangement practical, incentives must exist for your VAR or OEM. The incentives can range from a revenue-sharing agreement to the ability for the VAR or OEM to charge the end user for the support. In a limited number of cases, the VAR or OEM is willing to do the support because having your product complements other products that they sell.

## Cooperative Support Through User Groups

Developing a user group is a powerful way to support your entire user base. The main idea of the user group is to empower your users to build their own cooperative support organization. Effective user groups conduct annual (or semi-annual) conferences, distribute newsletters, and trade tips about product use. Officers are often selected by the user base on a one vote per license (or per site) basis and act as coordinators of the groups and liaisons to your company.

If your users haven't started one, cultivate it yourself. First solicit opinions from your users as to what the user group should do. Then have them nominate officers. Work with the officers to develop the initial programs (i.e., conference, newsletter, seminars, . . . ) and help them execute the premier of each. After a year or so, bow out so the users can take over. You will still supply instructors and speakers for the group's seminars and conferences, articles for its newsletters, and money to supplement its membership dues and fees for programs. However, when the group starts to govern itself, you give up control. This works well for both parties. If you maintain a good working relationship, you will maintain contact with an excellent source of market feedback, but you won't have to be involved in day-to-day activities. Your users gain a strong voice in the product and support direction of your company. Working together as partners, you meet your mutual goals.

A word of caution: once you empower your users, you relinquish some control forever. Once they start to control their own destinies, they will want to continue to do so. That's not necessarily bad. A strong user base is always good for both sides. The issues arise if your user group wants to move in one direction, and you want to move in another. For instance, your users might want to bring similar (competing) products into their trade fairs, and you want them to show yours exclusively. Be ready to negotiate.

Working with a user group is a give-and-take proposition. You contribute speakers, money, and education. Your users provide references, product ideas, and cheerleading support. By helping organize a strong user group, your company and product end up stronger because you are forced to answer to the market. Borland International is among those companies that have proven most adept at spreading their gospel via user groups. In fact, Borland even conducts a yearly retreat to which it invites the presidents of various independent user groups. The retreats energize the presidents, who return to their own groups with additional information about Borland products.

## The Training Aftermarket

If your product becomes the next software blockbuster, don't be surprised if other companies produce training packages or seminars for your users. Personal Training Systems (PTS), for instance, produces audio cassette tutorials for major microcomputer software that include disk-based exercises. A dozen more companies provide videotape training. Dun and Bradstreet and other companies have seminar tours that reach most large and medium-size cities. Since these companies derive their revenues from student fees or sales of their packages, they typically gravitate towards software packages with large installed bases (i.e., WordPerfect, Lotus 1-2-3, MS-Word for Windows).

The training aftermarket can augment your own training. But don't rely on aftermarket suppliers, because you have no control over them. If they do not do a good job, or if they stop supporting your product, your customer satisfaction will decrease.

# *Product Characteristics Determine Support Methods*

Complex products have more modules, more lines of code, and often more applications, therefore more bugs, more workarounds, and additional complexity in the user interface. In short, a complex product can be a support nightmare. To keep your customers satisfied, you need a strong quality control program that cleans up your software before it goes into general distribution.

You will probably also need to resolve many customer problems. Therefore, you should have well-organized procedures to take customer calls and send feedback to your development staff. In addition, have a quick method to reference and distribute information about known problems.

## Clarifying Your User's Support Needs

Not every software company deals with the same types of users. How you deal with yours depends on their level of sophistication.

Unsophisticated end users (e.g., somebody who is computer shy) need to be treated differently than advanced users. The unsophisticated user often refuses to try new things without permission for fear of "breaking" the system, therefore clogging telephone lines by calling you for help. (He's usually averse to using e-mail and bulletin boards.) Often, all he needs is somebody to answer a simple question, show him where to look in your documentation, or patiently walk him through his problem.

A sophisticated user, on the other hand, dives right in, often stretching your product by trying to apply it to a situation that you didn't envision. You need to help these users find ways to use your product as they wish—even if you feel that they are asking your product to do more than they have a right to expect. Sophisticated users are looked upon as the "experts" by the corporate community. They affect many purchase decisions. If you gain these users as allies, they will steer many purchases in your direction.

Your sophisticated users are perfect conduits to the market, providing you with valuable market feedback. When a sophisticated user makes a suggestion, evaluate its merit. It may provide the new capability that opens up a new market for you or provides a competitive edge.

## Complying With Standards

To reduce your support requirements, write your software in compliance with generally accepted standards, such as Microsoft Windows, X Windows, or Motif. First, many users are already familiar with the standard, making it easier for them to learn and use your product. Second, you can take advantage of common tools instead of reinventing your own. For instance, Microsoft Windows provides printer drivers for the most common PC printers. You can use Microsoft's drivers instead of writing your own. In addition to easing your support burden, you reduce your development time.

# *Practices That Work for You and Your Customers*

Question: *How many software engineers does it take to screw in a light bulb?*

Answer: *None. It's a hardware problem.*

Don't point your finger at other vendors. When a customer calls for help, he does not want to be told that it's not your problem, that it's the fault of hardware (or a conflicting software package) from the vendor. He does not want to be told to call someone else. If the customer cannot run your software properly, it is your problem, even if it's not your fault. Help him fix it. If necessary, call the other vendor yourself to work out a solution. You gain a customer for life. Who knows, the other vendor may become a marketing partner too.

There are other policies and practices that increase satisfaction, as well:

- *Always treat your customers courteously.* There is no excuse for bad attitudes or rudeness when dealing with customers. This goes for face-to-face, written or telephone contact. Did you know that the person on the other end of the line can usually tell if you're smiling when you talk with him? So smile. Your customer is more likely to smile back.

- *Meet (or BEAT!) customer expectations.* When you promise something, deliver. Whether it's e-mail or fax response within a specific number of hours or a phone response to a user question, make it happen in a timely fashion. If you won't make the commitment, tell your customer as soon as you realize it. Don't make him wait until the last minute; you will only destroy the goodwill that you have built. Dell has built a reputation on delighting customers. I know several customers who have abandoned Gateway 2000 to do business with Dell because Gateway failed to deliver on promised support.

- *Your customers get number one priority.* Answer phones promptly. Have adequate support staff available for peak demand. Don't hide behind secretaries or voice mail. If you must use either to handle calls, make sure you set the customer's expectation level at that time and that you call him back promptly. If you handle many calls, make sure that your telephone system can handle the volume.

- *Keep in touch.* Use your customer database to send periodical newsletters, interim updates with bug fixes, or support databases. Don't let them forget you.

- *Define a formal method of incorporating features, fixes, and suggestions from users.* Receiving the same suggestions from several customers should tell you something. Tally and track suggestions so you can figure out the best ways to enhance your product and customer service.

In addition, make sure that your own staff has the right resources available to provide the high-caliber support you want them to provide. They need access to systems to duplicate problems. If you license source code or if you make frequent changes to your product, you may need to provide source code to your support staff as well as an open line to the developers.

Many customers have difficulty describing their situations, making it tougher for your staff to help them. In addition, there is usually no visual communications to aid them. So when choosing your support staff, choose people with excellent communication skills, patience, and non-competitive personalities.

They should be people who can learn quickly, gauge a customer's mood, and go the extra mile to resolve the problem. Once they are on board, train them, reward them for successes, and integrate them with the other aspects of your business. Remember, they talk to your customers frequently and are great sources of market feedback.

## Measuring Your Success

One of the most important aspects of customer satisfaction is knowing whether your customer is satisfied. While there is a large amount of subjectivity to it, it can actually be measured in several ways. First, by asking your customer. Second, by keeping your own statistics.

Sending out questionnaires on an occasional basis (i.e., every six months) to a subset of your customer base will help you put together empirical evidence of your ranking. Don't change your questionnaire drastically from period to period; you will want to use the previous period as a benchmark for current results. Make the questionnaires easy to read and answer. Ask whether the training, documentation, and support are adequate. Ask what they like best and dislike most about your product. Ask for suggestions. If your aim is to enhance your post sales support, you can send out a separate, targeted questionnaire to people who have recently received help on your help line. It doesn't hurt to send out generic questionnaires to customers of several competing products to find out how you rank compared to them. However, it is usually best not to identify your company when you send out an industry-wide survey.

Whenever you have customers together—at training classes, seminars, or trade shows—ask them the questions or give them the survey to fill out. The key is to find ways to extract accurate information.

Finally, keep statistics related to your bugs, questions, and responses. Here are a few statistics that are used widely:

*Mean Time To Resolution:*
> The average time a customer must wait to obtain a solution. It shows how quickly you can solve a customer problem.

$$MTTR = \sum_{calls} \frac{(time\ call\ closed) - (time\ call\ opened)}{(number\ of\ calls)}$$

*Mean Time To Isolate:*

The average time it takes to isolate a detected problem so that it can be fixed. It indicates how easy it is to fix a problem.

$$MTTI = \sum_{calls} \frac{(time\ problem\ found) - (time\ call\ opened)}{(number\ of\ calls)}$$

Chart your statistics and post them them internally so your support staff can see how they are doing. Keep them aware of the progress. Make them part of the process and give them credit for the success.

## Don't Rest on Your Laurels

Creating a delighted customer base is an ongoing effort. And that's fine because when you do delight your users everybody wins. Your users can take advantage of all that your product has to offer while they promote your growth in good times and sustain your company during bad times. Your relationship with your customers is truly give-and-take.

# Getting Your Product Out the Door

Let's assume that you have been developing your product for a number of months, or even years. You may have even announced it already. In a short time, you will be ready to deliver it. It's time to put on another hat, that of production manager. You might think that production sounds simple if you have never been involved in software distribution: the buyer hands his money to the seller, and the seller hands over a diskette. At worst, you have to copy a few diskettes—not a big job. But it's not as simple as it looks. Before the product moves successfully from your warehouse to the customer, you must perform many tasks: these are traditionally called "production" and "order entry" or "fulfillment." If any step fails, you will lose sales or create unhappy customers. In this chapter, you start as the production manager, then manage order processing.

## *Goals of Production and Order Processing*

Your key production and order processing goals are:

1.  Ensure that the delivered product meets your quality criteria.

2.  Minimize the amount of time it takes to fill each order.

3.  Minimize the amount of resources you use in the process.

4.  Minimize out-of pocket costs.

5.  Collect valuable information about the customer.

The first two goals are key to satisfying your customer. Goals three and four aim to maximize profit. The fifth goal is for ongoing communications with your customers.

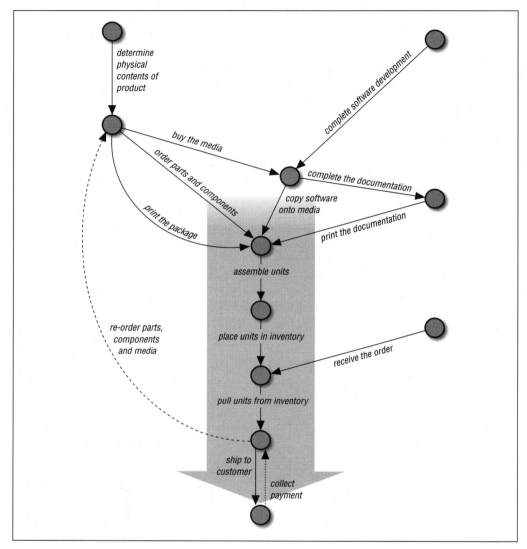

***FIGURE 13-1:*** *BASIC PRODUCTION AND FULFILLMENT ACTIVITIES*

To reach these goals, you conduct two distinct procedures: readying the product for release (determining what goes in, determining how many you need, ordering or producing the component parts, assembling and stocking the product) and processing orders (order entry, delivery, adjusting inventory, registering the user). Let's look at each task in depth.

# *Determining What Goes In*

Your marketing, planning, and product development teams have already answered many basic production questions. At this stage, you should be able to answer questions like: What platforms will the software run on? How should packaging be used to attract buyers? How big will the program be? Now, you must incorporate the answers into a new set of questions that further define your production requirements:

- Do I need to buy 3.5" floppies, 5.25" floppies, 8 mm tape, CD-ROMs, other media, or a combination of the above?

- How many diskettes will be in each package?

- Will I include documentation? If so, will it be paper or electronic? How many manuals will I need? How many pages? What are the printing requirements?

- What kind of packaging needs to be produced? Plastic clamshell, printed cardboard, vinyl, or heavy paper? What size? What type of printing? Does it need a protective "shrinkwrap" plastic cover?

- Is there anything else that needs to be in the box?

As you answer these questions, get input from your marketing, customer service, and development directors. Development influences several of the answers (such as how many disks, and how they are arranged); marketing is concerned about the physical characteristics of your product's package (appearance, size) and how it affects sales.

Once you have carefully defined the product to be shipped and decided how to package it, you need to create "bills of materials" (BOMs). The first step in this process is usually to assign a marketing part number (often called an SKU or stock-keeping unit number) for each product you will sell. For instance, your HP-UX version may have SKU 0001; your Solaris tape version, SKU 0002; your Solaris CD-ROM version, SKU 0003; your DOS/3.5" diskette version, SKU 0004; your DOS/5.25" diskette version, SKU 0005; and your DOS/3.5" competitive upgrade version, SKU 0006. You then define the parts of your BOM for each SKU by determining the specs, part numbers, and quantity for each item that will be included in the SKU.

Note that the SKU and the part number are NOT the same. (This is a very easy mistake to make.) The SKU is something that a customer can order. The part number refers to an individual piece of your product. Here's an example of how SKUs might map into your sets of part numbers:

```
SKU 001:  HP version of product, which consists of:
     pn 001-01-001   generic binder
     pn 001-01-002   generic warranty card
     pn 001-02-001   HP cover insert
     pn 010-02-001   HP tape

SKU 002:  Sun version of product, which consists of:
     pn 001-01-001   generic binder
     pn 001-01-002   generic warranty card
     pn 001-03-001   Sun cover insert
     pn 010-03-001   Sun CD-ROM
```

To make things easier to track, create some kind of order to your part numbers. In this example, the first three digits represent the kind of thing (packaging=001, software media=010); the second two digits represent target systems (01=generic, 02=HP, 03=Sun); the last two represent a specific item.

## Cross-discipline Issues in Production

Other issues determine how you will assemble your product and how much each unit will cost. Examine these issues to decrease your cost of production:

* What needs to be included to make installation foolproof? (Understanding this question decreases the number of units returned.)

* Can the software be compressed to fit on fewer diskettes? (Fewer diskettes decrease production costs.)

* Package design: four color, two color, or black and white? Photos? (Package design determines production cost, the perception of the product by the market, and the lead time for ordering printed parts.)

* How quickly will a new or interim release happen? (Your release schedule determines order quantities and procedures.)

## Incorporating Printed Materials

Once you have determined what should be in each package, you can determine what you need to order (diskettes, tapes, clam-shells, envelopes, ... etc.) or print (labels, documentation, package face, warranty/registration card, license agreement, inserts).

Printing is among your highest variable cost for your finished product. Open any off-the-shelf software package and you will find several pounds of printed material and a few ounces of software. Corel Draw 3.0, for instance, includes approximately 1000 pages of printed material (some of it in color) with its compact disk and eleven floppies.

You must specify your printing requirements in detail, including how many colors, size and type of paper, and print quantity, as well as how you want it cut, folded, scored, and bound. Although there are print shops that can handle most of your printing, you might use different shops for different parts of your product. A quick printer may do your labels; a commercial printer, your documentation or inserts; and a screen printer, your shell.

In virtually every instance, you supply the printer with your instructions and camera-ready art work. Some printers can accept your art work in computer readable format. If you want to provide it electronically, be ready to submit it in EPS (Encapsulated Postscript) or another format that can be used by Macintosh-based pre-press packages.

The cost of printing depends on the type and size of the stock, number of colors, whether the art work bleeds off the side of the stock, whether it includes photographs, how many additional operations need to be done (cut, fold, score . . . ), whether there are any special processes (custom die-cut, coatings), and the quantity you have printed in a single print run. When you ask for price quotations, have them quote several quantities so you know the optimum quantity to order. It may differ for each printed item.

Additionally, the length of time it takes to complete your printing job depends on how many operations the printer must perform. He needs a full day to print each side of the stock to allow drying. Cutting, folding, and scoring operations cannot be performed until the ink is dry or you risk smudging the ink. That still doesn't mean it will only take a few days to complete your job. It may take the printer days to set up your job, and he'll schedule it according to his other work. You may have to wait for other orders to finish before yours gets to the front of the queue. Large manuals, for instance, may take a month.

Documentation is normally done by commercial printers. However, if you are only printing a small quantity, you might be able to do it yourself, either by laser printer or xerographic copy. Doing it internally is not cheap (approximate three to six cents for an 8.5" × 11" page), but it does not entail the start up overhead of a larger print run. It also ties up your people, systems, and printers, and has a home-made look. Generally, if you will be printing more than 100 manuals in a run, offset printing is a better idea. If you must do extremely small quantities, consider using the local copy shop instead of doing them yourself. Also, print up a nice two-color cover on a heavier stock.

There are also service bureaus that do electronic printing on high-speed devices such as Xerox Docutech machines. This is an excellent alternative if you prefer many small quantity runs (i.e., if your document comes in several varieties for several platforms). It reduces your internal bottlenecks as well as the large up-front cost of large print runs.

# Ordering and Producing Components

Since the shippable product is the sum of its parts, a product with one part missing cannot be sold. Therefore, it is absolutely essential to give your suppliers enough lead time so they can fill your order before you run out of stock. To ease the burden of ordering parts (purchased or printed) you may want to use an MRP (Material Requirements Planning) system. Your MRP software consists of a "parts number" module into which you load a unique identifier for each part (part 0001 for tech manual, part 0002 for warranty card, part 0003 for diskette 1, etc.), and a bill of materials module that associates each part with the materials and quantity that are needed to make the part (i.e., each diskette needs one diskette, one label, and the loaded software). On some predetermined schedule (i.e., monthly), you enter the amount of each item that you have in the warehouse—or in your back room, if you're small enough—as well as the expected demand for your product. The MRP system "explodes" your product by giving you a listing of its component parts, checking the need for each part against the current inventory and parts on order, then setting an order schedule to make sure you have all parts in hand when you need them. For MRP to be useful, each component (disk, book, insert, etc.) must have a unique identifier (i.e., a part number) associated with it.

# Determining How Many Units To Stock

According to production experts, you should keep enough inventory to meet demand, plus a small buffer stock to meet unexpected excess demand. Theoretically, as you order more parts (including printed material, which can be treated as parts), your per unit purchase price goes down, but your carrying costs go up. This is represented graphically in Figure 13-2.

Carrying costs and purchasing/production costs are based on quantity. Carrying costs include the cost of money, risk of obsolescence, shrinkage, cost of space, and the cost of taking inventory. Purchasing and production costs include cost of parts, assembly time, parts order processing, and receiving costs.

In the computer industry, the cost of carrying inventory is small because the variable cost per unit is small. The majority of your costs are in development and marketing. Especially in times of low interest rates, the carrying cost component is negligible compared to other issues.

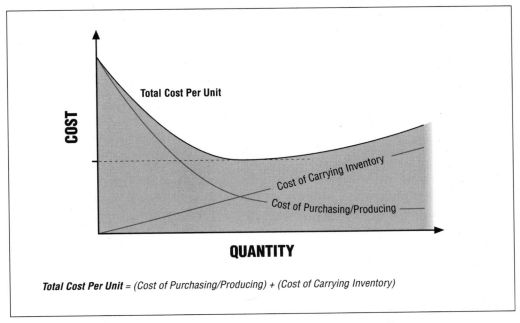

*Total Cost Per Unit* = (Cost of Purchasing/Producing) + (Cost of Carrying Inventory)

**FIGURE 13-2:** FINDING THE OPTIMAL PRODUCTION LEVEL

To make it clearer how these relate, see the following example. I have simplified "carrying cost" by saying that it's approximately the cost of money (i.e., the amount you could make if you invested the money elsewhere). Here are our initial assumptions about our product:

| | |
|---|---|
| Average monthly sales volume | 1,000 units |
| Printing Lead Time | 1 month |
| Parts Order Lead Time | .75 month (3 wks) |
| Printing Lead Time | .5 month (2 wks) |
| Unit Price | $50.00 |
| Unit Variable Cost | $15.00 |
| Carrying costs (interest) | 8% |

Let's start by comparing some simple scenarios:

| Ordering PATTERN | Average amount OF INVENTORY | Average cost OF INVENTORY | Average monthly COST OF HOLDING | Total annual cost OF HOLDING |
|---|---|---|---|---|
| 1000/mo. | 500 | $ 7500 | **$ 50** | $ 600 |
| 2000/2 mo. | 1000 | $15,000 | **$ 75** | $ 900 |
| 3000/3 mo. | 1500 | $22,500 | **$100** | $1200 |
| 4000/4 mo. | 2000 | $30,000 | **$125** | $1500 |

If you order 4000 units every four months (instead of 1000 per month) for a one year period, your total additional holding cost is $900. Contrast that with a typical economies of scale in printing and ordering parts.[*]

| Order QTY | Cost per UNIT | Total COST/1000 | Savings PER THOUSAND |
|---|---|---|---|
| 1000 | $15 | $15,000 | 0 |
| 2000 | $14 | $14,000 | $1000 |
| 3000 | $12 | $12,000 | $3000 |
| 4000 | $10 | $10,000 | $5000 |

By utilizing purchasing economies of scale, you can realize a significant savings. In our example, where we're selling roughly 12,000 units per year, ordering in quantities of 4000 yields a total annual savings of $60,000 ($5000 for every thousand units you buy). Economies of scale are very heavily in your favor because your carrying costs are relatively low.

Small companies might not be able to reach the optimal order quantity because they may not have enough cash to purchase enough inventory, or because demand is never great enough. For instance, printing prices decrease dramatically when you increase the number of copies. But if your sales volume is relatively small, you may not be able to take advantage of the most important discounts. It would be foolhardy to purchase thousands of printed pieces that you will never use. As you become larger, the theory gains relevance.

For small software companies, greater emphasis should be placed on how many units you expect to sell and how much money you have. You obviously want to meet customer demand, but your production rate may be constrained by your cash flow. It doesn't make sense to jeopardize your entire business to save a few dollars of variable cost. If the difference in cost means the difference

[*] Savings are based on quantity prices for printing and parts. Your actual costs will probably differ.

between a profit and loss, rethink whether you are in the right part of the market; if your profit projections are that sensitive, there's something wrong.

Not having enough inventory to fulfill demand is also costly. For each unit that you cannot ship, you lose a sale (or even a long-term customer). Your "opportunity cost" is equal to your revenue lost minus the cost of purchasing the unit. Rarely do you have a chance to gain it back—your buyer will simply purchase a competing product elsewhere.

In our example, if sales in June accelerate to 1500 units, and you are only ordering 1000 units per month, you will lose 500 sales when you run out of stock. This corresponds to a financial loss of $17,500 (500 units at $35 each). With larger ordering quantities, you may not lose any sales.

To prevent shortages, act as if demand is not identical from month to month. Then stock enough units to satisfy the demands based on high-end estimates. This extra inventory is called "buffer stock," and is your key weapon against losing sales due to underestimating of demand.

Now that you know how to order the stock, let's look at four scenarios based on our previous example. The key goal is to minimize your total cost of production and inventory by (1) decreasing the carry costs, (2) decreasing the unit production costs, and (3) decreasing the out-of-stock potential and the associated out-of-stock cost. You start with the following questions:

- How many units do you expect to sell during the period?

- How much money will you lose if you do not have a unit available for shipment?

- What kinds of savings can you achieve by ordering larger quantities?

- Can you save by assembling your units in larger quantities?

After answering the questions, plug your answers into a matrix to calculate your lowest total cost scenario. If you use a spreadsheet, you will be able to change scenarios and understand the implications of each change. Tables 13-1 and 13-2 compare two different ordering patterns; 13-3 and 13-4 compare different demand levels.

Demand is rarely even. So, when you produce your charts, take into account the way that your demand will vary due to trade shows, heavy demand season, or advertising.

**TABLE 13-1:** *DEMAND = 1000/MONTH; ORDER QTY = 1000/MONTH**

|  | Jan | Feb | Mar | Apr | May | Jun |
|---|---|---|---|---|---|---|
| **DEMAND** (IN UNITS) | 1000 | 1000 | 1000 | 1000 | 1000 | 1000 |
| **ORIGINAL # OF UNITS IN STOCK** | 1000 | 1000 | 1000 | 1000 | 1000 | 1000 |
| **AVERAGE INVENTORY DURING MONTH** | 500 | 500 | 500 | 500 | 500 | 500 |
| **COST OF CARRYING** | 50 | 50 | 50 | 50 | 50 | 50 |
| **COST OF PARTS** | 15,000 | 15,000 | 15,000 | 15,000 | 15,000 | 15,000 |
| **COST OF LOST SALES** | 0 | 0 | 0 | 0 | 0 | 0 |
| **TOTAL COSTS PER MONTH** | 15,050 | 15,050 | 15,050 | 15,050 | 15,050 | 15,050 |

* Expected Production/Opportunity Cost (Sum of months): $90,300

**TABLE 13-2:** *DEMAND = 1000/MONTH; ORDER QTY = 2000/TWO MONTHS**

|  | Jan | Feb | Mar | Apr | May | Jun |
|---|---|---|---|---|---|---|
| **DEMAND (IN UNITS)** | 1000 | 1000 | 1000 | 1000 | 1000 | 1000 |
| **ORIGINAL # OF UNITS IN STOCK** | 2000 | 1000 | 2000 | 1000 | 2000 | 1000 |
| **AVERAGE INVENTORY DURING MONTH** | 1500 | 500 | 1500 | 500 | 1500 | 500 |
| **COST OF CARRYING** | 140 | 50 | 140 | 50 | 140 | 50 |
| **COST OF PARTS** | 28,000 | 0 | 28,000 | 0 | 28,000 | 0 |
| **COST OF LOST SALES** | 0 | 0 | 0 | 0 | 0 | 0 |
| **TOTAL COSTS PER MONTH** | 28,140 | 50 | 28,140 | 50 | 28,140 | 50 |

* Expected Production/Opportunity Cost (Sum of months): $84,570

By increasing our monthly order, we increased the carrying cost, but we also reduced the parts cost for a total savings of about $6000. Now let's see what happens when demand increases:[*]

---

[*] For simplicity, we assume that since you are shipping all you can make, you will ship them evenly throughout the month. When demand exceeds supply, you would actually fill backorders (if any) immediately, then satisfy this month's orders. Your average inventory under these conditions would become less than 500 units. In fact, it would decrease on a monthly basis until it reaches zero—at which point, you're shipping the units as soon as you receive them.

**TABLE 13-3:** *DEMAND = 1200/MONTH; ORDER QTY = 1000/MONTH**\*

|  | Jan | Feb | Mar | Apr | May | Jun |
|---|---|---|---|---|---|---|
| **DEMAND (IN UNITS)** | 1200 | 1200 | 1200 | 1200 | 1200 | 1200 |
| **ORIGINAL # OF UNITS IN STOCK** | 1000 | 1000 | 1000 | 1000 | 1000 | 1000 |
| **AVERAGE INVENTORY DURING MONTH** | 500 | 500 | 500 | 500 | 500 | 500 |
| **COST OF CARRYING** | 50 | 50 | 50 | 50 | 50 | 50 |
| **COST OF PARTS** | 15,000 | 15,000 | 15,000 | 15,000 | 15,000 | 15,000 |
| **COST OF LOST SALES** | 7000 | 7000 | 7000 | 7000 | 7000 | 7000 |
| **TOTAL COSTS PER MONTH** | 22,050 | 22,050 | 22,050 | 22,050 | 22,050 | 22,050 |

\* Expected Production/Opportunity Cost (Sum of months): $132,300

The cost is much higher, mostly because of the sales you're losing.

**TABLE 13-4:** *DEMAND = 1200/MONTH; ORDER QTY = 2000/TWO MONTHS**\*

|  | Jan | Feb | Mar | Apr | May | Jun |
|---|---|---|---|---|---|---|
| **DEMAND (IN UNITS)** | 1200 | 1200 | 1200 | 1200 | 1200 | 1200 |
| **ORIGINAL # OF UNITS IN STOCK** | 2000 | 800 | 2000 | 800 | 2000 | 800 |
| **AVERAGE INVENTORY DURING MONTH** | 1400 | 533 | 1400 | 533 | 1400 | 533 |
| **COST OF CARRYING** | 140 | 50 | 140 | 50 | 140 | 50 |
| **COST OF PARTS** | 28,000 | 0 | 28,000 | 0 | 28,000 | 15,000 |
| **COST OF LOST SALES** | 0 | 14,400 | 0 | 14,400 | 0 | 14,400 |
| **TOTAL COSTS PER MONTH** | 28,130 | 14,450 | 28,130 | 14,450 | 28,130 | 14,450 |

\* Expected Production/Opportunity Cost (Sum of months): $127,740

If you would prefer to solve a single equation instead of filling in the charts, minimize:

$$\sum_{months} \left( \frac{interest}{12} \times cost \times \frac{stock + (stock - satisfied)}{2} + cost \times quantity + unsatisfied \times (revenue - cost) \right)$$

The terms in the previous equation are:

*interest*   is the "cost of money," expressed as an annual interest rate.

*cost*   is your purchase cost (manufacturing cost, assembly, etc.) per unit.

*demand*   is the number of units you can sell in a month, assuming that you have enough inventory.

*stock*   is your inventory at the start of the month. This equals the inventory at the end of the previous month plus the amount you order (*quantity*), if any.

*satisfied*   is the satisfied demand (number of units you sell), per month. *satisfied* and *demand* should be equivalent, unless you run out of stock; so we can say:

$$satisfied = \begin{cases} demand & \text{if } demand \leq stock \\ stock & \text{if } demand > stock \end{cases}$$

*unsatisfied*   is the "unsatisfied demand" (units not sold because of insufficient stock).

$$unsatisfied = \begin{cases} 0 & \text{if } demand \leq stock \\ demand - stock & \text{if } demand > stock \end{cases}$$

*revenue*   is the amount of money you receive for each unit.

*quantity*   is the number of units you purchase in the month.

It's worth noting that *stock-satisfied* is the inventory at the end of the month; so

$$\frac{stock + (stock - satisfied)}{2}$$

is your average inventory, over the entire month, assuming that sales are evenly distributed through the month. Another simplifying assumption in these formulas, and in the tables, is that "unsatisfied demand" is simply lost. In the real world, you would take some backorders, and ship these units when you have more stock. However, if you are in a competitive market, many customers will just buy from your competitor, rather than wait for your shipment. The number of backorders will be relatively small.

While solving the single equation simplifies the procedure, it offers less insight into stocking levels and cash flows, especially if demand changes over time.

## When You Have Multiple Products

If you support more than one operating systems or platform type, your inventory challenge is even bigger. A customer ordering software for his Sun won't be satisfied if you send him a copy on an HP tape. A DOS user might only have one type of floppy diskette drive. You can't send a 3.5" diskette version to load through a 5.25" drive. But you don't want to keep huge inventory levels of each type.

Again, estimate demand, but this time estimate it for each type of software. Then, based on your costs of carrying, parts, and losing sales, determine whether to:

1.  Combine products into one package: 3.5" and 5.25" floppies in a single box for DOS systems, TAR tapes with common manuals for several UNIX platforms, Windows and DOS versions together, etc.

2.  Stock totally separate inventory for each platform type.

3.  Assemble your product at the time of order, side-stepping the controversy completely. This raises other issues, like whether you can get the product to the customer quickly enough, and whether you have enough of each component.

Again, your cost structure leads your actions. If your product can be shipped on a single floppy diskette, putting both sizes in the box is probably inexpensive. If your product requires twenty, it may be better to separate them.

## *Assembling Your Product*

If you're like most software developers, your attitude towards assembly is probably something like this: "Assembly? I'm shipping software, not lawn mowers." But that's absolutely wrong. Although to you, your product looks like some files on a floppy disk, with a manual—something that hardly needs to be "assembled"—someone still has to take the floppy disk, put the label on it, stick it in a pocket in the binder, etc. Assembly is relatively simple compared to assembling a lawn mower or a dishwasher, but it's not something you can ignore.

How you assemble your product depends on how many pieces you have and how many you need to assemble. If you only sell two per month, assemble them with your spare resources. If you sell thousands per month, use dedicated people, or outsource assembly altogether. You may be able to find a company to assemble it for less than you can.

In-house assembly is easier, quicker, and less costly if you can assemble the product in advance so you can pull it off the shelf when the customer orders it. In most cases, you have already paid for the parts and they are sitting on the shelf anyway. You might as well have them sitting in units ready to ship. If certain parts are common to multiple SKUs, you can often assemble the common portions into almost-finished units that can quickly be completed when you know exactly how much you need of each particular product. For example, you might assemble a box, a binder with documentation, warranty cards, and business reply cards in advance; at the last minute, you slip in the software media (different for different platforms you support) and installation notes for that particular platform. With a procedure like this, you can ship quickly and with minimal effort; you also decrease the total inventory you keep on hand, since you don't have to stock as many of the common parts.

However, if you do assembly in-house, don't distract your development or marketing staffs by asking them to do it. They probably won't be happy about putting diskettes in boxes—and they will cost you a lot more than a few temporary employees would have.

## Putting Your Software on Disk or Tape

When your product development is finished, your technical team will have a *final* copy that can be designated "Release 1.0". You should immediately make a single master disk (or tape) and a backup. Then label them both uniquely.[*] The Master Disk is the one—and only one—that will be used to copy onto a shippable product. The backup will be whisked away and locked up for safekeeping. I know this step seems simple, but it is often overlooked, and, as a result, can account for confusion, leading to customer support problems and customer dissatisfaction. Setting up strict procedures prevents you from making foolish mistakes. It's just not smart to ship an old revision of your product with your most current (non-compatible) documentation. Nor do you want to send out anything other than your best work. When you release a new version, the older disks should be conspicuously labeled as an old version, and your new single Master Set should be used exclusively. Assign a new SKU, change the bill of material to reflect the new version, and purge your obsolete inventory.

## Duplicating Your Software

Duplicating your software is a time-consuming task that should be approached with care. If you are selling custom products to select customers, the process is straightforward because you can probably make each customer copy at shipment time. However, if you sell large quantities, whether on diskette, tape, or CD, the burden of software duplication can be great. There are three ways to handle duplication:

---

* The master disk might say something like:

```
MASTER DISK, Joe's Equation Editor
Release 1.0, 1-5-94, 11:30 AM
Disk 1 of 5
```

The backup would have all of the same plus "Backup Copy."

1. Duplicate the software yourself using your own time and development systems.

2. Obtain automated devices to do the task for you.

3. Outsource duplication.

Although duplicating the software yourself sounds attractively inexpensive, it is rarely appropriate; you usually end up diverting your staff from other important business and slowing down every other part of your company. It seems simple: you copy the software onto the media and label it. But if your software takes several diskettes, the process bogs down. In addition, the herky-jerky motion of installing the media, copying, de-installing, labeling, and installing a new one keeps you from getting any other productive work done and ties up your systems. If you must duplicate your software internally, use an inexpensive temporary employee instead of your expensive technical staff.

I learned this the hard way. A number of years ago, I suggested that my company distribute demo disks to our sales force so they could give them to prospects. It seemed like a simple task at the time. We had 15 salespeople, and I wanted to give them each ten copies. Since the volume was low, I decided to do it in my spare time on my desktop system. The preprinted labels and floppies arrived and I inserted them into my machine only to realize that each diskette had to be formatted. This took several hours. Then the information was copied onto the floppy from my system. The entire process took a full day and a half from my schedule. And I only produced 150 diskettes! Imagine how much time it would have taken if my software had required three diskettes each, or if I had to send out 1000 demos. Self production may be necessary when you're starting up and shipping only small quantities; however, it quickly becomes unwieldy as your volume increases.

For larger quantities, you're better off using a machine that does unattended disk duplication. It reduces your labor by 90% and is more reliable than hand duplicating. And machines are fast; they format and duplicate several hundred diskettes per hour. Some even label your disk. Of course, you must have the volume to justify the investment in such a device.

The best choice for most small companies is to outsource the entire process to third parties who have the unattended duplicating machines. While the cost per copy may be somewhat higher, you do not need to invest in the machines yourself, saving valuable capital resources. To find duplication machines or services, attend COMDEX or look in the back section of major computer industry magazines.

# *Processing Your Orders*

The day has finally arrived—your product is being released. Your development team breathes a collective heavy sigh and pats one another on the back for a job well done. Scores of shrinkwrapped cardboard boxes line the shelves of your warehouse, each with a copy of your software. At long last, you will be paid for your effort.

Your eyes are glued to the door in anticipation of the postman delivering your first mail orders, while you hover over the telephone, hand poised over the handset, ready to accept the first phone order ... "RING!!!" The order is placed and more wheels are set in motion:

1. Your order entry person sends the order to accounting, who checks the credit of the customer to make sure he can pay for the order. (You can set a minimum threshold, below which you will not check credit, say $50 or $100.)

2. The order is accepted by accounting.

3. The manifest is put together and the product is pulled from inventory.

4. The shipping information is sent to the shipping department, who sends the items to the customer by the appropriate shipping method.

5. The inventory is adjusted to account for the purchases.

6. If your inventory reaches your predetermined reorder point, your team assembles and packages additional units, and parts are reordered.

"Whoa!" you say. "This sounds like something from a Fortune 500 company; do I really need it for my one-product company?" Yes, you do. A small company is really no different from a large one in this respect. You have to accomplish the same result, so you must go through the same steps: the customer must receive his product; you must receive your payment and be ready to fill your next order. The only difference between large and small companies in this respect is that more orders are processed in the large company, so more people are involved. In a small company, a single person may be able to receive the order, check the customer's credit, pull the product off the shelf, and send it out.

## Taking Orders

It's important to make it easy for your customer to buy from you. This may mean you accept orders by telephone, mail, fax, or e-mail. Each has its own merits.

Telephone orders let you give direct feedback to your customer. You should confirm that the information you receive is correct, help the customer decide what features he needs, and make sure that the product, as ordered, is appropriate. You can also settle the payment method, and tell the customer when the product will be shipped. The major difficulties with the telephone are that you don't have any written confirmation of the customer's order and that you must accept the call as it comes in, not at your convenience. If you don't have enough telephone lines or people staffing the phones, you may lose the order.

Fax, e-mail, and mail orders offer several advantages. First, you can batch process them, making it possible to fill them at your convenience. Second, orders automatically contain written (or electronic) confirmations. The problem with these methods is that they are subject to misinterpretation if the customer leaves out important information or does not write clearly. You may, for instance, ship the wrong media type or send the order to the wrong address. Even if you provide standard order forms, not every buyer will use them. But those who do are likely to give you more complete information.

E-mail ordering, as of this writing, is still in its infancy. Although companies offer it (or are experimenting with it), the majority have not yet made provisions to accept e-mail orders as part of standard operating procedure. There are administration challenges related to credit card security and buyer identification. I suspect it will catch on soon, with UNIX software vendors leading the way.

Finally, you can hire an outside company to accept orders for you, and even ship your product. These firms take calls from your customers on dedicated or shared telephone lines and either send you the order information or ship the product directly to the customer. To find companies that provide these types of services, look in direct marketing magazines, industry publications, and your local yellow pages. They are listed as telemarketing (inbound) or fulfillment companies.

## Getting Paid

It's not enough to collect the information and send out your product. You must also receive payment. You have choices here, too. For purchases of high-priced software by corporations, be prepared to deal with a purchase order (P.O.)—a trackable, written commitment to purchase specific items at specific prices. (Your sales team should always issue a quotation that spells out payment terms before the customer issues his P.O.) If you decide you are willing to ship upon receipt of a purchase order, be prepared to invoice the customer, track the account receivable, and ask for money that has not been paid.

If your product has a low price, it is often in your best interest to accept payment by charge card. Credit cards mean that corporate customers won't have to obtain purchase orders; they can charge the purchase and be reimbursed later. Credit cards also provide an easy way for individual users to pay for software.

Charge card sales mean quick payment for you, because you collect from the company issuing the card (your bank, for VISA and MasterCard, or American Express or Discover). They, in turn, collect from the customer. It typically costs you several percentages of the total charge, but it's well worth it. You get the cash almost immediately and you don't have to pay the cost of invoicing or collecting delinquent accounts. Speak with your bank or directly to the national charge card company to obtain the privilege of accepting charge cards. They'll set up your account and show you how to take advantage of their services. Unfortunately, some credit card issuers require their customers (i.e., vendors) to maintain a physical storefront. This can make it difficult for software companies to obtain charge card acceptance privileges. If you have these problems, speak with industry groups such as your local Chamber of Commerce; The Software Publishers Association, or ABCD, the Microcomputer Industry Association. These and other similar groups may know about alternatives.

## Collecting Important Information

Information you collect from the customer is important. You care about more than the shipping and billing information; you must also collect information that helps you track customers and understand the market. You should always be able to find out how the customer heard of your product, either by asking him for a code number from the ad or mailer, or by asking him directly. In addition, you need to be able to collect "registration information" that tells you who is buying (or using) your software and how to contact him in the future. Registration information is critical because it points out high-probability customers for upgrades and new products, and gives you a cost-effective way to reach them.

If end users purchase directly from you, you can collect the information when they purchase, thereby starting the warranty and putting them in your high-quality prospect database. If your salesperson spends time with the customer, you can get the information from him.

If users don't purchase directly from you, you need to use another method, such as inserting a registration card in the box. The key to getting a high registration rate is to make it easy for the user. Preprint as much information on the card as you can so that the end user does not have to look up model number, serial number, or other information; prepost the card so he doesn't need to pay the postage; preprint your address on the face of the card; and provide check boxes to make answering your questions easy. Some companies even provide incentives like prize drawings if buyers send back their registration cards. Perhaps the most unique approach I have seen is from Delrina Technology. When you install their WinFax software, it asks whether you want to register automatically by modem. If the user types "yes", the software dials Delrina automatically and registers itself.

Don't leave information collection to chance; automate your order entry. When John User calls to order your software, the order entry clerk should have a script telling him to ask which system type the customer has, and whether she has the required amount of memory and disk space. This helps get the right software to your prospect, thereby minimizing customer headaches and product returns. For instance, if your product line includes versions of your software for Macintosh, DOS, and UNIX, asking these questions can ensure that you send him the right version. If revenue per customer warrants it, you can even keep a record of your customer's configuration for future use.

# *Delivering the Goods*

Shipping the product quickly is in your best interest. Not only does it satisfy the customer, it allows you to claim revenue and collect your money faster. There are a number of companies who will ship your product to domestic or international locations including UPS, Federal Express, DHL, Emery, Airborne Express, and the U.S. Postal Service. Methods, services, and prices differ among the carriers.

In general, the price they charge is based on the weight of your package, the distance it will travel, and how quickly it must arrive at its destination. For instance, a shipment from San Jose to New York City by UPS ground costs more than a similar shipment from San Jose to Kansas City. But there are other factors, too. UPS charges pickup fees of five dollars per week for an unlimited number of packages, while Federal Express charges several dollars per piece; the U.S. Postal Service charges a few dollars for each stop at your facility, regardless of numbers of pieces you send.

If you are looking to save shipping expenses, use standard ground shipping rather than air. A ten pound package shipped by ground can generally make it across the United States in about five to ten days for only $5 to $15. If you want the package delivered overnight, you will pay $30 to $50. Economy air currently costs $15 to $25. Also, consider negotiating with freight carriers to get discount rates.

When preparing your product for shipment, make sure you have an outer package that will withstand the jostling that the product will undoubtedly undergo during transit. To test your packaging, ship your product to yourself. That will indicate what shipments will look like when they arrive at your customers' sites. Also make sure the package is properly labeled. If you ship an expensive piece of hardware with your software, you probably want some insurance coverage. For a tape or floppies with documentation, it's less expensive to forego the insurance and replace any lost shipments by yourself.

## When You Rely on Volume Sales

Certainly the process that I have just described works for products sold directly to the customer. But what other issues affect your handling of orders when you sell through resellers, or have salespeople trying to bring in large orders?

The main difference between selling directly and selling through intermediaries (VAR's, OEM's, distributors, or resellers) is that they are motivated differently than end users. Therefore, they have different requirements when it comes to interacting with your company. While end users are interested solely in putting your product to use, intermediaries are interested in how they can make money with your product. This shows up in larger orders with different fulfillment requirements.

Distributors are willing to purchase a product from you and warehouse it themselves so they can quickly respond to their reseller customers. They are interested in negotiating a master agreement with a solid price and either a set delivery schedule or total number of units against which they draw. When they call you and tell you they want delivery, you had better be able to deliver quickly. If you cannot, they may sell competing products that they have in inventory. You will not recover such lost sales and your market share will erode.

Other resellers may buy multiple units of your standard product for shipment to a central location, then distribute the products to their own resale locations or ask you to ship directly to each location. In the latter case, your shipping procedures must allow multiple shipments from single orders. Again, you had better be able to deliver your product quickly or you will lose sales.

An OEM or a VAR probably doesn't need all the fancy packaging. In fact, it may want a single copy of the software and an electronic version of the documentation as well as copy privileges. This makes it easier for you. When your customer sells your product to the end user, he makes a copy for his customer and produces his own manuals. Then, on a quarterly basis, he tells you how many he has sold and sends you a check.

If you have external salespeople calling on prospects, they will usually get the purchase order and coordinate shipping arrangements with you. Since they are part of your company, their motivations are similar to yours; they don't get paid their commission until the customer's check is received. If everything goes smoothly, your salesperson gives you advanced warning of large purchase orders so you can prepare delivery. When the P.O. is received, you are ready to ship it. If there is a collection problem, the salesperson can also help collect.

## *Move 'Em In, Move 'Em Out*

In short, the process of producing and handling your product is not short at all. It involves other aspects of the company, such as sales, marketing, customer service, development, and finance, and cannot effectively be done without cooperation from these groups. If planned well in advance, it can be easy to get your product into the hands of the customer. If not, you will hear complaints from customers and employees alike.

# PART 3

# Finances and the Young or Growing Company

# ~14~

# Large Profits with a Small Staff

## *The Doomsday Scenario*

Although there are many ways for small software companies to make money, there are even more ways to lose it. The Software Publishers Association (SPA) estimated that the average small software company (those with revenue under $5 million) lost money in 1992. At the same time, large software companies (revenues over $30 million) had average operating income equal to 16% of revenues. Seems a bit unfair, doesn't it?

Don't throw your business plan out the window, just because other small companies aren't making money. There are plenty who are. And yours can be one of them—if you avoid the major traps. To help you avoid a big one, let's examine a key finding of the SPA (Software Publishers Association): large companies bring in more revenue per full-time equivalent employee than small companies do.

The median revenue per employee for large companies is $180,000, versus $103,000 for small companies, a difference of 74% (shown in Figure 14-1). Sure, the ability to bring in customers has an extremely large impact. So does research and development cost. However, the SPA's numbers, which were based on a survey of their members, show that small companies spend amounts similar to large companies on sales and marketing (38.7% of total revenue versus 35.4%) and research and development (16.5% versus 11.6%).[*] Costs of goods sold are almost identical. The culprit is general and administrative expense. Relatively speaking, there are too many people on payroll who do not directly bring in money!

If you're currently running a small company, with say ten people, you're probably ready to dispute my claim that personnel levels are too high. Everyone on your staff is working 12 hour days, six days a week to get your product

---

[*] Software Publishers Association, "In Software Industry, Size and Profitability Go Hand in Hand" (press release), September 21, 1922.

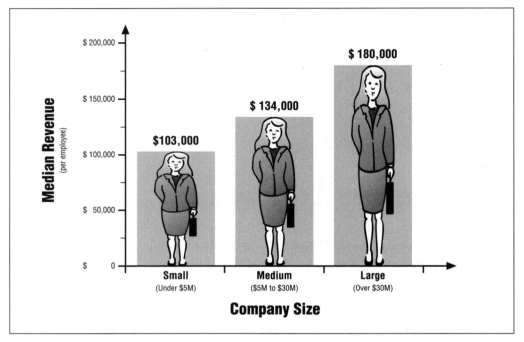

**FIGURE 14-1:** REVENUE PER EMPLOYEE

developed and marketed. How can you possibly get more done with current staff?

That's the whole problem. You can't. To make a business run, you need a critical mass of expertise and enough "hands" to do the job. The expertise is expensive, and your budget can be eaten up by hiring just a few full-time people. Therefore, you have to gain the expertise without staffing up, so you can increase the effective productivity of your entire team.

The numbers speak for themselves. A ten-person firm with sales of $103,000 per employee can spend up to $1,030,000 without losing money. If the same firm can sell $180,000 per employee, it makes money, as long as it spends less than $1.8 million total—a difference of $770,000. These days, $700,000 still pays the salaries and overhead of quite a few people, with dollars to spare.

The key, then, is to reach high revenue levels before staffing up. In a closed system, this is the ultimate catch-22. Fortunately for business owners, the world is not a closed system.

# *When Paying More Costs Less*

One nice thing about the maturing computer industry is that there are modern guns-for-hire out there, people who have participated in successful software businesses (and sometimes unsuccessful businesses) who work as outside contractors for companies in need of specific expertise. They are your catalysts from the outside who can help increase your revenue per employee. These hired guns can help you with legal, marketing, accounting, or other must-do tasks while minimizing the hiring of full-time staff, thereby increasing your profitability.

Getting back to our ten-person company example, let's assume that the company was started by three of you, each drawing salaries of $80,000. Just to pay your own salaries would cost $240,000 or 23.3% of revenues (assuming $103,000 per employee). The figure is way out of bounds compared to the 11.6% that profitable large companies are paying for their general and administrative budget. So you either must bring down your salaries (something you may not be willing to do), or bring up revenues without adding people. If you can increase revenues to $180,000 per employee, you automatically decrease the cost to 13.3%, a figure that is likely to allow a reasonable profit.

"So how do the outside contractors help? You can hire an employee at a much lower hourly rate than the cost of a contractor." That's the issue in a nutshell. The outside contractor costs more *per hour* but not necessarily more in total. They only work when you need them, and you don't have to find new projects for them once the task is done. Since you pay them only when they're working for you, you save money immediately. You also save because you're not (directly) buying benefits, paying social security, renting office space, etc., for the contractors.

Suppose that using an outside marketing consultant for 12 days at $1500 per day helps you change your marketing to save 5% of your marketing expenses while increasing revenue by 5%, both conservative numbers. Your ten-person company would save $19,900 (5% × 38.7% × $1,030,000) and your revenue would increase by $51,500 (5% × $1,030,000). Your $18,000 investment yields $70,400—not bad for a small (5%) influence.

Using external contractors works for several reasons:

- Outsiders add expertise in an area in which your internal expertise is lacking or non-existent. Even if you have a great technical background, you need to handle legal, accounting, production, marketing, and sales tasks. Doing it yourself can result in wasted hours learning how, and wasted money as you spend it unproductively on mailers that don't work, contracts that don't protect you, etc.

- External people have ready access to people and resources that you do not. Public relations people, for instance, can reach editors that you cannot. They can also do it efficiently because they know where to go and they are well received.

- Companies that specialize are already set up to support activities that may be distracting or burdensome to your own staff. Advertising agencies have dedicated media buyers, artists, and copywriters. Seminar firms have developed registration systems. Telemarketing firms have scores of telephone representatives.

- Specialists have better tools than you have to do specific tasks. It's only natural to invest in the items that are most closely aligned with your specialty because they pay back more quickly. That's why lawyers have the law books, public relations people have the publicity-checking services, and CPA's have the tax codes at their ready disposal.

- Some individuals may have previously worked for your competition, customers, or suppliers, putting them in the unique position of having several perspectives of the industry. They keep their perspective fresh by associating regularly with others in your industry. While you can't ask them what your competitor is doing, you can expect them to act with a broad understanding of what's going on.

There are also reasons not to use external contractors. Maybe, your ego is too big to accept outside help. (I didn't say they were good reasons.) Maybe, your goal is to build a big company. Maybe, you want to emulate large corporations.

If you want to emulate large corporations, don't be shy about using outside help. They use it too. Sun uses external contractors to orchestrate their seminars as well as maintain customer systems. Microsoft uses external public relations and advertising companies. Even IBM uses consultants to supplement its external staff to gain additional industry insights. Most companies use external lawyers and accountants either to supplement their own or instead of hiring their own.

*TABLE 14-1:* AREAS IN WHICH OUTSOURCING IS DONE

| MARKETING | Customer SUPPORT | Product DEVELOPMENT | ADMINISTRATION |
|---|---|---|---|
| Telemarketing | On-site Service | Product Design | Legal |
| Seminars | Call Desk Support | Writing Code | Accounting |
| Trade Shows | | Tuning Code | Production |
| Advertising | | Porting Code | Physical Plant |
| Public Relations | | | System |
| Market Information | | | Administration |
| Direct Mail | | | |

## A Tale of Two Entrepreneurs

Not everybody has wonderful experiences when they deal with outside contractors. Dan Heller, president of Z-Code Software, is so disenchanted that he won't do it again. When he first started Z-Code, he contracted with an outside software publisher to market his new UNIX e-mail product, Z-Mail. The publisher didn't sell anything. Heller believes it was primarily because the publisher did not care about his product. According to Heller, "no one else is going to care as much about your product as you do. You either have to accept that, or you don't have other people sell it." Dan's business is now doing well, but he's doing it without the aid of external contractors.

Chris Ryland, president of Em Software, has had good luck dealing with outside vendors. His company, founded in 1989, develops add-in products for Quark XPress, a Macintosh-based desktop publishing package. Chris develops his software himself. He contracts with a local technical writer to write his documentation and outsources his marketing and sales to a company that specializes in Quark extension products from various vendors. Chris has been able to profit from his relationships by concentrating his own efforts where he is more adept (developing software) and leaving the other tasks to those who can do them well. He's a working, one-person software company. Absolutely everything is contracted out.

## What's It Going To Cost?

There are many compensation models for outside contractors. They vary according to type of work and experience of the subcontractor (whether company or individual). Sometimes vendors will try to offload the risk to the subcontractors by paying only on contingency. The majority of good subcontractors won't work this way. If your product doesn't work properly, if you can't give them the right support, if you mislead them, or if you run out of money, their chances of getting paid properly are too slim. Therefore, expect to

## ☞ *Getting the Most From Outside Contractors* ☜

To make sure that you properly utilize external contractors, pay attention to these details:

- Use a contractor you know; there will be fewer surprises. If you can't use someone you know, use the grapevine: get an associate to refer you to someone. Get references from entrepreneurs and other software companies who have used any potential contractors, and check them.

- Get the right one for the job. Whether individual consultant or large company, contractors have their expertise. Make sure that the contractor you select has the skills to meet your requirements.

- Have specific goals in mind. For instance, you might want her to find out how many electronic equipment manufacturers are prospects for your product, what they need, and how they feel about products that compete with yours. Communicate these goals to her, and make sure that she buys in to the goals. If the contractor agrees to the goals, there can be no confusion about her mission.

- Commit enough resources to make the project a success. The worst thing you can do is tie the hands of your contractor by assigning a mission, yet keeping him from being successful because you or your staff won't give him full cooperation.

- Maintain a two-way relationship. Consultants and subcontractors are yours while you are paying them. Take advantage of them by learning from them while you are working with them. Give them information that will help them do their jobs well. You may be working with them in the future.

- Stay close to the project. Good contractors often work on several projects at once and may be swayed toward other projects. Be the squeaky wheel to make sure you get the attention you deserve.

- Choose somebody who is willing to teach you. The more you know about what they are doing, the better you can work with them. For instance, many good telemarketing firms will either make your calls for you, or help you set up your own in-house department.

"put in a piece of skin" by committing to a set payment schedule. (The exception is when you sell through the channel, in which a company will resell product that they buy from you—i.e., a distributor, computer store or publisher. But these really aren't subcontractors; they're customers.) Here are a few common compensation models for external contractors:

- Lawyers usually charge by the hour for corporate work. ($100 to $250 per hour).*

- Accountants also charge by the hour. ($75 to $150 per hour)

- Advertising agencies either charge a percentage of the ads that they place or set fees. (Hourly fees: around $40 for administrative help up to $180 for a partner).

- Consultants usually charge by the day or by the hour. In a small percentage of the cases, marketing consultants are willing to take part of their compensation in commission, but virtually always require some non-contingent compensation. ($1,000 to $2000 per day)

- Public Relations companies charge by the month for full programs or by the hour if you want them to accomplish specific tasks like writing a press release or developing a press kit. (Hourly fees: $50 to $150 per hour; monthly fees: $2,000 and up).

## *Bringing Home the Pay You Deserve*

If you have ever worked with venture-funded companies, you may have noticed that venture capitalists make liberal use of outside consultants to make sure that the companies in which they invest are profitable. Contrast venture capitalist methods with those of many entrepreneurs who often wait until too late to capitalize on outside expertise. Many of these executives delay their own paychecks to furnish funding for the business. In many cases, the business never achieves the revenue levels that allow repayment of the deferred compensation, so the executive loses it forever.

Don't forego your paycheck to hire people when you can utilize outside contractors effectively. By utilizing the contractors, you will boost your profitability and increase your management flexibility, leaving you in a better position to bring home the pay you deserve (or, if not what you deserve, at least increase what you can afford).

---

* Some lawyers do work on a contingent basis, but only if they expect a large payout at the end. They rarely do so for corporate work.

# Prospering by Keeping
# Expenses Low

There are two factors that make up your profit: revenue and expenses. To maximize your profit, minimize your expenses.

## *All Corporate Functions Involve Overhead*

*Overhead* denotes the fixed expenses of the business: typically items, activities, and people not directly attributable to specific sales or unit production. This usually includes product marketing, research and development, and administration. These and other overhead personnel provide vital functions, functions you can't live without, and costs are, of course, associated with each one.

It is fairly obvious that one cannot write software without programmers, answer support questions without people trained to do so, or develop marketing plans without somebody who can understand marketing concepts. Less obvious, though, is the exact level of staffing required. Appropriate staffing levels vary greatly from company to company, depending on factors such as product type, target market, and management capabilities. Microsoft's need is immense. They have many products and many employees doing various tasks around the globe. By contrast, the neighborhood computer consultant's need is minuscule. But he still needs to find new customers and file tax returns, which costs money and takes time away from consulting. Your needs are probably somewhere in between. Let's examine how managing your company expenses can increase your profits.

# *Overhead Grows While You're Not Looking*

According to The Software Publishers Association,[*] the differences in profitability between different software companies are driven by differences in fixed costs. Large costs in these categories result in decreased profit and sometimes losses.

While these functions are necessary to your business, you must be careful that the costs associated with them do not overtake your organization. Unfortunately, costs often start growing before management notices. Your overhead increases slowly as your requirements climb, and accelerates as your business grows. In good times, overhead blossoms because you pay less attention to costs and more attention to getting the job done quickly and easily. When you try to cut costs during bad times, you'll consider many of these costs untouchable. Once a person joins your staff, you'll find it difficult, if not impossible, to cut his position. You naturally feel that you can't get the job done with fewer people. Or if it's clear that a position is no longer needed, you're naturally reluctant to lay off a loyal employee. None of us wants to lose our job, see our friends or associates out of work, or make our own tasks tougher to accomplish. Given that cutting overhead is difficult, it's clear that the best way to get rid of overhead costs is to avoid them in the first place.

# *The Quickest Path to Lower Expenses*

Since personnel is the single largest cost in most organizations, the key to keeping your overhead down is to keep down your overhead staff. To do so, you must distinguish between necessities and luxuries, before luxuries appear to be necessities. When I began Marketing Masters, I would like to have had many people on staff, including people dedicated to public relations, telemarketing, and strategic marketing. But I started the company without any of these; I didn't even hire a secretary. It was tough to do, too. Being in a small company, one wants camaraderie, the security (whether real or imagined) that comes from having other people around, and the ability to bounce your ideas off others who can add a dimension to your thoughts. However, I realized that I could accomplish the work by myself if I supplemented my efforts with those of *external* strategic partner companies. I set up my company to take full advantage of other companies with specific expertise. In this way, I could provide better service to my clients without high overhead. I went even further in cut-

---

[*] Software Publishers Association, "In Software Industry, Size and Profitability Go Hand in Hand" (press release), September 21, 1992.

ting costs by setting up my initial office in my home, an important savings for a startup business.

The low overhead route, however, has its disadvantages. If you go without a secretary, you'll end up typing letters at times when you should be writing code, selling your product, or managing staff. At some point, the opportunity cost of your time exceeds the cost of hiring a secretary. You might also be sacrificing growth in order to keep your cost structure low. Without the large team to provide much of the ancillary services, a company must concentrate efforts in a limited number of activities, thereby reducing growth. These are the management tradeoffs that you face when making staffing and budgeting decisions.

Managing a small company is dramatically different from managing a small portion of a large company because of the tradeoffs required by the different overhead structure. Large company managers take for granted the amount of resources available with just a phone call—resources that cost quite a bit. Most small companies don't have such resources. Many of the best and brightest managers from large, established companies have failed in small business ventures because they couldn't adjust to working without the abundant overhead structure.

## Adjusting Overhead Costs

Every time you add a person to your staff, your costs rise, and not just by the amount of their salary. Larger staffs require more support and more supplies. People take up space, require furniture, and make phone calls. Each of these items has associated costs. In fact, many managers estimate that your associated costs approach 100% of the salary of the new employee! No matter how hard you try to keep costs down, you will be burdened with a significant amount.

Let's examine a hypothetical new hire with an annual salary of $50,000. The new employee may be a software developer who must interact with a number of outside companies, or be a marketing person. In either case, expenses will jump with his hiring, as shown in Table 15-1.

**TABLE 15-1:** EXPENSES ASSOCIATED WITH HIRING

| Type of Expense | Overhead Cost | Assumptions |
| --- | --- | --- |
| Taxes and Benefits | $10,000 | Taxes and benefits typically equal 20% of $50,000 salary |
| Management | $10,000 | One manager for each five employees ($50,000 / 5) |
| Travel | $12,000 | $1000 per month |
| Telephone | $2400 | $200 per month |
| Office Space | $2800 | 140 square feet @ $20 per s.f. |
| Office Equipment, Software, and Supplies | $1000 | Includes amortization of systems plus license fees plus miscellaneous supplies |
| Total Overhead Costs | $38,200 | |

In this example, the overhead cost for our employee is almost 80% of his base salary. The expense break-down changes depending on what functions the employee performs. You may think you can get away without several of these costs. Some managers say you cannot; others say that you'll merely make up the overhead elsewhere. We have not even included some large overhead costs such as relocation expenses, headhunting fees, or the resources used to find and hire your new employee.

Certainly, you won't add every cost for every new hire. For example, you won't rent 140 square feet of space when you add a single person. On average, though, you will increase your need accordingly; perhaps you'll add 700 square feet when you hire five people, because your current office cannot handle the additional bodies. Any way you look at it, your personnel overhead costs will catch up with you at some point.

Generally speaking, it is wiser and easier to avoid adding operating costs than it is to reduce them. Reducing overhead with a layoff can be traumatic. Those who are laid off must deal with the financial implications and the effect on their self esteem. Those who remain often feel betrayed by their employers and become concerned for their own well being. Layoffs are usually difficult, too, on those who make the decision to decrease staffing. You probably know somebody who has been laid off recently; there have been many layoffs in the computer industry over the past few years. IBM, Apple, Digital, Prime, among other companies have recently gone through massive "early retirements," "redeployments," or outright layoffs. In all of the downsizing decisions, corporate decision-makers felt that overhead had gotten out of hand. As we mentioned earlier, it's very easy to add overhead costs, but difficult to reduce them.

---

### ☞ *Cutting Costs During Good Times* ☜

Since overhead costs tend to expand during good times, don't let down your guard. When times are good, it's easy to say that you'll hire a few extra people to help you through the crunch. But the requirement never seems to go away. When the hard times return, your high cost structure will hurt your competitiveness and profits.

Each time you feel the urge to hire a new employee, ask yourself the following questions:

- Why do I need to hire this person?

- What will my cost be if I hire?

- What will happen if I do not hire?

- What will my cost be if I do not hire?

- How long will I need the services of this person?

- If the need is temporary, will I be able to discharge the person after the need is satisfied?

- Can I get the job done without hiring somebody? If so, how?

---

## Reducing the Most Harmful Costs

Hidden costs are the most damaging costs. As the name suggests, hidden costs are expenses that may not be obvious to you when you make your budget. It's easy to overlook expenses like postage, long-distance phone bills, and office supplies. But if your hidden expenses are too high, you'll miss your financial targets or you'll be forced to drop important projects due to lack of capital. Hidden costs are not always large, but cumulatively, they can have a significant effect on your profitability.

The costs themselves are not the problem. The fact that they are hidden is what kills you. Logically then, to keep hidden costs down, make them apparent. Sometimes hidden costs arise when you reduce a different cost. For instance, you may get rid of an internal cost only to find an unexpected increase in the cost of some outside service required to perform the same task. A common example is the hidden expense of increased facsimile use when a company attempts to reduce express mail costs. A 30-page document can be sent by overnight courier for less than $10. Sending it by fax may cost $6 to $9, but that is hidden in your other bills: since most long distance calls cost about 20 cents per minute, that same document, faxed at two pages per minute average speed, will cost $3 in long distance charges. If you send it to one of your own offices, you will also have to add about $3 to cover the cost of the fax paper. Most fax recipients make a copy of the faxes they receive because they do not like the feel of the thermal paper that most faxes still use. Add another $1.50 to cover the five cents per page copies. If a $20,000 per year secretary has to stand by your machine, that's another $1.50. You've spent $9 for the fax. Although the scenarios and numbers might change, the fact remains: you incur a significant number of expenses during the typical business day that you don't notice. There's nothing wrong with spending $9 to send a fax, but there is something wrong with thinking that you have saved $10 when you have only saved $1.

The key to finding hidden costs is to look at every activity your business performs and then figure out which supplementary activities are typically performed in conjunction. Long-distance telephone supplements sales activities. Programming tasks require electricity to run systems. Copiers require electricity, paper, toner, and someone to make the copies.

Because it is often easy to overlook or underestimate costs, you could add a fudge factor to your estimates to simulate your hidden costs. However, the fudge factor does not help you to reduce or understand hidden costs. It simply makes allowances for them in your profit and cash flow projections.

## *Candidates for Your Hidden Cost Search*

There are a few areas in which companies typically overspend their budgets. As a result, lots of activities tend to stop at the end of the budget year, as managers attempt to stay within their budgets. Having people sitting around idle because some department is almost out-of-budget is clearly a hidden cost you can't afford; you can avoid it by understanding what the costs of doing business really are, and building those costs into your budget plans. Watch for these areas (listed below) for hidden costs when you do your planning.

*Personnel*

Administration, accounting, marketing, and development.

Example: The cost of systems administration. If you have a dedicated systems administrator, you probably have a pretty good feel for what it costs. If, on the other hand, your development staff performs its own system administration, you're probably losing a lot of development time to reconfigurations, backups, software installation, and other related activities. By having your developers do system administration, you may think you're getting something for nothing, but you're not; you're really paying through the nose. (At one point, the burden became so bad at Multiflow that the engineers in our operating system development group hung signs on their doors saying "I'm not a system administrator.")

*Legal, accounting*

Charges from outside contractors to file forms, negotiate contracts, or advise about tax issues.

Example: You add an out-of-state employee. You'll be subject to that state's business taxes. It may not cost you any more in taxes because you would probably have to pay a similar amount if she lived in your home state, but it will cost you several thousand dollars per year to do the extra accounting, file the extra forms, etc.

*Outside Services*

Marketing, outside programming, or temporary personnel.

Example: Extra people to help ship product during times of extraordinary demand, a public relations firm to help launch your product, extra programmers to fix bugs. This category is likely to balloon in good times, eating up your profits.

*Travel*

Unexpected trips and elevated costs on individual trips.

Example: Last-minute trips that your sales person makes to keep a large deal from falling into the hands of a competitor; unexpected invitations for your officers to speak to important audiences.

*Printing and supplies*

Waste because of overstock.

Example: Printing costs are based on quantity; ordering larger print runs usually saves money. But the cost per piece won't go down if you waste your money by purchasing more pieces than you can use. Order what you need. For every print job, evaluate the cost/quantity issue carefully. You'll conserve cash by not overbuying.

*Telephone*

Underestimation of long distance.

Example: Every time you add a new person or begin a new program, your telephone costs will rise. If you publish an 800 number, it will rise even more.

*Luxury items*

Soda, coffee, client entertainment, extravagant office furniture.

Example: Lots of companies in the computer industry provide free soft drinks to personnel. Do not forget to add the annual cost of $200 to $300 for each person.

*Computer related*

Time associated with down systems or support.

Example: Every time your electricity goes out or your shared system crashes, your development staff is out of business. If they are on salary, you're paying for them whether or not they can work.

## An Example of Hidden Costs

Seminars are one of the most effective ways to sell to large accounts; yet while they reduce the cost of direct sales, they still cost money. Having produced seminars for many companies, I have noticed that most have no idea how much seminars really cost them, with cost of personnel most likely the expense left out of the equation. The following example shows how costs can hide, even in the most effective programs.[*] Our assumptions are:

1. Seminars will be held in 12 U.S. cities; average attendance will be 75 people.

2. To attract attendees, use direct mail; average response rate will be 2%.

3. Only 75% who register for the seminars will actually show up.

Taking these assumptions together, you will need to mail 60,000 pieces to get 1200 registrants who become the 900 attendees required to reach your 75 attendee per seminar goal.

*TABLE 15-2: IN-HOUSE COST OF SEMINARS*

| Seminar Activity | Total Cost | Cost Type |
|---|---|---|
| List rental and label production (60,000 names at $.15 each) | $9000 | Hidden |
| Design seminar promotion and mechanicals | $1500 | Hidden |
| Printing and folding (60,000 pieces at $.20) | $12,000 | Visible |
| Mail house services (or internal processing) | $1500 | Hidden |

---

[*] Thanks to Jerry Chichester of Effective Marketing, Inc. for providing the estimates.

| Seminar Activity | Total Cost | Cost Type |
|---|---|---|
| Bulk rate postage (average $.18 per piece) | $10,800 | Visible |
| Telephone and labor costs for 800# registration ($3 per call) | $3600 | Hidden |
| Personalized confirmation letters ($2 per letter) | $2400 | Hidden |
| Telephone reconfirmations in advance of seminar ($4 per call) | $4800 | Hidden |
| Meeting room rental ($600 each) | $7200 | Visible |
| Refreshments for attendees ($10 each) | $9000 | Hidden |
| A/V equipment rental ($150 per show) | $1800 | Hidden |
| Travel and living for one administrative support person ($600 per city) | $7200 | Visible |
| Two man-months of preparatory labor | $8333 | Hidden |

The total in-house costs, excluding the costs of the presenter and preparation of the presentation, are $79,133, of which $41,933 is hidden; less than half the cost ($37,200) is visible. You may have already recognized some of the costs that I call hidden. Most people don't; but that's not the point. The better you understand your cost structure—the more hidden costs you drag out into the open—the better off you'll be.

## Not on My Budget, You Don't

Company politics interfere with your ability to keep your costs low because each of your managers wants to meet his own budget goals. At first glance, departmental budgets seem like a wonderful incentive to reduce company expenses—if everybody reduces his own costs, total company costs will decrease accordingly. Unfortunately, it doesn't always work that way. In the real world of business politics, a common technique for reducing one's department cost is to transfer expenses to another department. So you end up with managers who fight with one another and burden each other with additional expenses. The result: company costs often rise. Take our 12-city seminar example. An external seminar production company can probably orchestrate a similar tour for $50,000 to $60,000, $20,000 to $30,000 less than it would cost the company to stage its own seminar. However, there are often counter-productive incentives to organize seminars in-house. If a manager orders a $60,000 seminar from outside, the money is unquestionably coming from his budget. But if he runs the seminar in-house, he can transfer significant portions of the cost to other departments by utilizing administrative help from within the company. His battle cry: "If we all pitch in, we can have a great series that will propel us to market fame!" He wins by doing the work in-house because he does not have to pay for the personnel out of his budget—and might even become a hero on top of it. But overall, the company loses, because the labor still costs money, workers in the other departments become frazzled, and other managers must find alternative ways to get their own jobs done, often at higher cost.

The "not on my budget" mindset is not limited to seminars. It happens throughout your company. Development managers steal programmers from each other—sometimes an hour at a time. Marketing support uses development people instead of adding to its own staff. You may have done it yourself at a previous employer. The problem is not confined to large organizations. It happens any time a manager is asked to meet a budget goal.

You might react by handling the budget yourself, but that will only put another task on your loaded agenda. Instead, recognize the potential for increased cost, and get involved with your managers to suggest cooperative solutions that make sense from the company viewpoint. Provide incentives (stock options, bonuses, etc.) that reward your managers (as well as all employees) when company-wide costs decrease and profits increase.

## *Managing Changes in Expense Structure*

As time goes on, cost structure is bound to change. You'll add managers, move into new headquarters, change the methods you use to sell or migrate your software to new platforms. Each change may seem innocuous by itself, but the cumulative effect may burden your company with a cost structure that is too high. Therefore, it's important to examine your expenses periodically to reveal important trends:

- Are certain types of costs escalating at an irrational rate? If so, find out why.

- Have you consistently underestimated spending in certain areas? If so, come up with a better method to estimate these expenses for future periods.

- Has the growth in your expenses exceeded your growth in revenue? This is a serious trouble sign. Examine those areas that are growing fastest and those that make up the largest portion of your total costs. Find ways to decrease them.

Compare your costs quarter to quarter, month to month and year to year. Use prior period (i.e., Q3 1994 versus Q4 1994) as well as corresponding period from previous year (i.e., Q4 1993 versus Q4 1994) as benchmarks.

# Managing Your Cash Flow

It's human nature to dwell on making a profit when you're operating your own business. But you should concentrate just as hard on maintaining sufficient cash flow because that's what gives you the fuel to operate and grow. Although the difference between profit and cash flow may not be obvious at first, the distinction is important. In this chapter, I'll cover the importance of cash flow to your continued operations, how cash flow differs from profit, circumstances that impact your cash flow, and suggestions on how to manage your cash.

## *The Universal Business Requirement*

You don't expect to travel cross country by car without a full tank of gas to start and an occasional fill-up along the way. If you did, you would never reach your destination. Each time your gas tank fell to "E," you would be walking to the next fuel stop. Likewise, you can't run your business without cash; you need at least enough to get started, and more as you go along to pay your expenses. Just as gas fuels your automobile trip, cash fuels your business operations.

You might think that there is a simple answer: Simply make sure sales go well so money comes in. As expenses go up, just increase sales. Unfortunately, it's not that simple. Even if you can grow your sales dramatically, you may not be able to pay your bills. Even worse: success can cause more cash flow problems than mediocrity. This may seem counterintuitive, but it is true. Success can actually *cause* cash flow problems because success usually means growth—and growth requires money.

If your sales grow 10% per month (which is certainly a sign of success), you have to spend 10% more on parts, support, and shipping—but you have got to do it with the income you collected on last month's sales. Even worse, if you are being paid 90 days after receiving the order, you have got to operate using money from sales that happened a quarter ago, when your sales were roughly 40% less than they are now. And if you don't, you will get a bad reputation for being a company that can't deliver. As your growth rate rises, your cash flow issues can become more difficult to manage. As far as predicaments go, that's a good one; consider yourself lucky if your worst problem is 150% annual growth!

Your company is no more exempt from cash flow problems than Wang, Macy's, or Drexel Burnham Lambert. Each was a leader in its field, but succumbed to cash flow problems. Software companies are more susceptible than many other businesses because of the rapid pace of development, the changing marketplace, and a cost structure that is predominantly fixed. Therefore, to succeed, prosper, and even to exist, you need to make sure that you don't succumb to poor cash flow.

To illustrate how important positive cash flow is for any company, let's look at a few sample situations.

### Scenario A

It's June 30. You have $40,000 in the bank. You have recently sold software worth $20,000 and expect to receive the payments on these sales by July 15. Your payroll of $55,000 is to be paid on July 16.

In this textbook example, the resolution is simple. After you receive the payments from your customers, you will have $60,000—enough to write $55,000 worth of checks and still have $5000 left. But if a major customer fails to submit a $10,000 payment on time, you will be short. In this real world situation, you will have $5000 *less* cash on payday than you need.

### Scenario B

A market opportunity presents itself that will allow you to double your sales and dramatically increase profits within the next 12 months. To take advantage of the opportunity, you must hire three new people immediately at a cost of $20,000 per month. You won't receive a single dollar of revenue for at least six months. If your bank balance is currently at $20,000, will you be able to fund the $100,000 that you need over the next six months to take advantage of this opportunity? Not unless your incoming cash will support the extra expenditures.

Every month, you must make many decisions that depend on the cash you have available: Can you hire the new support person? Is there enough money to purchase a new workstation? If cash is tight, whom do you pay first? Virtually every aspect of your business is affected by your cash situation.

Cash flow is the sustenance of a growing business. If cash flows are good—a lot of cash coming in, and little going out—you can grow faster. If cash flows are poor, they may impede your growth or put you under altogether.

# *Cash Flow Is Not Profit*

Don't confuse cash flow with profit. Cash flow is *hard*; it's the amount of money in your checkbook at the end of the month—how much hard currency you receive minus how much hard currency you pay out. There's no debate about how to measure it. You've got money or you don't. Profit, on the other hand, is a very fuzzy concept and is subject to different interpretations, accounting methods, etc. You can be extremely profitable in the short term, but still go out of business because you run out of cash.

When you compute your profits, you subtract your expenses from your revenue. But, because of credit you extend to customers, you may not actually see the hard cash from your sales for months, so your revenue may not accurately state how much cash you receive during a given month. In addition, the way you account for expenses often widens the gap between how much your books say you have earned and how much money you have actually taken in. For example, depreciation on fixed assets such as office equipment and furniture (explained later in this chapter) delays much of your expense until future accounting periods, even though you must pay the bills today. In fact, creative accountants can find ways to raise or lower your profits legally through accounting techniques. These techniques, though, don't change your cash flow. Cash flow is what's in the bank (or your cash box) at the end of the day; your profit is the number at the end of your income statement, as Figure 16-1 illustrates. Decisions that optimize profits may hinder cash flow. In the following sections, let's examine how they differ, and how the difference affects your business.

## The Business Accounting Model

You run your personal finances largely on a cash basis. That is, at the end of the day, your bank balance is a fairly good indicator of your real position. To be sure, you have bills due and a paycheck next week, but by adding and subtracting a bit, you can come to your current position fairly readily and intuitively.

Most businesses can't run on cash accounting. The tax authorities won't allow it; they require another form of accounting, called "accrual accounting," if your business keeps any inventory or makes any long-term investments, including research and development. The government's rules help make sure the IRS gets its share of your profits, because they restrict the amount of leeway you have in stating your taxable income. In addition, you have to use methods that are acceptable to the financial community—which includes your bankers, investors, and other business partners. They subscribe to the basics of the tax authorities' accounting methods, with some minor adjustments.

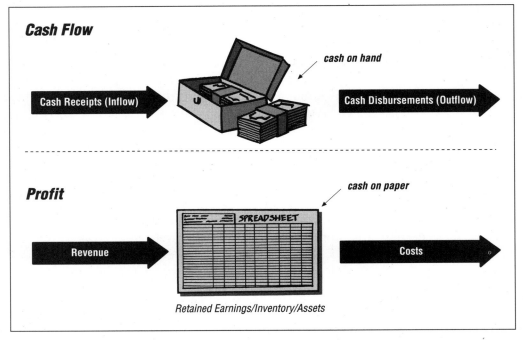

**Cash Flow**

cash on hand

Cash Receipts (Inflow)

Cash Disbursements (Outflow)

**Profit**

cash on paper

Revenue

SPREADSHEET

Costs

Retained Earnings/Inventory/Assets

***FIGURE 16-1:*** *CASH FLOW AND PROFIT*

The conceptual gap between cash accounting and accrual accounting is significant, and may be the most important (and difficult) transition for you to overcome; it requires a new, and often counterintuitive, way of thinking. Your income is no longer based on actual cash receipts and disbursements, as it was with cash accounting. Not only do you need to know how much you are spending and when, you also must recognize when an expenditure or revenue item gets posted to your books—which may not be when the money is spent or received.

There are many ways that accounting methods can change your tax status and affect your cash flows. The following sections describe a few common issues.

*Accounts receivable*

As we said above, in accrual accounting an important distinction is made between the time you recognize revenue (i.e., add it to your books) and the time you receive the cash. You often receive payment from your customer after you have delivered your product. Yet the IRS tells you that your income from the sale is taxable as soon as you ship the item. For example, assume that you have billed $200,000 for software shipped in December. You may not actually receive that money until March, but it is counted as current year income. As a result, you must come up with the cash to pay the income tax on the sale before you get the money from your customer. This can create cash flow problems, especially when your customers are slow to pay. The longer the delay in collection, the worse the problem becomes. If you are growing rapidly, the problem is even worse: you need cash to fuel your growth, and paying taxes on money you haven't received is the last thing you want to do.

*Inventory*

Extending the problem, items you purchase for inventory aren't considered an expense until they are actually sold to customers. That means unless the product is sold during the current period, the government taxes you on the dollar value of the inventory as if you had never spent the money. Assume you have just spent $50,000 to buy diskettes and manuals for your product. As far as the taxation authorities are concerned, you have $50,000 in an "asset" called inventory, not an expense. So the $50,000 looks like additional profit. It's taxable. If your business is not well capitalized, you will need to find the cash to pay the additional taxes or reduce your inventory towards year end, to bring your actual expenses more in line with your cash.

*The timing of inventory recognition*

Inventory is one of the more complex areas of accounting, affecting both profit and cash flow. As an example, let's examine two inventory accounting methods: FIFO (First In First Out) and LIFO (Last In First Out). If you use FIFO, you assume that the inventory you acquired first is the first inventory that you use for products that you ship. LIFO assumes you ship the inventory in the reverse order from which it was acquired. (There are other methods too, but LIFO and FIFO are the two extremes.)

Suppose that your software requires five floppy diskettes for distribution and that you sell 1000 packages per month for the entire year. Suppose further that the cost per diskette is $1 in January, and $1.50 in July, and that you purchase 40,000 diskettes in each of these months to satisfy anticipated demand for your product. The products that you sell during the first six months of the year use 30,000 diskettes (five per package × 1000 packages × six months) leaving you 10,000 diskettes for the second six months. At the end of the year, you have shipped 60,000 out of the 80,000 diskettes that you purchased and you have handed over $100,000 to buy the diskettes. Your actual cash outlay is the same, no matter which accounting method you use.

What about your profit? If you used FIFO, it would be $5000 more than if you used LIFO, because FIFO would state your diskette cost at $70,000, while LIFO states it at $75,000. The difference is whether you consider a diskette that is shipped on July 1 to be a $1.00 diskette or a $1.50 diskette. That's entirely up to you and your accountant.

When you account for other expenses that are attributed directly to the cost of goods sold, the difference between methods can be significant. But any way you look at it, the money you have "on paper" isn't the same as the money you have in the bank.

**TABLE 16-1:** *COMPARISON OF FIFO, LIFO, AND CASH FLOW*

| | FIFO | | LIFO | |
|---|---|---|---|---|
| **Cash Outlay** | | | | |
| January: 40,000 at $1.00 each | $40,000 | | $40,000 | |
| July: 40,000 at $1.50 each | $60,000 | | $60,000 | |
| Total cost of diskettes: | | $100,000 | | $100,000 |
| **Expense Recognition on Income Statement** | | | | |
| January–June: | 30,000 × $1.00 | | 30,000 × $1.00 | |
| July–December: | 10,000 × $1.00 | | 30,000 × $1.50 | |
| | 20,000 × $1.50 | | | |
| Total, January–December: | | $70,000 | | $75,000 |
| **Year-end Inventory** | | | | |
| | 20,000 × $1.50 | | 10,000 × $1.00 | |
| | | | 10,000 × $1.50 | |
| Total | | $30,000 | | $25,000 |
| **Summary** | | | | |
| Actual Cash Outlay | | $100,000 | | $100,000 |
| Accounting Cost | | $70,000 | | $75,000 |

Although the cash outlay doesn't change between the two methods, your expense recognition changes by $5000 (approximately 7%), thereby changing your profit. Of course, this also changes the taxes you must pay too.

*Amortization and depreciation*

The IRS requires you to make a distinction between expenses that can be written off in the current year, like copier paper or travel, and capital expenses such as equipment. When you buy a piece of equipment—say a $5000 computer system—you may pay for it immediately. But for business purposes, you must "capitalize it"—that is, treat it as if it were money in the bank, and "depreciate" the expense over the useful life of the equipment. The catch is that the IRS defines "useful life." According to the IRS, your $5000 computer has a useful life of five years or more, so you only get to charge the first $1000 as an expense.* The remaining $4000 is added to your "profit" for the year, and you will be expected to pay taxes on it as if it were income, rather than an expense. A similar computation is performed for intangible assets, like patents or trademarks—except that in this case, it is called "amortization."

After you have been in business a few years, you will gain the benefit of further depreciation from prior expenditures on equipment. This creates positive cash flow in the sense that you are able to charge deductions against your income (for tax purposes) that don't involve a corresponding cash outlay. The net effect of depreciation and amortization on cash flow is that it separates your actual disbursement of cash from the time you get tax credit for the purchase, thereby causing you to make significantly higher short term cash outlays.

## Your Accountant Can Guide You

All of these accounting practices can be quite perplexing to the uninitiated. It certainly can take some getting used to, since the taxable income perspective that drives most business accounting is much different from the cash flow perspective you need to run your day-to-day business. But you must get used to concentrating on both, because either one, if not monitored and managed, can cause problems for your business.

In a growing business, you will typically show greater profits than the corresponding cash flow. Your tax liabilities will only make the problem worse, because taxes are paid on your profits, not on your cash. Tim O'Reilly, the publisher of this book, says that in ten years of a successful business, the only reason he has had to borrow money is to pay taxes on profits that have not yet been received as cash. In summary, unless you already have a good handle on accrual accounting, get a good accountant and develop financial statements and spreadsheet models that will give you a regular sense of both your profits and your cash flow.

# *The Importance of Positive Cash Flow*

It's amazing how many ways cash problems can affect your business. Accounting practices, payment practices, and how money flows through the banking system can all impact the amount of cash you have available. Cash shortages can impede your growth, interfere with your credit rating, or put you out of business altogether. That's why positive cash flow (more cash coming in than going out) is so important.

---

* There are many accounting methods for computing depreciation—you may need to use several in the course of doing business. A full discussion of different methods is beyond the scope of this book; consult your accountant.

# You Need Cash for Growth

If you're like most high tech entrepreneurs, you're looking forward to a high growth rate in both revenue and profit. However, growing companies require even stronger cash flow than companies with steady earnings. Even swiftly growing businesses can fail if they don't have adequate cash flow. Osborne Computer, the makers of the original "luggable" PC's, died in 1983 after amassing over $40 million in debt. BusinessLand, the computer store chain, had cash problems too, which were solved only when it was purchased in 1991 by JWP. JWP ran into more trouble later, partially brought on by the cash flow problems caused by its purchase of BusinessLand. Both companies ran into their cash flow problems while in periods of rapid growth.

Suppose your company is successfully selling your software to a niche market. (Let's call it market A.) Your marketing director tells you about a new opportunity to sell your product into a second market (market B, of course). Should you do it? Not unless you handle the cash flow constraints involved. This is how it works:

You are currently making $10,000 per month in sales to market A. It will take a startup effort of $15,000 per month for six months to get into market B. Your marketing director expects each sale to take three months of effort. He anticipates $5000 in sales in your initial month of receiving orders with revenue increasing to $10,000 the following month before leveling out at $15,000 per month. Your cash flow for the first six months looks like the figures shown in Table 16-2.

*TABLE 16-2: ENTERING A NEW MARKET*

| Month | Revenue, Market A | Revenue, Market B | Startup Costs | Monthly Cash Flow | Year-To-Date Cash Flow |
|-------|-------------------|-------------------|---------------|-------------------|------------------------|
| Jan | $10,000 | $0 | $15,000 | ($5000) | ($5000) |
| Feb | $10,000 | $0 | $15,000 | ($5000) | ($10,000) |
| Mar | $10,000 | $0 | $15,000 | ($5000) | ($15,000) |
| Apr | $10,000 | $5000 | $15,000 | even | ($15,000) |
| May | $10,000 | $10,000 | $15,000 | $5000 | ($10,000) |
| Jun | $10,000 | $15,000 | $15,000 | $10,000 | even |

If you have no other costs, you would need at least $15,000 in the bank to last through the first three months of your new marketing effort. Actually, you would need a lot more; we've significantly understated your cash requirements. In the real world, you would not receive cash for your sales immediately. And, of course, there are other costs that we didn't include, such as cost of goods sold, personnel who will sell into the new market, and your normal operating costs. You would need a significant amount of additional cash—either from your bank account, creditors, financiers, or additional revenue sources—during the first six months to initiate your new marketing strategy.

Cash requirements grow larger if you attempt to grow faster. For instance, if you had attempted to get into multiple markets, add development people, or increase market share more quickly, you would have needed even more cash than in the example. You would have needed more parts to assemble your product, more people to sell, take orders, or provide telephone support. You might even have borrowed more money, which would have increased your interest expense.

Shrinking companies are also faced with large cash flow requirements as they confront tremendous pressures to cut costs as they shrink. If revenues decrease, your incoming cash flow dries up. Unless you have put a lot of money into reserve, you will need to cut your outgoing expenses dramatically so you don't run out of cash.

When it comes right down to it, many cash flow problems are caused, not by internal decisions, but by external forces such as banks, suppliers, and customers. To survive in this environment, you must become aware of situations that can cause you problems, so you can take steps to avoid them. This is true whether your company is growing, shrinking, or running at a steady pace.

## Price Changes Impact Your Cash Flow

Suppose you don't sell directly to the end user, but sell instead through the channel of distributors and resellers. The whole cash inflow picture changes. First, the terms you provide to distributors differ from those that you give to end users. Second, whenever you change your pricing, the effect ripples through your account balances and future collections.

When you sell to a distributor, it's almost as if his warehouse is yours. You assemble your product at your plant and ship enough to your distributor to satisfy his demand for the next 90 days. Each month, you examine his inventory level and replenish his stock to meet demand in the subsequent 90-day rolling period. You don't receive your payment until your distributor sells your product, so you must have a cash flow buffer until your distributor sends you the money. At least you are not waiting forever; the standard agreement is that your distributor pays you within 60 days of receiving your shipment, even if the units have not been sold.

- You sell your product to your distributor, King Kong Corporation, for $100. King Kong marks it up to sell to resellers (and subsequently to end users). King Kong's initial estimate of demand is 10,000 per month. So you enter into a standing contract with King Kong in which you deliver three months worth of inventory immediately (30,000), then replenish King Kong's inventory monthly so King Kong can maintain a consistent inventory to cover the demand for the subsequent three months. You grant King Kong 30-day payment terms, meaning they don't pay for units until 30 days after they are sold. (This "standing order" arrangement is a typical practice.)

| Month | You ship them | They sell |
|-------|---------------|-----------|
| Jan | 30,000 units | 10,000 units |
| Feb | 10,000 | 5,000 |
| Mar | 5000 | 10,000 |
| Apr | 10,000 | 10,000 |
| May | 10,000 | 10,000 |
| Jun | 10,000 | 10,000 |

As of March 31, you have shipped 45,000 units and have received payment for only 15,000. Payment for an additional 10,000 will be received in April. In addition, you have shipped 20,000 units for which you will not be paid until May or June. This amounts to $2 million in inventory that you are financing.

Now, here's where it becomes tricky. If you cut your prices, you must credit your distributor for the difference in price on all the inventory he already has in stock. You don't actually have to write him a check; the credit goes toward future purchases.

• On April 1, you cut your distributor price to $80. That means you must immediately credit King Kong $20 each for the 20,000 units in its inventory. Suddenly, you owe King Kong $400,000 in credits—the equivalent of 5,000 units (at the new, reduced price) or 50% of the next monthly shipment. In addition, the rest of the units are sold at the lower price. Instead of selling $1,000,000 worth of product in May, you sell $400,000—a cut of 60%—as a result of a 20% price decrease!

Conversely, if you raise your price, your distributor can execute a price guarantee, typically around 30 days, to purchase additional inventory at the older, lower price. Normally, he has 30 days to order, 60 days to accept delivery, and a guarantee that he can obtain the same number of units as he purchased during the preceding 90-day period.

- On April 1, instead of cutting the price, you raise the price to $120. King Kong will probably issue a purchase order in April for 45,000 units at the old $100 price to be delivered on May 30. Although it may happen earlier (if King Kong sells your units earlier), don't expect your $4.5 million dollar check until July 30.

So, to manage cash flow from distributor sales:

- Don't expect a price increase to spur business results in immediate incoming cash, because your distributors will buy as much as possible at the lower price and still not pay for it for 60 days. (The reasoning here is that they are buying more inventory than they really need immediately.)

- Carefully examine the cash flow implications of a price decrease. Understand whether you will be hit by a sudden charge back on products you have already sold—a situation that can cause immediate and painful cash flow problems.

- Even if you don't change your prices, expect incoming cash to lag deliveries by up to 60 days.

## Watch for Changes to Cash Flow

Your total cash flow is the sum of all the small inflows and outflows that happen on a daily basis. An administrative inconvenience here and a collection problem there can add up to big trouble if not carefully watched. Consider the following examples:

- Banks can tie up your money by waiting until deposited checks clear at the issuing institution before letting you have access to your funds. When your deposit consists of checks from various parts of the country, this can delay your ability to use your money for a week or more.

- When the economy (or a specific sector) is down, customers often try to stretch payments. Customers who would normally pay in 30 days wait 45 days to pay; those who normally pay in 60 days may take 90. If several large customers stretch payments, you may have problems. Some customers will cancel or delay purchases in bad economic times.

- Payments for large computer and software purchases often depend on *acceptance tests*, in which the buyer reserves the right to "examine" the product in use for some period before paying all or part of the balance. He pays you only when your product completes his tests successfully. In my experience, acceptance and subsequent payment rarely occur when the vendor expects. Depending on the software (or hardware) involved and the personality of the customer, the delay may be a few days or a few months. To guard against excessive delays, make sure that you write the acceptance criteria into your sales agreement and that the criteria against which you are judged are within your control. Don't let the customer delay your payment because his hardware doesn't work or because he is simultaneously testing other products.

- Administration of purchase orders often delays payments. In my years in the industry, I must have come across dozens of large payments that were delayed because somebody was not available to approve a check or because a clerk misplaced the paperwork. If you deal in large purchase orders and don't get at least a few of these, I would be surprised.

No matter what type of product you have or what market you sell to, assume that you will not collect all the money paid to you and that a significant portion will be received late. Plan your expenditures with this in mind. If you don't, you may run into short-term cash flow problems that could easily have been avoided.

## Anticipating Cash Requirements

Cash flow is affected by your ability to predict the future. While you don't need to be Nostradamus, the better you are at understanding your future revenues, expenses, and cash flows, the easier it will be to have enough cash on hand.

Suppose your company's known expenditures are $100,000 per month. If you have estimated that your monthly revenues will be $120,000, you're covered in most circumstances. However, suppose you have to spend an unexpected $30,000 during April, or that your revenues dip to $90,000 during May. In either case, you may have a potential cash flow problem.

**TABLE 16-3:** *UNEXPECTED CHANGES IN CASH FLOW INCREASE RISK*

|  | Projection | If Receipts Dip | If Expenditures Increase |
|---|---|---|---|
| Cash Receipts | $ 120,000 | $ 90,000 | $ 120,000 |
| Cash Expenditures | 100,000 | 100,000 | 130,000 |
| Net Cash Flow | $ 20,000 | (10,000) | (10,000) |
| **Trouble?** | No | **Yes** | **Yes** |

To prevent cash flow trouble, examine your expenditures and revenues closely. Try to figure out which portions are subject to the most change. Try to estimate the probability of a change. Then plan for what you will do when problems do happen. It's easier to arrange for a credit line when you don't need money than when you do.

Cash flow issues will arise. The real question is when and how. Figure out what you will do in advance of the problem to minimize its impact on you.

# *Computing Your Cash Flow*

There are two common ways to examine your cash flow. You can look at your previous cash flow to understand how your position has changed. You can also forecast your upcoming cash flow to determine what your requirements will be. To look at your previous cash flow, compute it directly from your income statement. To forecast your upcoming need, you will need to make some assumptions and develop a cash flow forecast (pro forma cash flow summary). Both types of analyses are important.

## Your Statement of Changes

All public corporations develop a yearly statement of changes in cash flow from their yearly income statements; it's a Securities and Exchange Commission (SEC) requirement. As a privately owned company, you don't have to develop a statement of changes, but it's a good idea; the exercise will help you to recognize problems before they become critical. The idea is to take your original cash position, then show all the changes during the period so you can see your cash position at the end of the period. A sample statement of changes is shown in Figure 16-2.

Notice that the depreciation is added back on the statement of changes in cash flow. That's because the statement started with the net income from the accounting statements. As we have already seen, depreciation is a non-cash expense. Therefore, it was subtracted from net income even though no cash changed hands. We add it back to compensate for the previous subtraction.

## Your Pro Forma Cash Summary

An accurate cash forecast will help you prevent a cash shortage. To put together your cash forecast, you will need to make a few predictions: How many units you will sell? When will you sell them? How long it will take to receive payment? How much money will you need to spend? Then map the figures on a matrix from which you can compute your net cash need during each period. You will probably want to use a spreadsheet program so you can make adjustments to see how sensitive your cash flow needs are to changes in circumstances.

A sample format for your cash flow forecast is shown in Figure 16-3. When completing your forecast, remember that you are interested in when cash changes hands, not when sales, purchases, or billing happens. At the bottom of

```
                    Sample Software Corporation
                  Statement of Changes in Cash Flows
                     Year Ended December 31, 1994

Increase (Decrease) In Cash
in thousands
----------------------------------------
Cash flows from operating activities:
    Net income                                            $2,540
    Adjustments to net income:
        Depreciation                          $  880
        Decrease in merchandise inventory        120
        Increase in accounts receivable        (210)
        Increase in accounts payable             350
                                              -------
        Total adjustments                                  1,140
                                                          -------
Net cash provided by operating activities                  3,680
----------------------------------------
Cash flows from investment activities:
    Payment for purchase of building           (50)
    Payment for purchase of equipment          (12)
                                              --------
Net cash used in investment activities                      (62)
----------------------------------------
Cash flows from financing activities:
    Proceeds from issuance of common stock      500
    Dividends paid                                0
                                              --------
Net cash provided by financing activities                    500
----------------------------------------
Net increase in cash                                        4,118
Cash beginning of year                                         25
Cash end of year                                            4,143
```

**FIGURE 16-2:** *STATEMENT OF CHANGES IN CASH FLOW*

each column, compute the sum of the inflows and the sum of the outflows for the period. The net difference is your cash surplus (or cash need, if negative). It's important to make sure that your time increments are small enough to pinpoint trouble spots so you can arrange to have enough cash. (Most companies use one month as the basic increment.) Your forecast should also cover a long enough period to take into account seasonal trends. If you're looking for bank or venture funding, you will probably need to submit a credible monthly forecast to your financier that shows your projected cash flows for the next two-year period. Startup companies would be wise to make similar projections.

```
                  Sample Software Corporation
                      Cash flow forecast
               January 1995 through December 1997

                      Jan Feb Mar Apr May Apr Jun Jul ...


   Receipts
        Cash sales
        Payment of Credit Sales
        Loan Proceeds
        Other
   Total Receipts

   Disbursements
        Direct labor
        Direct materials
        Equipment
        Salaries
        Rent
        Utilities
        Advertising
        Insurance
        Loan Payments
        Taxes
   Total Disbursements

   Total Cash Flow (Receipts - Disbursements)
   -------------------------
   Beginning Balance (previous month ending balance)
   Ending Balance (beginning balance + month total cash flow)
```

*FIGURE 16-3: TEMPLATE FOR A CASH FLOW FORECAST*

# Managing Your Cash

The best way to make sure you don't run out of cash is to manage it. There are three important aspects to managing cash flow:

1. Making sure you have enough working capital to start, and resources to get more cash along the way

2. Managing the amount of money going out the door

3. Developing procedures to spur timely receipt of cash from external organizations and individuals

If you find yourself with excess cash on hand for a short time, you will want to invest it wisely while making sure it will be available when you need it. We'll leave a discussion of your investment options to other authors.

Just about every action you take has some effect on a cash flow. Let's look at one common business decision. You may want to purchase a $100,000 computer to use for the next three years. However, if you buy it, you must pay the entire $100,000 immediately, which might leave you short of funds for other projects. As we've noted, the government won't give you much help because the tax authorities make you capitalize the system, thereby delaying the bulk of the associated tax benefits until future years. So your first option is to delay the purchase, thereby delaying the cash payment. Of course, if you really need the system, this option is not the best.

If you lease the computer instead of buying it, you won't have to pay the entire amount up front. Instead, you pay a fixed monthly fee for a specified period of time. At the end of the lease, you either continue the lease, buy the computer at a prespecified price (often a set percentage of the original price or "fair market value"), or send it back and owe nothing. Your total out-of-pocket costs of leasing are generally higher than purchasing, but the smaller up-front cash outlay often makes it the best alternative. However, you should realize that there are other consequences to a lease. Because you don't own the computer, it becomes a debt on your balance sheet and cannot be used as collateral for loans.

You can also time share from somebody else's system. If your software runs on UNIX, you can dial into the system or connect via the Internet. If you need a PC, you will have to go to the system yourself. This option also lowers initial cash outlay, but may be difficult to arrange or lack adequate security. No matter which option you choose, you will need to balance your need for cash with your need for profits and convenience.

The remainder of this chapter covers the three cash management methods.

## Obtaining Adequate Working Capital

Working capital is the term for the money you keep on hand to handle everyday cash needs. It's easy to spend more than you have because you always need an additional developer, an additional page of advertising, or double your booth space at your most important trade show.

What happens if you don't have working capital? Will the new developer be willing to work for you if he doesn't get paid? Will the magazine accept your ad without payment? Will the trade show organizer reserve your booth if you don't pay in advance? Unlikely. Unlikely. Unlikely.

Don't put yourself in a position where you must stop development or inadequately market your product because you run out of cash. Start with enough money to get you to the point where you have sufficient revenue flowing in and have additional backup cash sources lined up. The relative cost of overcapitalization is small; but undercapitalization exposes you to great risk.

### Arranging lines of credit

The best time to arrange lines of credit or loans is when you don't need them. Banks and other financiers are always more willing to "risk" their money on a company that they perceive entails no risk. Set up your lines of credit in advance to reduce the possibility of future problems. When cash flow problems arise, you will be ready to act swiftly to neutralize them. (Chapter 17 describes how to obtain financing.)

### Other sources of capital

You may be unable to obtain venture financing or a loan from a bank. If so, use a creative approach to obtain cash flow. Perhaps you can consult on the side while developing your product. Maybe you can obtain a technology sharing agreement in which your partner pays part of your costs or provides a cash infusion. You might even be able to get advance payment from a major customer to use as working capital. The best time to arrange these special relationships is before you get into trouble, not when trouble strikes.

### Expect trouble

Speaking of trouble, it will happen, just as sure as you are going to have a disk drive failure at some point. Plan for it by having extra cash to use for emergencies. You rarely can predict when a competitor will introduce a new product that decreases your sales by 50%, or when a power outage will cause you thousands of dollars of damage and lost production. In either case, your cash flows will change—possibly permanently. Be ready to adjust.

## Keeping Cash From Going Out

The easiest way to control cash flow is to minimize the cash that moves out the door. Reducing outflows solves half of the cash flow dilemma. There are several ways to decrease cash outflow: buying only what you need, predetermining your payment terms, delaying payments until they are due, and prioritizing your payments.

### Buy only what you really need

Before you purchase anything, ask yourself whether you really need it. If the answer is "No, but it would be nice," then you shouldn't buy it. In particular, don't purchase something just because you might need it later; your situation may change and eliminate the need. I know a young entrepreneur who bought 40,000 sheets of letterhead, enough to last for several years. By buying in quantity, he got a great price—but half of his stock became worthless because the company moved before they were used. In the end, buying so many sheets was a bad decision; he could have used the money elsewhere. It is particularly important to delay large capital purchases as long as possible; such purchases require a lot of cash, without giving you any immediate tax benefit.

It is also unwise to enter long-term contracts in which you spend a great deal of money based on expectations of future revenue. These long-term contracts tend to become cash hogs, draining valuable money from company accounts. Avoid them.

### Set up acceptable payment terms in advance

Whenever you need to make large expenditures that jeopardize your cash flow, pre-arrange payment terms that both you and your supplier can live with. Since Marketing Masters does a fair amount of subcontracting, we try to work out payment terms with our subcontractors who meet their cash flow needs while allowing us some room to move in case the client is delinquent on payments. In this way, we don't have to worry about making the next payroll or paying our rent.

### Pay on the due date

If a supplier offers you credit with no interest or penalty attached, take it and don't pay until the payment is actually due. This increases the cash you have available for emergencies, and may even allow you to put some into interest bearing accounts for a short period. For every $10,000 on which you can collect interest of 5%, you gain $500 per year. When interest rates are low, on the other hand, it's not unusual for computer retailers and office suppliers to offer extended terms such as "90 days, same as cash."

Paying on the due date, instead of before it, is a standard practice of large, successful firms. If IBM issues a P.O. for your software that has 0-day payment terms, you know you won't receive a check from them for two months. Why should you pay them for equipment 30 days before the money is due? Play by the same rules as they do. Don't pay the bill the day you get it. That's not when it's due. Pay on the due date. (By the way, that does not mean pay *after* the due date. If you consistently pay your bills late, you will ruin your credit rating.)

If your credit terms include an interest charge, you can use your purchase as if it is a short term loan. For instance, a computer supplier may offer you a three year payment option at 10% interest on a $5000 system. By accepting the offer, you have effectively received a loan for $5000 without having gone to the bank. Take care, however, not to overburden your company with high-interest loans because the interest cost and delayed payments can cause future cash flow problems. The rule of thumb is to pay off your high-est-interest loans first.

---

### ☞ *Pay Taxes First, Payroll Next* ☜

If you get into a jam, prioritize the order in which you make your payments. The normal pecking order is: federal government first, then state and local government, personnel, important suppliers, secured creditors, unsecured creditors, investors.

Since the government makes the rules, it gets paid first. If you fail to pay your taxes on time, you will end up paying them anyway, but with a penalty, or you will go to jail. This holds for income taxes, social security, and payroll withholding. It's a good practice to put payroll taxes and deductions into a separate account on pay day. You will be sure that the money is available when you need to pay the government, and reduce the penalties you incur due to mistakes or cash flow problems.

Usually, your state and local governments are next in line. If you don't pay them, they can close you down, then your employees. There are two reasons your employees get high priority: (1) they are your most important asset; and (2) you legally have to pay them next.

After you have paid your employees, pay your most important suppliers. You don't want them to cut off your future supplies because you can't pay. Similarly, you don't want secured creditors to take their collateral (often workstations, furniture, or other equipment). Your unsecured creditors should be paid next. They get low priority because they have little leverage over you. They aren't important to your future operation. Nor can they fine you or take away equipment. Your investors only get money if there is any left. This might seem unfair, especially since you probably feel some kind of duty to your investors, but it isn't—it's business. Investment is risky by definition.

---

## Keeping the Cash Coming In

Controlling your cash inflows is much tougher than controlling the amount of cash you spend, because many of the decisions are made by others. First, you're dependent on the market for your product. If you don't sell as many units as expected, or have to cut price, your incoming cash drops. Second, when you sell your product, the buyer might not pay you on time, even if you do have a contractual agreement stating payment terms.

Even though your ability to receive cash is largely out of your hands, you can affect it by increasing sales (covered in the marketing section) and by collecting payments on time from those who owe you money.

### Dealing with purchase orders

Purchase orders (P.O.'s) are often used by corporations to track purchases and payments. The customer issues a purchase order to your company stating what is purchased and under what terms (price, delivery, shipment . . . ). It usually "freezes" a certain amount of budget money with which the customer will pay you. If you don't negotiate special payment terms before the P.O. is issued, you will be governed by its standard terms, often "net 30 days" (which can mean 30 days after shipment, delivery, installation, or acceptance—depending on who is interpreting the term).

I have found that most corporate purchasing agents are willing to modify standard terms for large orders, allowing payment in increments. For example:

> 10% due with purchase order
> 80% due with shipment (FOB shipping point)
> 10% due upon installation and check out

Modifying the payment terms gives you your cash earlier, but you still have a vested interest in getting the customer up-and-running. You don't get your final payment until he is satisfied.

If you accept standard P.O. terms, make sure that the P.O. clearly identifies whether the payment is based on shipment, delivery, installation or acceptance.

### Prepayment discounts

If cash flow is a problem for you, you might consider offering a discount for prompt payment. Terms like "2/10 net 30" are common in these cases. 2/10 net 30 means a 2% discount if paid within 10 days, otherwise payment due within 30 days. Unfortunately, some unscrupulous companies take the discount even when they do not pay within the approved discount period. Prepayment discounts are also an expensive way to collect money. That 2% discount for 20 days use of cash is an effective annual rate of approximately 35%. That's what you're paying to get the money early. A less costly way to offer an incentive is to offer free additional software when they have paid in full.

### Cash in advance

While it is somewhat unusual, some companies are able to demand full prepayment before delivery. Those that can usually have a unique product with capabilities that cannot easily be duplicated, or have products that incorporate a service. These companies can justify prepayment because once the service is rendered, they have no collateral or leverage to get payment. Companies that provide products or services to events (such as trade shows) often require advanced payment. If you have ever displayed at a trade show, you have witnessed it from the other side. It is not unusual to pay tens of thousands of dollars to various vendors before the show starts.

### Collecting via credit card

If you sell directly to end users and if your price is no more than a few hundred dollars, consider using credit cards as a means of collection. You will be charged a fee by the credit card company for each transaction, typically 2% to 5% of purchase price. This charge is well worth it, because the amount of money due you (your accounts receivable) drop dramatically, it is less costly to collect and sometimes sales even go up—all of which are beneficial to your cash flow.

Contact your local bank (for MasterCard or Visa), American Express, or Discover to set up to accept charge cards. If you are unable to find a source willing to allow you to accept payment via credit card, contact a local business group or The Software Publishers Association to find out what options may be available through them.

### Try to buy situations

If you allow your customers to try your software before they buy, you are setting yourself up for major cash flow problems. Don't make try-and-buy situations your norm. Offer them only to your best prospects, and then, only if you trust them. Try-and-buy situations often lead to "Can I have more time?" which delays your payment. Whenever possible, offer a money back guarantee instead.

### Sometimes you must fight to collect

There are two conditions that may force you to use extraordinary methods to collect your money: when a customer simply won't pay or when your cash condition becomes dire.

If a specific customer owes you a lot of money for a long time, you can sit and wait and hope and pray that he finally pays, or you can keep on top of the customer until he cannot stand it anymore. Sometimes the customer still refuses to pay (or can't pay because he has not managed his cash flow properly). You can ask your lawyer to put pressure on him to pay. Although your lawyer has a bit more clout than you do—the threat of court action—he still may not collect, and you would be out legal fees, too. Alternatively, you can have a collection agency approach your customer for payment. The agency will typically have the check written to it and pay you a percentage of what it collects. The collection agency usually keeps about one-third of what it collects.

You do have leverage in collection disputes. You can demand return of your product. If the delinquent customer wants to continue to use it, he may be willing to work out a payment schedule acceptable to you.

If a reseller owes you money, you can put that reseller on "credit hold" by refusing to send him any more shipments until he pays you. If he wants to continue to sell your product, he'll pay you what he already owes first. This may take some guts for you to do, especially if he is a large reseller, but it may be necessary.

When your cash need gets dire, you can "factor your receivables." Factoring is when you sell your entire portfolio of receivables to a third party, who pays you cash and collects from your customers. You get a quick infusion of cash but less than you would if you collected yourself. Factoring companies usually pay 30% to 70% of the value of the portfolio. Factoring should only be a method of last resort.

# Financing Your Company

In a perfect world, your first sale would happen the day you completed your product, thereby beginning a long history of growing revenue and profit. This is the real world, however, so before you have a product to sell, you need capital to begin—human capital, hard currency, or both—as well as occasional infusions of cash on an ongoing basis. The cash pays for staffing to develop, assemble, and sell your product, as well as equipment on which to develop it. By operating a software company, you have an advantage: the amount of equipment you need is very low because you can develop your product on an inexpensive desktop system or time-share on a large system. But there's still the cost of staffing; and you need money to pay for electricity, phones (to locate and sell to your initial customers), and development tools.

Finding cash is an ongoing struggle. Even very successful companies spend lots of time working with their bankers and other investors. Fortunately, there are many ways to obtain funding. In this chapter, we'll look at your options.

## *Financial Needs Change With Time*

Your need for capital varies over time. If you have not yet started your business and only have an idea for a product, your cash requirements may be substantial because you're facing many months of labor before the product will bring in a single dollar in sales. Your needs are less if you have been developing the product after hours while you were employed elsewhere, especially if it is almost ready for demonstration and delivery. For most products, you will need money to start your marketing and sales effort, although a few companies can get away without large expenses to start marketing.

Once you get going, you should be able to pay for your efforts with cash. But the picture changes again in times of growth. You may need additional cash to fund the growth as you add people, equipment, and facilities. Each time you decide to expand by entering new markets or producing new products, you increase your need for cash. And if your market takes an unexpected downturn, you may need extra money to survive. To help you through the many stages, you may turn to outside sources (as opposed to your internally generated revenue) to find your cash.

*TABLE 17-1: YOUR NEED FOR CASH VARIES OVER TIME*

| Stage | Revenue | Expenditure | Need for Non-Revenue Cash |
|---|---|---|---|
| Development | None | Large | High: No income to pay for development |
| Initial Marketing | Low | High | High: Cash inflows typically not sufficient to meet expenditures. Cost to enter market may be great. |
| Ongoing Sales | Steady | Steady | Low: Inflows typically able to offset outflows |
| Growth | Increasing | Large | High: Cost of entry into new markets or cost of new product development may be great. Inflows may or may not offset outflows. |
| Problems | Decreasing | Any | High or Low: Cost of turnaround may be great. But lowering costs may lead to reduced outflows while maintaining positive cash flow. |

# *Where To Go for Money*

There are many ways to obtain the funding that you need to start up, maintain, or grow your business. Each one has its risks and its benefits. The most common are:

- Using your own money and "sweat equity"
- Borrowing money from a bank
- Getting funding from a government source
- Relying on friends, relatives, and neighbors
- Seeking equity investments from venture capitalists

Where you go for your capital depends on your goals. If you have started your company to become your own boss, for instance, venture capital is not for you. The venture capitalists who fund you become your bosses. If your goal is to become filthy rich quickly, venture capital (if you satisfy their requirements) may be the best option. Borrowing money from a bank allows you to remain the boss, but also increases your risk: you are solely responsible for the entire business plus the money you have borrowed. As you read on, you will have a better idea about the risks, benefits, and requirements of each funding source, as well as how to take advantage of the one you choose.

## *Bankrolling Your Own Business*

It takes lots of time and energy to look for external funding. For many entrepreneurs, this means it's more productive to spend your time looking for business instead. After all, if you have a good demonstrable product and the enthusiasm that allows you to communicate your vision to potential users, you can probably obtain your funding by selling to a few high-volume purchasers. Otherwise known as "sweat equity," you are actually funding your endeavor from your own sales.

There are several keys to doing it this way. First, your product must be close to completion and you must have a demonstrable version to prove your product is real. Then, you must be willing to get on the phone to the most qualified prospects to tell your story yourself. This is the perfect situation if you have developed your product after hours while working for somebody else. By the time you start your business, you have a real, marketable product.

You will also have to do many things by yourself until you get your revenue flowing: accounting, copywriting, developing, customer support, and general administration. The key is to cut corners wherever possible. Make sure you have at least enough cash to pay your personal and business bills while you wait for income from your first customers. It could be a long time before you see significant income: anywhere from a month to a year after you start, maybe even more. That may not be an issue if you are independently wealthy. If you're not, make sure you have enough ready money to last at least six months. Otherwise, you can get pretty hungry.

Many successful companies were started on sweat equity by entrepreneurs like Steve Jobs, R.H. Macy, Alexander Graham Bell, Michael Dell, and H. Ross Perot. They've done all right for themselves.

## *Structuring Loans To Suit Your Needs*

In the business world, going into debt is a solution, not necessarily a problem. Borrowing money allows you to finance projects that you might not be able to undertake otherwise. In general, you can obtain loans ("debt financing") from banks, savings and loans, or finance companies. (We'll call all financial institutions banks in this discussion.) Your loans are either long term (paid off over several years) or short term (paid off within a year). Long-term debt provides general funding for the company. Short-term debt often provides cash for specific activities or to get through difficult periods. You are 100% responsible for the money you borrow, so use debt only when you are sure that you can pay it back within the time frame agreed.

Interest on loans is often charged in the form of "prime plus," with prime representing the interest rate that the bank charges its best customers for loans. Your loan's interest rate will probably equal the current prime rate plus a predetermined premium, typically about 2% for a company without a long track record. If the interest on your loan is at a rate of prime plus 2% and prime for the period is 8%, you pay 10% on an annualized basis. Since the prime rate rises and falls with banking market conditions, this methodology puts the risk on you if your bank's prime rate rises while you are borrowing. You also benefit if the bank decreases its prime rate.

Of course, the bank wants you to take the risks, while minimizing its own risk. So your banker will require collateral, typically in the form of a lien on your receivables, inventory, or equipment. Sometimes a bank will ask for a personal guarantee, by having you "pledge" your non-business assets. I'll cover collateral later in this chapter.

## Long-term Borrowing

When you want to borrow money to fund your entire business operation, you need long-term money, which often requires you to present a business plan showing the long-term viability of your enterprise. The banker will examine your business plan, interview you to understand your business skills, and ask for collateral in case you default on your loan. His willingness to loan you money will depend on the amount of risk you represent to him as a debtor. It's fairly difficult for startup ventures to get substantial long-term loans; the most likely way to get such funding as a startup is to use your personal assets as collateral. For example, you might take out a second mortgage on your house. I'll be more specific about how to judge the collateral value of your home in a few pages.

## Bridge Loans

Obtain a short-term bridge loan if you need money to fund a specific project for which you know payout will happen in a specific time frame. For example, if a customer has given you an order for 1000 units to be delivered within 60 days, you can often get the bank to loan you the money to buy the parts, assemble the units, and ship them to your customer.

# Lines of Credit

Lines of credit are predetermined amounts upon which the borrower can draw at his own option, sometimes as easily as writing a check. Businesses with cyclical cash flow patterns often arrange lines of credit to make sure they have operating funds while cash flow cycles are near the bottom—sometimes for periods as short as ten to 30 days. Lines of credit often include a fee (even if no money is borrowed) in addition to the interest charge for the actual borrowed amount. Some banks charge a fixed fee; others, a fee based on the amount of available credit. The following is an example of the latter:

Fred's Software Company sells software to farmers to keep track of their accounts. Farmers tend to purchase seasonally, with the winter being a time of low purchases. Therefore, Fred's revenue and cash flow dips dramatically during the winter months. Fred Smith, the president, has arranged for a $500,000 line of credit so he can pay his bills all winter while waiting for the good summer months. Last year, he had an outstanding debt of $100,000 during January, $200,000 during February, $100,000 during March, and a paid-off balance in April. The company's established line of credit has a 12% interest charge with a .25% charge for unused balance. The costs related to the credit line were:

|  | Jan | Feb | Mar | Apr |
|---|---|---|---|---|
| #1 Credit Line | $500,000 | $500,000 | $500,000 | $500,000 |
| #2 Amount Borrowed | $100,000 | $200,000 | $100,000 | $0 |
| #3 Amount Available (#1 − #2) | $400,000 | $300,00 | $400,000 | $500,000 |
| #4 Cost of Borrowed Amount (#2 × 12% / 12) | $1000 | $2000 | $1000 | $0 |
| #5 Cost of Available Credit (.25% × 12 × #3) | $83 | $63 | $83 | $104 |
| Total Cost (#4 + #5) | $1083 | $2063 | $1083 | $104 |

As can be seen by the example, credit lines mean quick availability of cash for certain activities, as well as a price for the privilege. Over four months, Fred Software paid $333 for the privilege of having access to the line of credit, in addition to the actual interest on the money borrowed.

# Demand Loan or Installment Loan

Your loan can take the form of an "installment" loan or a "demand" loan. There is little flexibility with an installment loan. Your payment schedule is established up front. You may even receive a coupon booklet to show when each payment is due. The mortgage on your house and auto loans are typical installment loans.

With a demand loan, the bank has the right to demand payment of the entire amount at their discretion, but in most situations, the payments have been pre-arranged by agreement between you and the banker. You are typically billed monthly for the amount due. From dealing with banks, I have found that a demand loan gives the local loan officer or branch manager more flexibility in providing the funds. Several years ago, I had worked out a payment schedule in which I paid interest on a monthly basis. Every six months, I paid 10% of the principal so that it would be paid off within five years. By paying the principal biannually instead of monthly, I got an extra cash buffer during my initial six-month startup, and similarly in each subsequent six-month period. Of course, the total amount that I paid to the bank over the term of the loan was a bit higher because my average principal balance was higher, but worth it for me. Ready cash was more important.

# What Bankers Want

There is a common belief that bankers lend money only to those who don't need it. Bankers have earned the reputation because they're not risk takers. They only lend money when chances are high that they will see their money again—the same thing that you or I might do. A banker would be more likely to lend money to an established company that wants to expand its offices and buy new furniture than he would be to fund a startup. He can seize and sell the furniture if the first company doesn't pay him back. The startup has no assets for him to sell if payments are not met.

Banks don't like risks; and providing working capital to a startup company is extremely risky. To do business with a bank, you must show the banker that you can do business on his terms. He'll evaluate your product and your market so he can figure out whether your business is viable. However, few bankers understand the software business, and most are liable to reach the wrong conclusions about it. Therefore, you must present yourself and your idea in terms he can understand: financial and personal. That means you must show that your business plan is viable and your management team is capable of carrying it out.

Your business plan will give him much of the financial information. It will include information about your product and market, your competition, your expected revenues and costs for the next five years, your expected cash flows for the next two years, and information about your team. If you are already in business, it will also outline your financial success during the most recent years. Your business plan will also give your banker an idea of how well-organized you are.

Even more important is the personal aspect. He must feel confident that you and your team can carry out the task you tell him you will do. If he has no confidence in you, you will not get any money, no matter how good a business plan you present. He knows that once you walk out of the bank with his money, you're in control; and he's not willing to cede control of his money to somebody in whom he doesn't have confidence. Positive references from people that he knows and trusts help him make a decision in your favor. So do letters of intent from corporate customers stating that they will buy your product at a set price within a set time frame. You may even want to give him a demonstration of your product.* These are confidence boosters.

Once you pass these hurdles, he'll find ways to decrease his risk such as requiring collateral that he can seize and sell if you don't pay him back. He may ask you to keep your business account in his bank. He may also ask you to find a co-signer or require an up-front fee (i.e. closing cost) when you finalize the loan. Once the banker has determined how much risk you represent, he puts together a package to meet your needs while protecting his own investment. You may not always like the terms he offers. You will probably even negotiate with him to reach equitable terms. When the final agreement is reached, the risk will be yours, not his.

If you are rejected by a bank, find out why. He may see a flaw in your plan that you have not seen, in which case you should rethink your plan. Alternately, you may still want to proceed. Make adjustments based on his feedback; then return, or go see the next banker on your list.

## Guidelines for Working With Bankers

1. *Get an introduction.* A banker is more likely to do business with someone who has been referred to him by someone he knows and trusts. Talk to people who are running similar businesses, find out who their banker is, and get them to introduce you.

2. *Be prepared.* Preparedness shows that you have done your homework and are ready for contingencies. At minimum be ready to give details about how you will accomplish your mission. Have a game plan ready that states what you will do if sales do not proceed as well as expected. Understand

---

* Caution: Only give a demo if your product is stable and understandable to somebody in the banker's profession. Outside the computer industry, they don't understand development projects that are still unstable.

your cash flow issues and be able to communicate them. (A customer that understands cash flow is of utmost importance to a banker.) Make sure that you can convey the reasons that your new product will succeed as well as your knowledge of the competitive environment. Take with you any items required to show how your product will meet a market need. Be ready to answer unexpected questions, even if you must prepare for questions he does not ask.

Once the banker becomes interested in loaning you money, he requires a new level of detail: your business and personal income tax returns. The business return (if you have already been in business) shows him that the information you provide is reliable. The personal returns give him an idea about how much personal income you have drawn from the business to date and how much you need to live. Both levels of detail allow him to better understand the amount of risk he takes by loaning you money. The banker will also require appraisals on property that you use for collateral. Don't delay providing this information when he asks. It will only delay your loan.

3.  *Have a well-organized business plan.* For long-term business loans, walk in the door with your business plan ready. Without one, the likelihood of you receiving the loan is low. The plan must show that you have thought through contingencies and that your plan is doable.

4.  *Understand your banker's goals.* Bankers, like employees of other organizations, are compensated according to the way they accomplish their goals. If you know what their goals are, you will be able to negotiate well. Make it a point to understand what he can and cannot negotiate. Many banks charge an up-front fee equal to some percentage of the total loan (a.k.a. points). Many banks provide incentives to their managers and loan officers to extract these points even if they must take a smaller interest rate on the loan. (Another risk avoidance technique: they get their money up front.) If you know somebody who has negotiated a loan with your bank, call him to find out what works and what doesn't.

5.  *Put on your best image.* Treat your visit to the bank like an interview. Put on a suit and show that you can fit into the mold of businessman. It doesn't matter whether you wear a suit at your office. You're in his office now. Image and grooming are important at this time. As the old adage says, "You never get a second chance to make a good first impression."

6.  *Go to the right banker.* Banks have specialties. Some banks may be more likely to lend to small business while others are into consumer banking. Find out in advance which banks are your best targets. If you strike a bank that is

not correct for you, don't be afraid to ask that banker which bank would be more appropriate.

7.  *Be honest.* As in any business situation, don't try to suggest that you can do the impossible or unlikely. Be honest with your banker. You're trying to build a long-term relationship, and long-term relationships must be based on trust.

8.  *Don't waste his time.* An experienced loan officer or branch manager knows how long it takes for preliminary and subsequent meetings. If he allocates 30 minutes, fit your meeting into that time. Don't make him late for his next meeting. Do provide him with the important information to help him make an educated decision. Tell him your key points and let him keep a copy of your business plan so he can review it on his own time. Make an appointment for a follow-up discussion after he has read your plan and has had sufficient time to digest it properly.

9.  *Be on the same team.* Remember, your banker wants to find reasons to loan you the money, not to keep it from you. That's the way he makes his money. Work with him to put together an agreement that suits both parties.

10. *Build a long-term relationship.* A good relationship with a banker is a long-term relationship. You may need his help again in the future. Even if you don't borrow money from your bank immediately, get to know the branch manager. Say hello when you stop in, and let him know about large new accounts. If you feel that you will need large loans someday, you may want to borrow a small amount today, to establish credit with him. Put him on your mailing list so he feels like he is part of your business. If you become a great success, he can crow, too, as the person who loaned you the money to make it happen.

## No Need To Offer Your Firstborn Child

In order to protect their investments, banks ask for collateral from you. If you fail to repay the loans as promised, they will seize the collateral. Acceptable forms of collateral include houses, other real estate, stocks, bonds, or cash. Not all forms of collateral will be accepted by all institutions under all circumstances. Table 17-2 summarizes many acceptable collateral sources.

**TABLE 17-2:** POSSIBLE SOURCES OF COLLATERAL

| | |
|---|---|
| **Business Assets** | Cash |
| | Accounts receivable (the money that other parties owe you) |
| | Inventory (to the extent that it can be converted into cash) |
| **Personal Assets** | Cash and securities |
| | Stock |
| | Second mortgage on home |
| | Mortgage on some other asset |
| | Cosignature from a "second source" of payment |

Banks prefer liquid assets as collateral because liquid assets make it much easier for them to collect their money if a borrower defaults on his loan. A liquid asset is one that is either cash or easily converted to cash (hence the term liquidate). The less liquid the asset, the more collateral the bank demands. This provides the bank with a hedge in case it is forced to dispose of the asset at a lower price than expected. When a bank does liquidate a non-liquid asset, it keeps the portion of the proceeds that you owe the bank (including all interest to that point) and gives the remainder to you.

Fair Market Value is the amount of money that will be received by the seller if the asset is sold, and is important when you use non-liquid assets as collateral. Suppose you decide to use your home as collateral and present it to a bank whose policy is to allow up to 80% of the real estate fair market value to be used as collateral. If you paid $200,000 for the house and its real estate price appreciated to $240,000, your collateral value may look like this:

| | | |
|---|---|---|
| Home purchase price | $200,000 | (A) |
| Down payment | 40,000 | (B) |
| Original mortgage amount ((A) − (B)) | 160,000 | (C) |
| Amount paid toward principal since owning the house | 15,000 | (D) |
| Outstanding loan amount ((C) − (D)) | 145,000 | (E) |
| Current market value (FMV) | 240,000 | (F) |
| 80% × FMV | 192,000 | (G) |
| Collateral value (80% of ((G) − (E))) | 47,000 | (H) |

Now suppose that your home is in New England, which endured a lengthy real estate slump. The collateral value of your home, if bought at the peak of the market in 1986 for $200,000 with a $40,000 down payment, may look like this:

| | | |
|---|---|---|
| Home purchase price | $ 200,000 | (A) |
| Down payment | 40,000 | (B) |
| Original mortgage amount | 160,000 | (C) |
| Amount paid toward principal | 15,000 | (D) |
| Outstanding loan amount | 145,000 | (E) |
| Current market value (FMV) | 150,000 | (F) |
| 80% × FMV | 120,000 | (G) |
| Collateral value | 0 | (H) |

In our second case, even though you have already paid $55,000 toward the house that you purchased for $200,000, the bank will not accept it as collateral. If you default, the bank will lose $25,000 because it will have to sell the house for $120,000 while paying the mortgage amount of $145,000. The banker doesn't see this as a good investment, even if the bank already holds the mortgage on your home. Check into the value of your real estate and its expected value as collateral before you make an assumption that it will provide an adequate source of collateral for your needs.

If you allow the bank to use two different types of collateral, and you fail to pay as promised, they'll seize the collateral in whichever order they want. Generally, they'll take the easiest to liquidate. Thus, if you give them a $10,000 savings bond and a house, the bank will sell the bond first if they have to foreclose on your loan. If a balance still remains, it will liquidate the house. Again, the bank is trying to protect its own investment. Obtaining sufficient collateral is a sensible way for them to alleviate their risks.

## Getting Help From Uncle Sam

In some cases, businesses cannot arrange adequate bank financing because they have not been in business long enough, don't have adequate collateral, or are considered too risky by the bank. This may be the time to rely on the United States government.

One way is to obtain loan guarantees from the Small Business Administration (SBA). These SBA guarantees act as collateral for your bank. To start the process, you usually ask a bank for financing. If they think you have a sound business plan but insufficient collateral, ask to speak with one of their SBA loan officers. (The SBA is represented at most major banks.) You will go through the whole procedure again with the SBA representative. If he likes your business case, he'll guarantee your loan. If you fail to repay the bank, the SBA pays the bank out of government funds, thereby decreasing bank risk. The major cost of participating in an SBA guarantee program is filling out paperwork while the loan is outstanding. Getting an SBA grant can be a long, arduous process; you should be prepared to wait a long time and visit the SBA office several times. Before starting, ask yourself whether SBA financing is a reasonable alternative:

1. Determine if you can wait three to six months to receive your funding.

2. Determine why you were turned down by your bank. If you have a solid business plan, but simply lack collateral, you're a good fit.

3. Ask yourself whether you are willing to report to the SBA frequently. This can distract you from other functions of your business. If you plan to use SBA financing guarantees, it's best to include a budget for additional accounting expenses so you can offload part of the associated workload.

Another alternative is a federal SBIR (Small Business Innovative Research) grant. Federal SBIR grants are made by federal agencies (notably Department of Defense, Department of Energy, NASA, and ARPA) to provide money for companies and individuals to develop a technical product, process, or technique (typically basic research or applications for existing technology). In the past, most of the grant money has been provided to further military research, but the government is now more interested in commercial applications.

To receive an SBIR grant, you must apply formally by detailing the technical merits of your proposed project as well as how you will use the funding you receive. The application process is long and the number of awards is small compared to the number of companies who apply. In addition, you will be competing for funds with research scientists and engineers who know how to obtain SBIR grants to fund their projects.

## Your State Can Help, Too

Most states are eager to help fund new businesses because they create new jobs. In fact, many states have departments specifically to provide funding for small companies. Depending on the state and the department's charter, it may provide funds directly (as venture capital) if you can find matching funds, loan you money, or a combination. Some states provide special loan guarantees on either an ongoing basis or from time to time to meet state economic goals. Similar in structure to SBA guarantees, these state guarantees usually have different options and requirements.

For instance, in 1991, the Connecticut Development Authority established the Connecticut Works Fund (CWF) Preferred Lender Guaranty Program. This program guaranteed up to 20% of the outstanding loan balance for loans up to $25,000,000, with the *first* 20% lost (in case of a default) being the responsibility of CWF, shared with the bank. Once 20% of the loan was lost, the bank bore the rest. (SBA guarantees typically prorate the government's share of the loss from the start; they do not provide first loss coverage for their entire amount.) For companies to obtain loans under the CWF program, the borrower must have been unable to obtain conventional financing and they must create at least one job for every $20,000 that they borrowed. The CWF program was meant to help kick start the economy in the state, because it had been devastated during the preceding years by a decline in real estate, a banking crisis, and the contraction of federal defense programs. On an ongoing basis, Connecticut has three organizations that are meant to provide capital for small companies or companies with technology or growth opportunities. Find out what programs your state offers.

## Borrowing From Friends and Family

My best advice about obtaining loans from family and friends is "Don't!" There is too high a probability that it will break up your family. The business may be a bust and you will lose their money. Worse, it may be a success, and they'll feel that you haven't given them a fair deal. It's tough to win when you inject a financial deal into a non-financial relationship.

Now that I have made my feelings clear, you may decide to ignore me. If you do, at least protect yourself from potential problems. Make sure that everything is put in writing, including the amount of the loan, interest rate, payment schedule, and what happens in case of a default. (This is like a prenuptial agreement.) Be perfectly clear that this is a loan and that they do not own a piece of your business. Ask your lawyer to draw up an agreement based on standard practices. Even though you are dealing with loved ones, this is a business matter, not a family matter.

Another alternative is to have a relative cosign for a loan from a bank. In this case, make sure your relative understands that whatever he puts up as collateral is subject to loss. If he co-signs and offers his home as collateral, his home cannot be sold until your loan is paid off, because your loan becomes a second mortgage on his house.

## Equity Financing: Selling a Piece of the Business

Debt financing is not appropriate in all situations. In some cases, equity financing is a more suitable alternative. With equity financing, you sell a percentage of your business to somebody else who shares the risks and rewards with you (as opposed to debt financing where you own the entire business, take the risk, and reap the rewards). For example, Barnie Software Corporation has obtained its funding by selling stock (a form of equity). Barnie Jacobs, the founder, contributed $20,000 of his own money and runs the company on a daily basis. Victor Capital bought a 50% interest in the company for $80,000, making Barnie Software's total capitalization $100,000. Barnie's risk is limited to $20,000 plus his time, instead of the entire $100,000 (as it would be if he had borrowed the money from Victor). But Barnie has given up one-half the decision making authority to Victor as well as one-half of the profits.

You can get equity funding from a variety of sources including:

- Venture Capitalists—firms or individuals who are in business specifically to provide funding to companies in exchange for equity.

- An "angel"—an individual who invests his personal money in your company. Typically, angels are not in the venture business.

- Your customers—when a company sees a promising new technology that it can use, it sometimes provides funds to develop the technology. These funds can be provided as purchases with advanced payment or an equity stake.

- State funding agencies—some funding agencies take a royalty or ownership stake when they provide funding for companies.

- Other computer or software companies—those that have products that are compatible with yours or companies for which your product is a natural extension. (Companies outside the computer industry may be interested in a similar way.)

Equity financing can be very tricky; get your lawyer and accountant involved to help you determine your valuation (and any tax issues) and put together the agreements.

## *Making Your Fortune Through Venture Funding*

If your aim is to become wealthy and you don't mind being part of a corporate hierarchy, venture funding might be an excellent option. Venture funding means selling part of your company to a venture capitalist who is in business specifically to invest in high tech companies. (We'll refer to the individual as the venture capitalist and the company as the VC firm.)

Here is the way it works. The venture capitalist contributes his firm's money to use in your business. In return, the firm gets ownership interest in the business (often a substantial percentage), a pro rata amount of voting power (if it owns 60% of the company, it elects 60% of the board), and a pro rata share of the profits. The venture capitalist will work with you on an ongoing basis to introduce you to important contacts and guide you both financially and in business. He becomes an integral part of your team.

When you work with venture capitalists, you also have access to additional future money. Most venture capitalists assume that additional funding will be needed and try to make sure they have money available to help the companies in which they already have investments. Each time they contribute additional funds, though, your share of the business gets smaller.

The key to wealth in a venture capital funded business is the cash out. Let's say that Acme Business Capital (ABC) is funding your venture. It pays $2,500,000 for 50% of your business. This sets a *de facto* market value on the business at $5,000,000 ($2,500,000 divided by .5). Your share of the business is now worth $2,500,000, too. Suppose, five years from now, your company has an initial public offering (IPO) by selling 50% of the total equity for $20,000,000. The value of your business is now $40,000,000; your percentage ownership is now 25% (50% of 50%), and is worth $10,000,000 (25% of the new $40,000,000 value). The numbers work differently for all companies, but the methodology is still the same: as your company gets revalued, your share of the business is revalued also. When it goes public, a market is created for your stock, so the venture capitalists cash out; you can sell a portion of your stock, too.

If your company is sold to another corporation, you automatically cash out. In addition, by going public or selling the company, your company obtains even more cash. Scott Cook, for instance, founded Intuit in 1983. In 1993, Intuit went public, selling 1,000,000 shares at about $15 per share. Since Cook owned 40% of the company after the offering, his shares had a value of $6,000,000. Shortly after going public, Intuit shares rose to $30. Cook's shares had risen to a total value of $12,000,000.

Before you get starry eyed about how you're going to make your fortune in the market, understand that not everybody gets rich with venture funding. Many companies never make it to cash-out stage. More importantly, you must have a compelling case to get venture funding. Most venture capitalists receive dozens of business plans every week from companies in search of funding. Only a small percentage ever get funded. Once you receive funding from venture capitalists, you will be pressured to perform well. Because only about one of five companies succeeds, the company that does succeed must make up for the money lost in the other four. Given the amount of money at stake, you can expect a lot of pressure to win, and to win big.

## Betting on the Batter, Not the Bat

Unlike bankers, venture capitalists are used to dealing in technical products. While they may not be as technically versed as you, they have had experiences with a number of other technical companies and have seen successes and failures. Most members of venture capital organizations have strong financial backgrounds.

They also know that the difference between success and failure in technical companies is more often due to the management team than to the product. Therefore, they would rather fund a top-quality management team with a medium-quality product than a mediocre management team with a great product.

Let's look at it another way. If you had $100 to bet on a batting contest between major league superstar Barry Bonds and Little League washout David Radin, on whom would you bet? Bonds, of course. Even if I was allowed to use the latest technology to double my batting capability, you would still bet on Bonds. The decision facing the venture capitalist is similar. They put their money on the batter, not on the bat. If the batter doesn't like the bat, he can always get a new one, just like a company's management team can produce new products or attempt to target new markets.

## Venture Capitalists Want You To Succeed

Despite rumors to the contrary, most venture capitalists are not trying to take control of your company. They're simply trying to make a lot of money, very quickly. That's why they're willing to risk funding you instead of putting their money into blue chip stocks. The blue chip companies are less risky. But your company has a greater possibility of extremely high returns in a short time period. Sure, the venture capitalist shareholder has the option to ask the board of directors to take certain actions, and he may even have a seat on your board. Don't confuse that with control. You control the day to day operations of your company. Their control is exerted by persuading you, the management, to do what they want. You will find that most venture capitalists participate mainly by providing support, guidance, and contacts.

There are cases in which the board of directors of a venture funded company ousts its management, such as happened to Rod Canion at Compaq and Steve Jobs at Apple. Running a venture funded organization takes a different skill set than running large publicly held corporations. Some founders can bridge the gap. Ken Olsen made it for thirty years at Digital before retiring. Ross Perot ran EDS until he sold out to General Motors. But many simply step down when the business gets large. If the founder recognizes it's time to go, he does so gracefully, and often with a large severance package. For many the next challenge is a new startup. If, on the other hand, you become unresponsive to the suggestions of your board and the needs of your stockholders, you will be asked to leave early. This is a tough decision for a board to make. After all, they originally decided to fund your company due to confidence in your management team. If they must take control from you, they must admit their original decision was flawed.

Venture capitalists know when to stop throwing good money after bad; their goal is to make money, not fritter it away funding companies that have missed their opportunity. This may seem cold-hearted, but they're just trying to protect their money. Don't be surprised, though, if they give up hope before you do, particularly if your company is poorly managed. Unfortunately, they're probably right; they have been through this before (most venture-funded companies fail; that's why it's called "venture") and probably have a better sense for when it's time to throw in the towel.

Remember, when you work with venture capitalists (or partners of any type), you must develop an ongoing relationship that works for all parties. Sharpen your political skills. If you can't, stay solo.

## Where Does Venture Money Go?

Only 15% of the deals funded by venture capital provide funds for startup and early stage companies. Most venture funds are allocated to companies who have already developed their products. In fact, almost one-third of the businesses who get venture funds have already received venture financing before. This is partly due to the relationships that the management teams at the funded companies have already cultivated with the venture capital community. Venture capital firms also use their money to protect other funds that they have already invested by putting additional money into companies that they have already funded. In addition, those who have already been successful in other venture-funded companies can point to the track record of their management team, a record that often demonstrates Class A management.

Consider this: Digital Equipment Corporation received venture funding. DEC begot Prime and Data General. (That is, ex-DEC managers started the companies.) Apollo was formed by former managers from all three companies. Ex-Apollo and Prime executives (along with a key technical founder from Motorola) founded Stellar, which later merged with the venture-funded Ardent to form Stardent. Finally, Stardent begot AVS, Inc. How many of these corporations attracted venture funding? You guessed it—all of them. Venture money seems to follow certain executives around the computer industry.

VC firms also travel in flocks. They have their own internal network that can help you attract additional money. Suppose, for instance, that one VC firm decides to fund your company, but you need additional funds from other sources. Your friendly neighborhood venture capitalist can call several of his friends to join the funding effort. This helps you both. You get the money you need as well as access to additional business expertise and contacts. Your current funds provider gets an additional trusted opinion about your company and management team, as well as a like-minded associate on your board of directors. He also gets to share the risk because his money will not be alone in your bank account. The funds provided by other venture capitalists will act as leverage in making his investment worth more.

Does that mean you're out of luck if you haven't received funding in the past, or are not well connected to the venture capital grapevine? No. But you may have to look elsewhere. According to Bruce Blechman and Jay Conrad Levinson, authors of *Guerrilla Financing*, a company that is either in startup mode or in an early stage of development can more easily obtain funds from individual investors than from traditional VC firms. They say that over 50% of the money from individual investors goes to early stage companies; over 82% goes to financings of less than $500,000.[*] This is a stark contrast to traditional venture deals, where most money goes to later stage companies and most deals are in the multi-million dollar range.

## Getting in the Door . . . and Staying There

According to the principles of Venture Founders Corporation, venture capitalists reject most proposals after a 20 to 30 minute scan, with many others rejected after a two-hour review.[†] Only ten percent are investigated in depth. But two-thirds of those are subsequently rejected due to perceived uncorrectable flaws in either the management team or business plan. This leaves only 3% that are considered fundable—and then, only if terms can be worked out. This begs the question, "With the odds so low, how does one actually get venture money?"

First you need to reach the people with the money. Narrow your sights to VC firms that make sense. Look for those that:

- Are not fully vested; they have money available for new projects.

- Make investments in companies that are in your stage of growth. If you are in startup mode, limit your search to companies willing to fund startups. Most VC firms restrict their funding activities based on their own goals.

---

* Jay Conrad Levinson and Bruce Blechman, *Guerilla Financing*, Houghton Mifflin, page 153.
† Dingee, Smollen, and Haslett, "Characteristics of Successful Entrepreneurs," in Stanley Pratt, *How to Raise Venture Capital*, (New York: Scribner, 1982), page 20.

- Can offer funds in the quantities you need. If you need $100,000, you won't attract a VC firm whose minimum investment is $1,000,000.

- Are willing to invest in your industry segment. If you have a software company, the VC firm must be willing to fund software companies.

Stanley Pratt, editor of *Venture Capital Journal*, suggests getting introduced to the appropriate venture capitalist by an intermediary who has helped that VC firm connect successfully with a venture-seeking company in the past; perhaps an accountant, banker or lawyer.[*] If you don't know anybody who can introduce you, you can send out a two- to three-page summary of your team's credentials and plan; then follow up by phone. Be selective. Don't do a blanket mailing to every VC firm in the world. You will not only waste time and money, you will also expose your idea too broadly, tipping off potential competitors.

Once you're in the door, you need to demonstrate that you understand your market, you're a good decision maker, a good long-term partner, and that your team can carry out your plan. Most importantly, you must show that you have a top-notch management team. During the courtship, the VC firm will investigate you and your company. You should investigate the VC firm too. Speak to executives at companies that were previously funded by the VC firm, both successful and unsuccessful. Ask about the venture capitalist's management style. Find out how he reacts under good and bad circumstances. Remember, once you decide to do business with him, the venture capitalist is not just another customer, he is your partner.

Congratulations. The venture capitalist just handed you a check. Now the real work begins. Stay as close to him as you can. Learn from him. Exploit the talents of his firm. Work with him (and for him) to make his money productive. If you have kept your promises and you need more funding later, he'll help you get it. He'll also provide as much support as he can to help your company earn money.

Now, suppose that you decide to leave the company. Don't burn your bridges. If you have already shown management competence and have executed your responsibilities as promised, you may now be one of those executives who have venture money following you around. And you may need it in your next endeavor.

---

[*] Stanley Pratt, "Guidelines for Dealing with Venture Capitalists," *How to Raise Venture Capital*, Scribner, page 87.

# PART 4

# Special Information for Startup and Fledgling Companies

# Finding a Place To Hang Your Hat

According to John Swanson, founder of Swanson Analysis Systems (SASI), "Starting a company in my home worked very well for me. The cost was right and the commute was even better." As a fledgling entrepreneur, he started SASI in his home in Elizabeth, Pennsylvania, 30 miles from Pittsburgh. Now, SASI is a $28 million company with over 175 employees. Today, SASI's main office in neighboring Houston, Pennsylvania is not opulent, but it provides a comfortable place to work.

Whether your company has one person or a dozen when you start, you need someplace to conduct your business. If chosen properly, it helps you to carry out your tasks efficiently with minimum discomfort. If chosen poorly, it can cause you extra work and increase your expenses.

## *Maintaining Comfort on a Budget*

You are in the software business, not the hair styling business. You don't need to impress your clients with lavish atmosphere. In fact, very few clients will ever walk into your offices. Don't spend your money on expensive office space or luxurious furniture. Spend it where it will do you more good—producing your product and building your market. Even the largest companies started in spartan quarters. Apple started in a garage.

If you don't have room in your garage or basement, don't worry. There are other ways to save money when you're getting started. The following hierarchy will help you keep your important startup funds working at maximum efficiency:

1. *Use existing facilities.* If you have a spare room, a clear garage, or access to a building, use it. These choices are inexpensive and the commute is short. You may even be able to write it off on your taxes. (Not all home offices are deductible. Check with your tax advisor to find out whether yours qualifies.)

2. *Use shared office facilities.* In most medium and large cities, there are shared office suites available. For a single monthly charge, you get an office, furniture, and telephone. They usually provide use of a conference room, copier, and fax (sometimes with an additional price attached). You even get access to a typist/receptionist.

3. *Move into an incubator.* Incubators are shared facilities that are set up by state and local governments expressly to aid small companies in their startup phases. Incubators offer the same amenities as shared office suites. In addition, they often include access to legal, accounting, and marketing people as well as other services helpful to the startup company.

4. *Sublet office space.* In most towns there are companies who are leasing offices that are too big or that they cannot afford. I know a small company in Pittsburgh that found luxury office space downtown by subletting from an accountant that lost a major account. The accountant even provides telephone answering and typing at low cost. A Hartford-based computer marketing company subleases from one of their clients. In addition to the spacious accommodations, they get free telephone service and voice mail.

5. *Find inexpensive fringe space.* If you look hard enough, you can find odd spaces that other companies simply cannot make good use of. Bell Atlantic opened a small Connecticut office in an industrial park where another company went bankrupt. Virtually every real estate company has one or two properties for which it cannot find a renter. If you can find such a property, you can often strike a favorable deal.

# Incubators: All the Comforts of Home

Incubators are office/industrial facilities that have been set up specifically to help young and growing companies. They provide a nurturing atmosphere and many of the amenities that you need, without making you buy them on the outside. Although incubators vary, here are some of the common amenities and services that they provide (sometimes as part of your lease, sometimes at extra cost):

- Inexpensive rental rates

- Flexible leases (amount of space, length of lease)

- Trash collection, security, janitorial services, electricity

- Answering services or centralized voice mail

- Insurance through group plans

- Notary public on premises

- Conference rooms (so you don't need your own)

- Fax machine

- Telex service

- Secretarial service

- Travel agency

- Catering, luncheonette

- Access to professional services (i.e., legal, accounting)

Some, but not all, incubators pose size and length of stay restrictions to limit the number of companies that can apply for space. Many add unique features. Science Park, in New Haven CT, has a branch of the U.S. patent library depository, and provides access to the Yale University gym, library, and computer center. They also participate in federally funded grant programs and business outreach programs that help their tenants find money to fund their businesses.

It's not always easy to find incubators—there is no special listing in the yellow pages. To find one near you, speak with your state or city department of economic development, chamber of commerce, or nearby universities.

## *Finding Your New Quarters*

If you spend a few days searching for the right office, you are likely to find something that suits your needs for the right price. (Price depends on your local real estate market and is normally measured in dollars per square foot.) Start with buildings that you know suit your needs. Call the management and ask if they have any office space available. Ask for referrals when you are unsuccessful. Call commercial divisions of real estate brokers. Of course, use the classified ads.

During your search, make sure that the building is zoned properly. If you plan to do development work or sales there, make sure it is zoned as "commercial." To assemble and ship your product, you may need "light industrial" or "mixed use" zoning. You may be able to get away with using your home as an office if you have one or two employees and very few visitors. As you grow, though, you often become an inadvertent nuisance to your neighbors. To reduce the nuisance factor, most communities enforce zoning restrictions in residential neighborhoods when home businesses create excess traffic or require multiple parking spaces. Contact your municipal planning and zoning department to find out whether you can legally use your building for your proposed business.

If your town does not have a planning and zoning department, find out from your municipal offices whom to contact.

If you decide to approach a real-estate broker for help, make sure your specifications are set in advance to save the broker time. Real estate brokers are paid on commission. They would rather sell or rent large properties than work with companies who only need a few hundred or thousand square feet.

To get the best deal, know the market. Call your local chamber of commerce to find the local vacancy rates and average prices of commercial property. If you find a loose market, you can probably negotiate. If rental space is tight, it becomes more difficult. Just like when you are buying a house, don't get your heart set on one specific office. If the agent senses "you just gotta have it," your ability to negotiate will be hurt. Of course, make sure that the space meets your specifications. It should have the right electrical and telephone connections, enough office room, space for conferences, postage/shipping, and storage. Also, make sure that you can run your network wiring between your machines. If you are located where there are no restaurants, you may even want room for a small refrigerator, microwave oven, and coffee maker.

Try to get by with a small, inexpensive space. As a startup, there is nothing more important to you than maintaining extra cash buffer. Too large a space eats into your buffer. If you are concerned about outgrowing your space, inquire about obtaining an option (or first right of refusal) on adjacent office space. Some owners of multiple properties are even willing to let you move into a bigger property during your lease term without penalty on your original lease.

## Balancing Current and Future Needs

When your company outgrows your startup office, you may feel inclined to find grandiose space in luxurious surroundings. Don't go to extremes. Overbuying office space drains your cash resources, decreases your flexibility (should changes in your market happen), and reduces your company value (in case you need to seek additional funding).

Imagen, an early leader in the laser printer industry, found out the hard way. After being cramped for three years, it moved to offices that were much larger and had room for significant additional expansion. The expansion never happened, and the Silicon Valley real estate market collapsed, making it difficult for them to find other tenants. Imagen was left paying top dollar for unused space. The difference in rent was the difference between profit and loss for several years.

Many companies stay in their startup offices until they bust at the seams. If you can do this, you can accumulate cash to buffer unforeseen circumstances. We started Marketing Masters in a bedroom in my home. As we grew, we needed additional space for equipment and files and more telephone lines. The lack of privacy caused by the increase in people through the office concerned my wife. So instead of finding expensive office space, we built a new office in the basement with more room, better electrical and phone facilities, and more privacy. We did not have to change telephone numbers or print new stationery because the address stayed the same. The basement served us well for over two additional years—and saved $10,000 to $20,000 in rent. If there is no reason to move, don't.

## Planning Your Space

The amount of space you need depends on the number of people you employ, whether you will host visitors in your offices, and the work habits of your people. According to Jay Brotman, principal of Svigals Associates, an architectural firm that has set up high tech clients, the key to determining your space is to understand your method of operation. If you don't yet know how you will operate, find a firm that is similar to yours and use it as a model. Jay has provided the following numbers to be used as a guideline (not a rule) when planning your office.

*TABLE 18-1: OFFICE PLANNING GUIDE*

| | |
|---|---|
| Executive office | 150 to 225 square feet (sf) |
| Standard private office | 120 sf |
| Semi-private office | 100 sf per person |
| Cubicle | 40 to 80 sf per person |
| Conference room | 20 sf per person (based on meeting size) |
| Reception/waiting area | 140 to 250 sf |
| Storage | At least 50 to 60 sf for the first ten people—add 50% every time you double the number of people |
| Work/copier/coffee area | 40 to 120 sf—depends on your specific needs and whether you need sit down space |
| Rest rooms | In most cases, already in existing facility |
| Parking | One space per person in suburbs; in the city, access to public transportation |
| Power | Clean (lights and computers on different circuits) |
| Lighting | 50 to 60 foot-candles; parabolic lighting or up-lighting preferred for computer users |

| Ventilation | 30 to 50 cubic feet per minute (cfm) of outdoor air per person |
| Air conditioning | Air conditioning an absolute requirement for computer businesses; The amount of air conditioning needed de- pends primarily on the computer equipment you will be using. |

## Deciding Where To Settle

If you are currently running a business or just starting one, your location may not be an issue. It's best not to make it one. If, however, you do need to choose a location, here are a few important criteria.

Sales offices should be placed close to your markets. If your clients are in the automotive industry, a location near Detroit is an obvious advantage. For an defense industry product, proximity to Southern California and the Washington, D.C. area are among your high priorities. Rubber companies are concentrated in Ohio; pharmaceutical companies in New Jersey. Close proximity to your markets decreases your travel costs and increases the amount of attention you can pay to your prospects and clients.

Use your location to decrease your cost of doing business. In general, it is less expensive to maintain an office in the midwest or south than in New England or California. Suburbs are less expensive than downtown locations. During the past decade, JCPenney, United Parcel Service, and GTE, among others, have moved large numbers of people from the industrial northeast to Texas, North Carolina, or other less expensive states. Their moves were prompted by the cost of doing business and the cost of living. If you are already in a high-cost area and don't want to move, find ways to minimize your expenses within your area. Consider moving to a municipality with lower taxes or to a building with lower per foot costs.

Maintain access to an appropriate labor pool. Certainly there is a large pool of computer programmers in San Jose, California, and in Bedford, Massachusetts. However, eastern Massachusetts and northern California are not the only places that you can find large numbers of software developers. They are now in almost any major city. Some cities are particularly strong, including Seattle, Detroit, Raleigh/Durham (North Carolina,, Los Angeles, Dallas, and Pittsburgh. Labor shortages did not keep Intergraph from being successful in Huntsville, Alabama or Gateway 2000 from making it in Sioux City, South Dakota. Certainly, if you are just starting out, you probably only require a few people anyway.

Some companies may try to shortcut location issues by hiring telecommuters. Even though telecommuting is becoming commonplace, most workers still work in a traditional office environment. (By the way, this book was written, edited, and produced remotely with files passing electronically between the author, the editor, and the publisher.)

Don't underestimate your need to travel. Whenever possible, locate your offices near a major airline hub and near major highways or rail systems. The software business will take you all over the country (or world).

## The Single Factor Above All Others

In the final analysis, the factor that always seems to have the most weight is where you want to live and work. There is nothing wrong with putting this above the others. After all, you are developing your business to enhance your life, not living your life to have a business.

# Using a Business Plan to Attract Funding

Your business plan defines your business concept, outlines your opportunities and risks, estimates your costs, and forecasts your future financial positions. Although self-funded companies can get by without a written business plan, most companies eventually encounter a situation where they must commit their business plan to paper. For instance, you need a business plan when you ask a banker to loan you money or when you seek equity financing from an investor. If you don't have a good plan, you won't get your money. Alexander Dingee, Leonard Smollen and Brian Haslett, of Venture Founders Corporation, suggest spending 150 to 300 hours to develop your plan.[*] You will need to be intimately involved; this is one of the tasks you can't farm out to a subcontractor. After all, the document is supposed to represent *your* ideas. There is no way that somebody else can develop it without your input. That means you will spend up to eight weeks of your own time, or that of key members of your management team, putting together your business plan.

## *Keeping Investors From Shutting the Door*

Before you start searching for investors, you should realize that most venture capital requests are rejected. It's worthwhile to think long and hard about whether there are alternatives. Mike Movolli, who founded Orion Systems in 1989, knew that his first UNIX-based imaging product would not be ready until 1993. But he couldn't wait four years to feed his family. Besides he needed money to fund the development of his product. So he and his developers worked as outside consultants to other companies to earn money to pay the bills and start up the product. But not everybody can be a consultant. Some companies must seek outside funding. So when you go looking for your money, you will probably be up against a number of other companies that are

---

[*] Dingee, Smollen, and Haslett, "Characteristics of Successful Entrepreneurs," in Stanley Pratt, *How to Raise Venture Capital* (New York: Scribner, 1982), page 20.

asking for money from the same people as you. Only a small portion will receive it.

Most proposals for funding are quickly rejected, on the basis of a quick scan through the business plan. So to be seriously considered for funding, your business plan must be *better* than the majority. It's in your best interest to think it through first, so you can be among the best. Why do you deserve to get the money? What proof can you offer that you will satisfy lender or investor requirements? What strengths does your management team bring to the table? What are the biggest risks and weaknesses? If you can answer these questions thoroughly, and with confidence, you stand a better chance.

A gratifying by-product of putting together your formal business plan for somebody else is that you clarify your own ideas. You may come across flaws in your plan that require you to rethink your strategy, or you may come up with new ideas to help you reach your goals.

## What Investors and Lenders Want To See

To maximize the effectiveness of your formal business plan, consider who the reader is. Then write it to satisfy him. Answer the questions that *he* will ask. Give him the information that will make it easier to make a decision in your favor.

Let's recognize that your business plan is different from your operations plan, even though they are highly interrelated and often composed concurrently. While an operations plan (and any relevant documents) helps you run your business, your formal business plan is a marketing document that helps you attract funding (loan or equity). Since not all funding sources are looking for the same things, you need to tailor yours to the person who will receive it.

You may be looking for an equity investment from a venture capital firm. An equity investor is interested in future profits. He'll take a long hard look at your projections to determine whether they are in line with the return he needs on his investment. If he thinks your future is bright, he'll seriously consider investing money in your company. For him, the past is not as important as the future. The amount of return an investor requires changes over time and varies from investor to investor. For the most part, though, venture capitalists are looking for above-average rates of return on their money. After all, investors can get average returns by investing their money in relatively risk-free investments. You're paying a premium to get your investors to take a risk with you.

A banker (or other lender), on the other hand, is mainly concerned about whether you will be able to pay him back on time. He only cares about profitability to the extent that you stay in business long enough to satisfy his loan. He dwells on your debt repayment history and your cash flow forecasts for the period of the loan. If you are seeking a $50,000 loan that will be repaid over the next two years, he will hardly look at the information you give him about what will happen three years from now. His eye will be trained on your 24-month cash flow projections. He wants to make sure your company is stable enough to make it to month 25 without a late payment.

Both types of readers care about the abilities of your management team. Before they are willing to give you money, they must have confidence in you.

## Components of a Formal Business Plan

When putting together your business plan, you should try to maintain accepted conventions to make it easier for the reader to find important information and analyze your plan. Appendix A lists several sources that can give you detailed recipes for your plan. Here, I'll briefly address the main components.

*Executive Summary*

This is a summary of your business plan that conveys its most important points. The Executive Summary must make the reader want to read the entire plan. Include a brief description of your company (and history if you have one), a synopsis of your market, distinguishing features of your product, a brief profile of your management team, a summary of your financial projections, how much money you are seeking, in what form you want it (debt or equity) and what you will use it for. Your Executive Summary should be one to three pages long. Write it last so you can capture the information from the rest of your business plan. Make it appealing and convincing, so the reader will want to investigate your plans more thoroughly.

*Your Business and Industry*

Explain your business opportunity by briefly describing the current condition of the market and industry as well as showing where your product fits in.

*Product(s)*

Describe the capabilities and advantages of your product. Highlight the distinctive features and discuss proprietary positions such as patents or trade secrets that would give you an advantage in the market. (But don't give away your secrets.) When writing this section, keep in mind that you don't want the reader to buy your product; you want him to understand why somebody else will want to buy it.

*Marketing*

Clearly define your market (who your customers are; why they buy). List actual or potential customers. Describe the size of the market in both units and dollars as well as market growth and trends. Identify the competition and show both strengths and weaknesses. If you take your competition lightly, you will reduce your credibility; your investors are looking for a management team that understands the types of challenges it faces, not one that disregards factors that can threaten profitability. Assess the market and estimate your market share and sales. Describe how you will achieve your sales goals including distribution, pricing, and promotion policies. Tell who you will target initially and how you will identify them.

Be specific. Lack of an adequate marketing plan or inability to convince the investor that one exists is one of the most likely reasons for rejection.

*Product Development Plan*

If your product is not yet complete, report the status as well as any development that must be done to make your product marketable. Include the dates that you anticipate the product to be completed (for Alpha/Beta tests) and ready for distribution. Discuss the difficulties and risks you anticipate. Outline the development costs as well as the budget you have allocated toward the costs. Indicate who will oversee the development process and that person's background in related tasks.

*Operations Plan*

How do you plan to run the business and get the product out? Discuss the labor force required (size and special skill sets), where you will do it (geography and facility), advantages your labor force or location provide (i.e., your location permits lower costs, or a key member of your team is the leading authority in a specific technology), what equipment you need, how you will obtain it (lease or purchase), and any special circumstances that will affect your operation.

*Management Team*

Provide brief outlines of the significant career accomplishments of your management team. Diagram the expected management role of each person on that team. Show the salaries that are to be paid to each member; include expected ownership interest. Identify board members along with their backgrounds. Assess your requirements for management assistance or training. If you have selected professional service providers (i.e., lawyer, accountant, advertising agency), identify them.

This section is extremely important. Investors back the management team, not the product or the market. If you cannot win them over in this section, you will not win them over at all.

*Financial Plan*

Include profit and loss forecasts for three to five years, cash flow projections for three years, and pro forma balance sheets (reflecting your expected assets and liabilities in the future) at startup and after six months, one, two, and three years of operations. Existing businesses should include current balance sheets and income statements for the previous two years. List the assumptions that you used to generate the numbers on your forecasts. A sample balance sheet and income statement is shown in Figures 19-1 through 19-3. A cash flow projection worksheet can be found in chapter 16.

## How Business Plans Are Evaluated

Getting approval from an investor is like walking through a mine field. You must get entirely across the field to be successful. Getting the investor to read past your executive summary does you no good if he rejects your proposal because of an inadequate marketing plan. Likewise, if he doesn't believe your financial projections, it doesn't matter if he liked your marketing plan. Thus, the plan you submit must be solid in every section. As you write it, keep the following points in mind:

- Your main objective is to convince the reader to provide funding. His main determinant is whether he feels you have a management team that has developed a good idea and has the ability to run the business profitably. To do this, you must provide a solid plan that is well conceived and bullet-proof. The more money you are looking for, the more bullet-proof it must be.

- Believability is key. Don't stretch truths or make projections that cannot work. If the reader cannot believe your business plan, why should he give you his money?

- Don't submit half-baked ideas or plans with errors (grammatical, mathematical, or typographical). It shows lack of attention to detail.

- When developing your marketing section, do your research. Talk to people who are in your target market to assess whether your product will really be purchased. Include details that show you have done your homework and know your market cold. Most proposals are rejected because the reader considers the marketing plan inadequate.

- In your financial section, state all your assumptions in detail. This allows your investor to make sure that your assumptions and financial capabilities are reasonable.

```
                    Sample Software Corporation
                          Balance Sheet
                        December 31, 1994

Numbers in thousands
--------------------------
Assets
--------
Current Assets
      Cash                                    $ 25
      Liquid Securities                         10
      Accounts Receivable              160
      less: allow. for doubtful accts.  (7)    153
                                       ----

      Inventory                                140
      Pre-paid expenses                         12
                                              -----
total current assets                          $ 340

Fixed Assets
      Land                                       0
      Buildings                       120
          (less accum. depr.)          40       80
                                      -----

      Equipment                       120
          (less accum. depr.)          60       60
                                      -----

      Furniture/Fixtures               25
          (less accum. depr.)          10       15
                                      -----

total fixed assets                            $ 155

Intangible Assets
      Patents                                   25
      Trademarks                                 5
      Goodwill                                   0
                                              -----
total intangible assets                          30
                                              -----

Total Assets                                  $ 525
                                              =====
```

**FIGURE 19-1:** *BALANCE SHEET: ASSETS*

```
Liabilities and Owner's Equity

Current Liabilities
     Accounts Payable                           $100
     Wages Payable                                40
     Short-term loans                              2
     Current portion of long-term loans            4
     Interest Payable                              1
     Taxes payable                                 6
                                                -----
total Current liabilities                         153

Long-term Liabilities
     Mortgages payable                             80
     Notes payable                                160
                                                -----
total long-term liabilities                       240

Equity
     Common stock                                 100
     Retained Earnings                             32
                                                -----
total equity                                      132
                                                -----
Total Libilities & Equity                       $525
                                                =====
```

**FIGURE 19-2:** BALANCE SHEET: LIABILITIES AND EQUITY

- If there are certain financial highlights that will help you make a stronger case, highlight them. Such highlights might be cash flow break-even level (particularly important when you are looking for a loan), profits as a percentage of revenue, and maximum cash requirements.

# *Making Sure the Proposal Does Its Job*

You and the key members of your management team will be spending many hours developing your plan. Spend your hours productively. Speak with your accountant to check that your pro forma projections, profit and loss statements, and other financial documents are in an acceptable format. Have him critique your assumptions, too.

Then, once your executive summary is complete, show it to an independent business person whose opinion you trust. Let him tell you whether you have provided enough information in a convincing manner to make an investor or lender read the rest of the plan.

```
                    Sample Software Corporation
                         Income Statement
                    Year Ended  December 31, 1994
                              (000)
----------------------------------------------------------------

Revenues / Gross Sales                              $2,180
Cost of Goods Sold                                     530
                                                    -----
     Gross Income                                    1,650


Operating, Marketing & Financial Expenses
     Salaries and Wages               760
     Rent                              24
     Utilities                         2
     Advertising                      450
     Depreciation                      5
     Interest                          3
     Miscellaneous                    10
                                     -----
          total operating expenses                   1,254
                                                    -----

Net Income Before Taxes                               396
Federal Taxes                                         154
                                                    -----
Net Income After Taxes                               $242
                                                    =====
```

**FIGURE 19-3:** *INCOME STATEMENT*

Include a table of contents to make it easy for the reader to find specific items. The easier it is for him to read it, the more likely he will.

To help you put together the details of each section, consult with your accountant, lawyer, or appropriate advisor—or pick up a book that illustrates how to put together business plans and financing. (Look in the appendix for some ideas, or go down to your local library or bookstore.) You will also need to include a disclaimer statement because you are legally prohibited from soliciting investments without a prospectus. You can get one from the same source.

Even after you have put together a top-notch business plan that makes a terrific case for somebody to finance you, you will need to meet with the financing party. This may be the final hurdle before you begin to negotiate. For more information on dealing with bankers and venture capitalists, see chapter 17, *Financing Your Company.*

# *You Can Succeed Without a Business Plan*

Last year, a friend of mine in Vermont started his own business. He wasn't willing to move when his former employer decided to pull out of New England. Although the local economy was in a recession, he realized that his sales skills were still valuable to many companies, so he went out to find one or two clients for whom he could provide specialized sales services. In a short time, he found his first client. The client gave him a small job that kept him busy part time and paid his rent. During the remainder of the business day, he went out to drum up more business, parlaying his first project's success into repeat business and additional clients. My friend now has nine people working for him and expects continued growth. He didn't have a formal business plan, but he didn't need one. In fact, if he had taken the time to put one together, he might not have been as successful.

The opposite is also true. A small software company in southern California had three formal business plans during its two years of existence. But the founders were so busy putting together their business plans that they did not take the time to make any of them work. A formal business plan does not assure success.

Eventually, you will probably need a business plan—or at least a document that communicates the essence of your business—if you look for external funding. If you are looking for several hundred thousand dollars or more in financing, you will need a very complete plan, including a marketing section, operations section, and financial forecast. If you are only looking for a few thousand as a loan (and if you have sufficient collateral), you may be able to get away with a simple financial forecast.

# Growing Your Staff

The better your staff, the more productive your company—and the more profitable. But finding, selecting, and retaining staff are among the most perplexing challenges that face any manager. Small companies are particularly susceptible to poor or inadequate staffing because each individual is such a large portion of the whole. By properly sizing your organization and building it with top-quality personnel, you will fuel profit growth and reduce problems.

## *Should You Hire?*

Hiring decisions should be made in light of your corporate goals. Are you looking to maximize long-term profitability, or do you need to conserve as much cash as possible to keep afloat? Are you planning a major expansion—and if so, does that expansion really fit your other goals? Empire-building for its own sake is never healthy, and no small company can afford it.

Before hiring, you must realize that there's a distinct tradeoff between quality of service and short-term profit. You've got to wrestle with this, and decide which is more important in light of your company and its goals. A lean staff often lacks the throughput to get enough work done. No matter how well you service your customers, some will be unhappy. Your personnel will often resist additional workload. They may feel overworked or under-appreciated. Both customers and staff will complain that you need more people. They may be right, but you will still need to face the fact that personnel cost is your largest single cost and by resisting the temptation to hire unnecessary people, you increase your profits.

Moreover, adding people does not always increase productivity. Many tasks cannot be easily broken into pieces. Personnel management becomes more time consuming. For each additional person you hire, you will greatly increase the amount of communications that must take place within your company, often straining you and your staff to accommodate the differing perspectives of your personnel. As Figure 20-1 shows, the more people you have, the more talking takes place. Confusion and miscommunications become more likely, and it gets harder to make decisions.

***FIGURE 20-1:*** *COMMUNICATION BECOMES COMPLEX AS ORGANIZATIONS GROW*

In short, don't hire somebody just for the sake of growth. Hire when there are valid business reasons and when there is no question that you will be better off. If you hire somebody you don't need, you hurt yourself and the new hire.

## Some Considerations for Hiring

Even though different types of jobs require different types of skills, there are some items that always need to be considered when you plan to hire a new person, no matter what his expected position will be. These items will help you fit him into your organization and help determine how you manage him.

*Span of Control.*

Even if you are among the best managers, you can't have everybody report directly to you—there is only so much time in a day. So expect to hire one additional manager for every three to seven people you hire. Sure, you have heard about managers who have 10 to 15 people reporting directly to them. They're easy to recognize. They have glassy looks in their eyes, have a line of people waiting unproductively to see them outside their offices, and say things like "Please send me e-mail so I don't forget."

### Composition of the task

Some types of activities can be broken into component parts to be performed by groups of people. Others cannot. A good example is software development. For large projects, you can break the code into modules with each person assigned to a module. The modules would then be integrated at the end. Other programs cannot easily be broken out, requiring the work to be done serially by one person.

### Experience needed

Some jobs can be filled by individuals who can be trained as they work. Others require specific expertise that has been previously developed by the person you hire. Some types of work require knowledge of nuances that only experience can provide. Make sure you find a skilled professional to fill these jobs instead of trying to mold somebody who does not quite meet standards. Startup companies, in particular, are not good training grounds.

### Teamwork

When you divide the labor you might increase productivity. However, your staff loses a degree of the perspective related to striving for the same goals throughout the organization. You need to strike a balance between the two based on your goals and the individuals you hire.

### Ulterior motives

No matter how strongly you believe that you are able to keep politics out of the office, it is impossible. Each person on your staff has his own goals. If the goals don't coincide with yours, it makes your management job more difficult. Jack may be threatened when you hire Paul. Jack may have wanted you to hire one of his friends; or he may feel that Paul will be better than him and become his manager, thereby blocking his promotion path.

### The cure may be worse than the ailment

In many cases, having too many people on your staff is more destructive than than having too few. Excess staffing creates profit problems as well as internal political problems related to under-utilized personnel.

## Ask Questions Before You Hire

It's not always easy to tell whether the time is right to add a person to your staff. Sure, you have been working 80-hour weeks. So have your current employees. But that doesn't necessarily mean that adding an additional person will relieve your burden. Nor does it mean that the extra person will increase your profit. So before you add that extra person, ask yourself some questions to help guide your decision.

- What do other companies in your industry typically require? By comparing your staffing levels to companies that have similar products or sell to similar markets, you can better understand how to stay competitive. Concentrate on the profitable competitors. You don't want to emulate companies that are not making money.

- What position does your company occupy in the industry? A small competitor has an advantage if it is lean, cost effective, and can react quickly to changes in product direction and market factors. Large companies cannot react as quickly, but can take advantages of economies of scale. Your cost per unit is less if you produce and sell more licenses. Therefore, you have higher gross margins with which you can hire additional people and still make the same money.

- Can you get by on current staff? If so, what kinds of problems will result? If not, what will it take to get by? Personnel decisions are always made by balancing the costs and benefits of hiring against the costs and benefits of maintaining status quo (not hiring). If you maintain status quo, you might not meet important deadlines; your burned-out employees might quit; you might be unable to support customers; or the quality of your product might be reduced. You might decide to delay the hire because, despite these worries, the cost of adding a person might still exceed the benefits. Hiring a new person will cost money and take staff-time for training. You need to decide separately for each individual whether it makes more sense to hire or wait. Remember, if you wait, you can still hire later. But if you hire, it's difficult (and costly) to change your mind after the person is on board.

- Are you willing to share the rewards? Each time you bring somebody on board, you take another slice from the profit pie. Is the pie big enough for all of you to eat? If you are looking for experienced people, will they be satisfied with the amount that you have allocated for them?

- Are the right people available? I know of one company who looked for two years for a certain type of individual, only to find out that he is a figment of their imagination.

- What does it take to get the job done? What are the costs of not getting it done? What are the costs of paying too much to get it done?

- What do you expect to happen during the next year, five years, ten years? Since hiring each person indicates a long-term commitment, and changes in personnel direction take place very slowly, does hiring fit in with the situation? Temporary personnel and consultants are excellent solutions to satisfy short-term requirements.

- Will you be able to keep a new hire busy during his entire work day; or will he need to find makeshift work to keep himself busy? If you can't keep him busy, the cost of the work he accomplishes goes up.

- What is your financial situation (i.e., your cash position)? Can you afford to pay the staff on a consistent basis? Will it cause you financial hardships in other areas? Do you have enough sales to support the increased staff on a continuing basis? Can you financially justify the people you have on staff or want to add? Will the benefits outweigh the costs?

- What are your long-term goals? Will you be robbing your retirement or your child's college fund to bring on additional staff members? Are you willing to do that?

- Do you have the skills to manage the people you bring on board? Do you want to manage? If not, do you have others with the desire and capabilities to do the management?

- Have you included enough budget for overhead associated with the new person? Every time you hire a person you add costs for office, telephone, telephone lines, taxes, benefits, supplies, and the personnel cost involved with taking more time to communicate with the additional people.

## *The Impact of Turnover*

Every time somebody leaves your company, it creates a new hiring decision for you. Do you replace the person who has left, or redistribute the work? If you decide to hire a new employee, you must take time to search, train the new hire, and scurry to catch the balls that may be dropped while the new person learns the job. In the meantime, you might miss delivery schedules, put projects on hold, or lose business. In short, turnover is time consuming and costly.

According to many human resources specialists, a person won't change companies unless there is both a "push" and a "pull." The push refers to an aspect of somebody's current job or employer that makes him want to leave. The pull is whatever he sees elsewhere that attracts him to a new position. For instance, somebody may want to leave your company because he doesn't like his boss. That's his push. If a competitor offers him a job with a raise in pay, that's his pull. He'll say goodbye. You could move him to a new boss with whom he gets along. But do it before he becomes disgruntled and starts to listen to recruiters.

You can't control the external factors that attract your employees to other positions. But you can do your best to eliminate the factors that can push them away from you.

# Common Reasons People Quit

To avoid pushing your employees out the door, take care of their needs. To do that, you must listen, keep them informed, compensate them adequately, and give them something to look forward to. Yet even when you do your best, some people will still leave. Here are some of the reasons that people leave.

*Poor communications*

When communications between you and your people break down, they are more likely to resign. When you don't listen (or when your employee *thinks* you aren't listening), your employee feels frustrated that he is not being heard or that you don't understand him. When you don't share important information, he thinks that you are treating him as a second-class citizen. Either situation can cause a serious personnel problem.

*Poor management*

When workers lose confidence in the people who are making decisions that affect their lives and livelihood, they become wary and leave. In fact, it's not unusual for many people to leave at about the same time. Lack of confidence in management is contagious. Even though things might not be better elsewhere, your employees can only see the management problems within your company.

*Lack of personal growth*

Many of the best employees have high aspirations that cannot always be achieved within your company. Suppose, for instance, that Jill, a software developer, wants to lead a software development group, but you only have four software developers, and can't justify another full-time manager. If Jill, or some other employee, does not feel that she will reach her personal growth goals within your company, she will find a company in which she can.

*Compensation issues*

You need to pay your employees enough to survive and pay them comparably to what they would make elsewhere. Not only base salary—also bonuses, percentage increases, health care, insurance, profit sharing, and retirement benefits are visible measures of how well you are treating them.

*Industry issues*

In some cases, a person simply wants to get out of your industry or industry segment because he believes that opportunity is better elsewhere. In 1990, a friend of mine left a company where he programmed in Ada so he could become a software developer of Windows applications. He felt that the Windows market afforded him more long-term opportunities than he had as an Ada programmer.

*External issues*

Sometimes the person moves for seemingly unrelated reasons, such as a change in his family situation, a health problem, or a desire to move to a different city.

## Preventing People From Leaving

Personnel management is an art. What works in one situation may fail in another. But there are several basic steps that human resources professionals and corporate managers believe will help reduce turnover:

*Keep communications open between you and your employees*

A happy employee is one who feels that he has control over his destiny. If he is in the dark about decisions that affect him, or if he doesn't feel he is being heard, he becomes concerned about lack of control. Make sure you let each employee know what you expect from him. Give him feedback when he does a good job. Comprehensively review his performance at least once a year. Solicit feedback from him. Employees who know they can approach you with problems are more likely to let you know how they feel about their jobs. They also submit more suggestions that just may help you increase your sales or profits. Improve your personnel management skills by reading *The One Minute Manager* by Kenneth Blanchard and Spenser Johnson or other books about constructive feedback and communications.

*Provide growth opportunities within your organization*

Henry Ford said it best: "When you come right down to it, most jobs are repetitive." According to Chris Ryland, President of Em Software, most software developers can do things three times. The first time they learn how to do it; the second time they do it the way they wish they had done it the first time; the third time, it's easy and relatively painless, but they don't learn a whole lot; the fourth time it's boring. People get bored doing the same thing year in and year out, especially if they are ambitious or bright. You need to provide them with opportunities to grow, so they don't become bored, and so they can reach their own aspirations. You can give them traditional promotions, use job rotation to expose them to new areas, or assign them to special projects that show off their skills.

*Grant merit incentives*

Reward your employee for a job well done by providing additional remuneration tied to achievement—a bonus when he reaches a specific goal, a commission for a sale, or a prize for winning a contest. Some managers simply treat an employee (and guest) to dinner if the employee has recently worked particularly long hours or has put forth extra effort to get a job done. When you tie a goal to an incentive, you create additional desire to achieve it.

### Provide a comfortable working atmosphere

A comfortable working atmosphere promotes good work habits, helps workers maintain their health, and increases peace of mind.

### Provide a stable environment

Be consistent in what you tell your employees and what you expect from them. Suppose, for instance, that you have been pushing your staff to complete a project by May 31. Don't chastise them if the software is not completed on May 15. That's not their target. Worse, don't vacillate on decisions. There are few things that frighten people more than when the boss keeps changing his mind.

### Provide golden handcuffs

Many companies provide incentives to stay put by allocating stock options or pension plans with vesting periods that are only executable after employees have been with the company for a predetermined length of time. In a typical retirement plan, for example, each employee becomes vested 20% per year (he can access 20% of the contribution if he leaves) until he reaches 100% after his fifth full year with the company. If the employee leaves before he is fully vested, he stands to lose a lot of money. Similarly, stock option plans allow the employee to purchase a certain amount of stock at a good price at set intervals (i.e., 500 shares after six months, 1000 shares after 1 year . . . ). If the employee expects the stock to increase in value, he wants to stay around long enough to cash in on his options.

### Be responsive to the needs of your staff

When Thomas Watson Senior was building IBM, he built great loyalty by being responsive to the needs of his people. If an employee was hospitalized, Watson (or the employee's direct manager) would show up in his hospital room. If a family member died, he would send flowers. He always made sure that his employees were well taken care of. In fact, at one point, a number of IBM employees from New York State were injured on the way to an IBM event in New York City when their train crashed. As soon as Watson found out, he dispatched doctors and medical equipment to make sure that the riders were taken care of.

### Be honest with your team

Don't lose the loyalty of your staff because they don't trust you or don't believe in what you stand for. If they *want* to find reasons to continue to work for you, they will. Your honesty is an important contributor to their desire to stay.

# *Finding Acceptable Personnel*

One of the tricks to building a first-class organization is to find the right individuals. That means you must know what you need and what you can offer.

1.  *Evaluate your requirements.* Before you hire somebody, you should have a list of requirements against which to match your candidates. This is particularly important because being a "good guy," a friend or good at "activity A" does not necessarily mean that a candidate will be good at "activity B". So write down the attributes that you need in your next hire. Include the activities that he must be able to perform as well as previous experience that will help him meet your goals. If there is advancement opportunity, include your thoughts about how somebody might grow in the position, too.

2.  *Determine your remuneration range.* Understand how much it will cost to get the type of person you need and compare that to how much you can pay him. Include salary, bonuses, commissions, insurance, taxes, and overhead costs. To find out typical salary ranges, talk to industry groups, local chambers of commerce, headhunters, and people in positions similar to the position you are trying to fill. Then be flexible. It's better to pay a little more to get the right person than to pay a little less and get the wrong person. The money you pay to the wrong person will be thrown away. To find out typical pay scales, refer to publications that publish annual salary surveys such as Information Week (each spring), UNIX World (May issue), EE Times (late summer), and Electronic Buyers News (each December).

3.  *Define your geographic preference.* If location is important to you, make it part of your hiring criteria. If the person will spend a large portion of his time on the road, or if he will be working on a solo development project, you may decide that geography is not important. But in most cases it is. Remote employees are tougher to manage and more costly (in travel and telephone expenses). If you need him in your office, make sure you restrict your search to people who live within commuting range or are willing to move. Don't forget to add money for relocation.

4.  *Don't forget the future.* Whenever possible, hire a candidate that will grow with your company. You might even relax one of your requirements to attract him. But don't relax your requirements too much. He still needs to perform the job at hand. If you don't get your jobs done in the present, you won't have a future.

## Sample Job Descriptions

The best job description includes all the important criteria with which you will judge applicants, with the information sorted by what you *need* and what would be helpful. The better you define your criteria, the less likely unqualified candidates will apply. Here are two samples.

> We are seeking a programmer to help us develop a new graphically oriented engineering software product. The candidate must have two to four years of development experience using C++ on UNIX platforms. Knowledge of X Windows, Solaris, Ultrix, and SCO UNIX a plus. Minimum education is a bachelor's degree in computer science or engineering. This person will work in our R&D department where he will develop graphical products using C++ on Sun workstations, port the software to SCO and DEC platforms, tune software for maximum performance, and interface with users in beta test mode. The position is in Sunnyvale, CA and the pay range is $40,000 to $60,000.

> We are looking for a senior account manager to handle large account sales in a four-state region in the midwest. Our preferred candidate would have five to seven years of success selling to large corporate accounts, with new account experience a must. Knowledge of corporate purchasing processes is required as well as knowledge of the territory including MI, IL, IN and OH. The candidate must have experience selling software with a base price of at least $100,000 per license. The candidate will be located in either our Detroit or Chicago office and will work independently of technical support. A technical degree or proven track record selling without large amounts of technical support is required. Annual quota will be in the $2 million range with a compensation package consisting of a base salary ($35,000 to $45,000) and a competitive commission.

## Knowing Where To Look

It's time to hire somebody. Now, all you have to do is find him. Instead of looking under rocks, look in the places where you are more likely to find the most qualified candidates. By narrowing your search early, you will reduce the time it takes from your own schedule. And if your time is a particularly precious commodity, use recruiters. Let's look at the methods used most.

## Networking With People You Know

Networking—asking your personal associates if they know candidates who fit your requirements—is the safest way to find new personnel. You will be getting information from people whom you trust. To start networking, pull out your card file (or personal database) and call the people you know who may fit the job profile. If you have not spoken to somebody in years, this is a good time to renew acquaintances. Find out what he has been doing recently; who he is working for; how life is treating him; and, of course, whether he is looking for a new challenge. Tell him that you are trying to hire somebody and thought he might have an interest or know somebody who does. Be candid. You're not committing a crime. You are looking for somebody to whom you can offer an exciting opportunity.

What if he's not looking for a new challenge or the timing is not right? Ask him if he can put you in touch with somebody who might be a good addition to your team or somebody who can give you a good recommendation. Call the person that he referred. Keep trying with other people in your card file.

You would be surprised at the people who'd be interested in joining your team even though they seem settled in their jobs. Your closest associates, in particular, may be willing to take a chance with you because they already know your style and are familiar with your company. It's less risky for them to talk to you, just as it is less risky for you. The further out you get from your string of associates (i.e., people with whom you don't have prior history), the riskier it gets. But it is never any riskier than any other method. It's time consuming though. You may spend 20 minutes on the phone with each person, time that adds up quickly.

Better yet, keep your associates informed about your company. Send them an occasional note to announce new products or new members of your team. Let them know when you have penetrated an account that they have been personally involved with—perhaps their spouse works there or they worked there in the past. If they are impressed, they will contact you when they are ready to change jobs. They will also send people to you when they think a good match exists—even when you don't ask.

## Recruiters

Recruiters, also known as headhunters, do the leg work to find qualified people for you to hire. They try to locate suspects based on your hiring criteria, do initial phone interviews, and pass the resumes of the qualified candidates to you for evaluation and further interview. There are two basic types of recruiters: retainer and contingent.

Retainer recruiters are paid a fee to search aggressively for a candidate for a position. You present your recruiter with your criteria and he searches for qualified candidates. Normally, retainer recruiters will even do preliminary face-to-face interviews and only send you a few highly qualified individuals from whom you can choose. This simplifies your work immensely. But you pay the retainer recruiter whether or not you hire somebody he presents. Retainer recruiters are a good choice to find a high-level manager or somebody with specialized talent.

Contingency recruiters are paid a percentage of the wages of the new hire if, and only if, you hire somebody that he presents. This is good and bad. It's good because you don't risk any money if he is unsuccessful. It's bad because he has a greater incentive to present you with marginal candidates who look good on paper. By increasing the number of candidates he presents to you, he increases his odds of placing a candidate.

If you think of the retainer recruiter as a gatekeeper who tries to keep out unqualified prospects, the contingency recruiter is the bloodhound who searches for people who meet your basic specification and lets you do the majority of the qualifying. Many recruiters do both types of searches.

Before employing a recruiter, interview him in the same way that you would interview a candidate. Make sure he is somebody who you want on your team and that his ethics coincide with yours. Speak to people for whom he has recruited in the past and select the recruiter based on his expertise and contacts. (Recruiters have specialties—i.e., marketing, programming, UNIX, CAD, manufacturing . . . )

"Oh no!" you say. "If I wanted to spend time interviewing, I would interview candidates for the job." First of all, checking out recruiters is less time consuming than checking out candidates. You do it all on the phone. Additionally, if you spend the time during your first hire to find a good recruiter, you will be able to use him later too. When staffing a branch office, I used one recruiter to find half of my employees.

## Running Classified Ads

If you're looking for a candidate with credentials that are easily found, you might run a classified ad (or post a notice on USENET) to solicit resumes. It costs less than a recruiter, but takes much more of your time because you will end up sifting through piles of resumes, most of which won't be acceptable. It's also pretty tough to find out what you're actually getting. Anybody can make himself look good on paper; and you won't have a personal recommendation to help you select. Ask for references and check them thoroughly.

## Attracting Candidates From the Competition

One of the best places to look for candidates is in your competitor's company. Ask customers for names; examine name tags at trade shows; look in industry articles. Then call the person who seems to fit your criteria.

There are many reasons that somebody would want to move from one competitor to another: better technology, better working atmosphere, better city (cost of living, livability, or family within driving distance), worry about a current company's future, a chance to make friends at the new company. In short, somebody might be willing to switch for the same reasons that somebody else might leave your company.

## Hiring Directly From Schools

If you are willing to spend time training your new employee, consider hiring directly from a school. You get a person that you can mold to fit your needs and who has not yet developed a lot of bad work habits. A new graduate is generally less expensive, too. While he may take a long time to become productive, his education often includes the latest techniques. A new graduate often exposes these new techniques to your experienced staff.

Table 20-1 summarizes the differences among the most commonly-used recruitment sources.

*TABLE 20-1:* HOW RECRUITMENT SOURCES STACK UP

| Category | Personal Contact | Competition | Classifieds | New Graduate | Recruiters |
|---|---|---|---|---|---|
| Time to Hire | Short | Short | Long | Long | Avg |
| Time to Productivity | Avg | Short | Long | Long | Avg |
| Industry Knowledge | High | High | Avg | Low | High |
| Safety of Correct Hire | Safest | Safe | Risky | Riskiest | Safe |
| Ease of Reference Checks | High | Low | Low | High | High |
| Employee Costs | Avg | High | Avg | Low | Avg |
| Hiring Costs | Low | Low | Avg | Avg | High |
| First Qualifications Provided | Yes | No | No | No | Yes |

# *Tips on Evaluating Candidates*

The most important document in the hiring process is the resume. It says a lot about the person applying for the job if you read it correctly. It summarizes the applicant's work experience and education, but it can paint an inaccurate picture. Use it as the first step in evaluating candidates, but go beyond it when making your decision.

Resumes should be written clearly. A poorly written resume can alert you to poor work habits and disorientation. A person should be able to state clearly the important parts of his work background.

Standard format for resumes is chronological, with the latest position listed first. Most of those written in alternative formats are trying to hide gaps in work history, an excessive amount of movement between positions, or inability to hold a position. However, a non-standard format doesn't mean that the person is not worth hiring. Your thorough evaluation will unveil the reason.

Look for indications of the applicant's ability to get the job done. Picture your ideal employee and compare that to the applicant. If you need specific work experience or technical background not listed on the resume, he is not a likely candidate, even if he has many other experiences to offer. A misplaced person is just as useless as an unqualified person. If you are looking at multiple candidates, develop thresholds that the qualifications displayed on the resume must pass before you are willing to hold a personal interview or phone discussion.

When you do speak with the person, ask questions that arise from your examination of the resume. Can the candidate supply you with references? Is he willing to do so? Does he properly answer the questions that you ask or does he sidestep the issues?

There are many people who look good on paper but do not perform. Attempt to get more complete information after you receive the resume and speak with the candidate. Ask for samples of his work. Call his references. If the references hedge, find out why.[*] Be thorough. Your most important asset is your staff.

---

[*] As a matter of corporate policy, some employers only verify dates of employment and will not provide further information about any employee at any level. This is not really hedging. But it certainly doesn't help.

# *Staying Within the Law*

Federal and state laws are very strong when it comes to how employers treat employees. The are stiff penalties for disobeying the laws; they can include fines and jail sentences.

Personnel laws generally cover how you treat your employees, how you hire and fire them, the types of insurance coverage you must keep, and the methods in which you withhold payroll taxes. Seek the advice of an attorney or tax professional to make sure you stay within the law.

Here are a few items from my personal check list:

- Are employee expectations in agreement with conditions that they will encounter?

- Do I treat my employees fairly? Do I insist that promotions and raises be based on merit?

- Have I withheld the appropriate taxes and paid them into the appropriate account on time?

- Have I provided all insurance coverage required by law?

- If I have problems with an employee, have I notified him of the problem along with a plan to correct the problem?

- If I must dismiss an employee, have I done so according to my legal (and ethical) obligations?

- Have I kept appropriate records about the employee to assure that I have an audit path if questions arise?

Remember, too, that discrimination is illegal in any personnel- related function. You cannot hire, fire, compensate, or promote one person over another based on race, sex, or other factors that do not affect job performance.

The following chart summarizes the different taxes, insurance, an other payroll deductions that may be applicable. The rules differ by state and local government. Check with your tax advisor for specific information.

***TABLE 20-2:*** *PAYROLL TAXES, INSURANCE, AND SUPPLEMENTARY DEDUCTIONS*

|  | Description | Liability/Contribution |
|---|---|---|
| Federal Government | Social Security | Employer/Employee |
|  | Withholding | Employee |
| State Government | Payroll Taxes | Employee |
|  | Worker's Compensation | Employer/Employee |
| Local Government | Income Taxes | Employee |
|  | Occupational Privilege Tax | Employee |
| Other Benefits | Medical Insurance | Employer/Employee |
|  | Dental Insurance | Employer/Employee |
|  | Life Insurance | Employer/Employee |
|  | Disability Insurance | Employer/Employee |
|  | 401(k) / Retirement Plan | Employer/Employee |
|  | Pension (other) | Employer |
|  | Stock Purchase | Employee |

# *Training Your Staff*

Even when you hire employees from competitors or for positions similar to their previous employment, you will need to train them in your way of business and indoctrinate them into your company culture. Don't shortcut this training cycle, because it helps you maintain your most valuable resource, your people. Understand how long it takes to bring the new hire up to a productive level. Help him achieve that level by providing guidance, reference sources, and any training that will help. As your organization grows, provide additional education so your employees can follow industry trends, discover new techniques, and grow into new responsibilities. When you build your staff, you make your single most important investment in long-term profitability. These are the people that will bring you new ideas, point out industry phenomena, and carry you to your goals. These are the people who will stick with you if times get rough and support you into better times.

# Tackling Legal, Accounting, and Tax Issues

You're about to build a business that will be worth hundreds of thousands or millions of dollars annually. Shouldn't you protect it from the start, even though you may not reach those lofty levels immediately? If I were putting together a new business today, the first thing I would do is make sure that I am surrounded by people who can best help me protect my interests, including a good lawyer and a good accountant. Lawyers and accountants keep us from making stupid mistakes. They watch out for our best interest when we begin new projects, and inform us when we need information about complex legal and financial issues. Good lawyers and accountants generally get paid well for their services, but their advice and actions recoup more than the amount that you pay to them. Ed Vielmetti of MSEN, an Internet access provider, says, "We like our lawyer to know what we're doing," an attitude shared by many good business people. Even though several thousand dollars in annual legal fees may seem large to you, your money, when spent properly, will pay you back many times over the life of your business. This chapter illustrates when you need to seek legal and accounting advice and the types of issues you will encounter.

## *Of Lawyers and Accountants*

Millions of pages of laws are put on the books each year; and taxes, accounting standards, and reporting requirements change frequently—in your local community as well as on the state and federal levels. You don't have time to track the changes yourself, but your lawyer and accountant can.

They also provide experience that you lack: your lawyer has been through many of the legal situations that you will encounter, and your accountant has frequent contact with federal, state, and local tax agencies. This experience will head off disasters that you're bound to create when you try to run your business without them.

Don't wait until you have legal trouble to pick a lawyer. That is both difficult and risky. You'd be under stress; you would have too little time to do it right; and you might not be able to get sufficient information to make a good choice. Besides, you want your lawyer to guide you when you're getting started. So find your lawyer when you first start out, or at least before you need him, so you can make your selection under advantageous circumstances.

Your primary goal when selecting your lawyer is to find somebody you trust, who has relevant business expertise, and will help you achieve your business objectives. A large law firm brings a significant amount of expertise to the table. However, large firms can be expensive, and are often unwilling to take a startup company because of the risks it creates for them: high probability of non-payment and inability to recoup overhead costs.

A small firm (with only one or a few attorneys) is often willing to spend more time and grow with you. The two most critical problems I have found with small firms are that you're depending on a single lawyer's expertise, and that you might not be able to contact the lawyer for long periods (if he's tied up with another case, or on vacation). A small law firm simply does not have the backup staff that a large firm has.

You should also select an accountant when you start your business. Your accountant can help you choose your corporate structure (corporation, partnership, etc.), show you how to set up financial controls, advise you on financing, and complete your tax forms. As time goes on, your accountant can help you obtain financing, invest your money, and even manage your accounts. Should you become a public corporation, you'll need a certified public accountant (CPA) to audit your financial statements for accuracy.

A good accountant gives you a distinct advantage. He will keep you from getting into trouble with the IRS and other tax agencies, and help you avoid unnecessary taxes, penalties, and interest. If he helps you prepare your taxes and you get audited, he can help you make it through the audit with minimum pain.

For both lawyer and accountant, select a local firm to make sure you get someone who knows both national and state requirements. If possible, find somebody who has worked with companies in the computer industry so they have a better feel for your situation. Don't give your business to your nephew who just received his degree. Let somebody else train him. You need experience. In addition, experienced advisers may be tied into other members of the business community that can be of help to you. Finally, give your business to only those whom you trust. You're giving them access to your most sensitive internal information and assets that are vital to your business.

# *Every Company Uses Legal Agreements*

During the ordinary business day, you make dozens of verbal agreements with the people around you. Most of them are simple: "If you write part A, I'll write part B." Occasionally, an agreement is important enough to put in writing. These agreements often involve high risk or people you don't know well, or are dependent on issues out of your control. By committing them to writing, you can protect yourself and your company in case an agreement runs astray. Not only do you have a written record to settle misinterpretations, you also have legal recourse.

The best way to assure that the agreement (contract) suits its purpose is to consult your lawyer. But, in the meantime, here are a few points to consider.

1. If the issue is complex enough to be easily forgotten or misconstrued, put it in writing. Use the written contract whenever you need to remind either party about the terms of the agreement. Additionally, since few employees stay with one company forever, the written document is a source of information whenever one of the responsible parties leaves his company.

2. To reduce miscommunications, write it simply.

3. Whenever possible, make the contract a complete agreement. Instead of referring to other documents, include them as attachments, or reiterate their contents in the contract.

4. Remember that there is a distinction between you and your company. If you are executing the agreement on behalf of your company, include your title. Otherwise, it may be misinterpreted as a personal contract.

5. Include provisions for something going wrong—termination, cancellation, or arbitration clauses. A termination clause states what happens when independent events affect the agreement (i.e., fire, earthquake, flood). A cancellation clause indicates the important dates, notices, and penalties that must be paid if either party fails to fulfill his promise. The arbitration clause provides a method to settle the dispute without going to court.

6. If you are not in full agreement with the document, do not sign it. Make sure that you have read it thoroughly.

Just because you don't put it in writing doesn't mean you don't have a contract. A valid contract needs three things: an agreement, an obligation on the part of one or more parties, and consideration—a payment of some kind (not necessarily money) that transfers from one party to the other. For example, you agree with Ajax Consulting that your company will use Ajax's utility within your new product and that you will pay Ajax a 5% royalty on all sales of your product. You maintain exclusive rights to Ajax's product. Whether you put it in writing or not, you have a valid contract because:

1. Both parties agree.

2. Ajax has an obligation to deliver its product to you. You have an obligation to pay royalties.

3. There is consideration: Ajax refrains from selling its product to anybody else. (Your first royalty payment to Ajax and your staff's effort to incorporate Ajax's code into yours are consideration too.)

There are many situations that might require a contract, including software license, employment agreement, subcontractor agreement, non-disclosure or beta-test. Let's look at each separately. While we do, keep in mind that litigation can be expensive. These agreements are put in place with the primary motive of eliminating litigation.

## Software Licenses

Your software license protects your rights to your intellectual property (your software). It states that you own the software (not the user) and governs what the user can do with it (i.e., how he can use, modify, or copy it). Often it delineates the warranty. In the cases where your customer does not have to sign an actual contract, it defines acceptance criteria. For instance, "Opening this disk packet indicates your acceptance of these terms and conditions." In most cases, your software license also states the limits of your liability.

## Employment Agreements

For most small companies, the best types of employment agreements are written offers that state the terms of the hire, including compensation, title, benefits, and other particulars. Although some companies rely on verbal agreements, such agreements are more likely to be misconstrued and end up with a disgruntled employee. The more details of the employment terms that you can put into writing, the less likely you are to run into problems.

Most of us use our own employee experiences in setting our employment decisions, a method that works well for the majority of cases. But occasionally you'll need to have direct help from your lawyer or accountant to deal with tax laws or labor laws such as COBRA or ERISA. Of course, you'll also need to understand federal and state employment practices governing worker's compensation, unemployment compensation, fair labor, and safety. Although you will probably receive information when you register your company for business, you may want to check your employment practices with one of your advisors.

# Rights and Obligations

In the computer industry, there are many paradigms under which people work:

- Salaried employee (you pay him a set weekly amount regardless of the amount of time he works during the week). Salaried employees are also called exempt employees because they are exempt from overtime payments.

- Hourly employee (you pay him based on how many hours he works). Hourly employees are also known as non-exempt employees.

- Independent contractor (he is his own boss, but works for you under a specific arrangement).

- Consortium (you pool resources—staffing, money or both—with others to bring out a product).

- Partner (you both own the company).

The value of what that person delivers or performs can be measured differently under various circumstances. Let's say somebody writes some software for you. Are you hiring her (1) to work a certain number of hours, (2) to complete a piece of *your* software to your satisfaction, (3) to write *your* software in its entirety, or (4) deliver a copy of a self-contained software package?

With this many paradigms from which to choose, it is easy to be misconstrue an oral agreement. Who owns the software, copyright, or patent? Who must support the product? When is payment due? Do you get the source code? If so, are you allowed to modify it? If a customer purchases but does not pay, does a royalty still apply? Even written agreements can be confusing.

I once paid a subcontractor to develop internal software for my wife's business. After the code was delivered, I found out that the subcontractor planned to sell the software as a package to hundreds of my wife's competitors, a situation that my wife and I found unacceptable. We felt that we owned the software because we financed it, developed the specifications, and "hired" him to write the software for our exclusive use. Worse, the software was slow, and he refused to provide the source code so we could tweak the performance ourselves. He claimed he owned the software and that as an outside contractor, he delivered a packaged product that just happened to be built to our specification. Our mistake was not specifying in advance who would own the rights to the completed software.

We ran into a problem with a single contractor. It gets more confusing when you use several. If your software is a combination of software modules from subcontractors and modules you license from other software companies, your licensing, payment, and ownership arrangements become even more complex. You need to remember the agreement you have with each party. It's much simpler (and less risky) to write a concise contract with each party to eliminate confusion.

As part of your agreements, make sure that ownership and modification rights are specified. If you will own the software once it is completed, state it. Also state whether you can modify the software at your discretion or whether you need permission. Source code should be protected, too. Stipulate in your contract how the code should be protected (for example, all copies of the code that leave the premises must be in object format, and all systems on which the source code can be loaded are protected by passwords or some other kind of protection). Then, make sure that you can abide by the source code protection agreement.

## Non-disclosures and Beta Test Agreements

When you want to disclose internal information to important customers, prospects, or associates, use a non-disclosure agreement to restrict them from revealing the non-public information for a specified time period. These are important in beta test situations, too, to keep information away from your competitors.

# *Tax Requirements Never Stop*

You are obligated by law to submit the proper taxes and forms to the Internal Revenue Service (and most states) whether they notify you or not. If you don't, you're subject to penalties and interest. Here is a list of some of the most common federal forms. Contact your tax advisor to get a more complete list of forms relevant to you and to help you satisfy your IRS and state obligations.

| Form | Purpose |
| --- | --- |
| Federal Form 940 | Employer's Federal Unemployment Tax Return |
| Federal Form 941 | Employer's Quarterly Federal Tax Return |
| Federal Form W-2 | Wage and Tax Statement |
| Federal Form W-3 | Transmittal of Income and Tax Statements |
| Federal Form W-4 | Employee's Withholding Allowance Certificate (not for submission) |
| Federal Form 8109 | Federal Tax Deposit Coupons |

| Form | Purpose |
|------|---------|
| Federal Form 1099 | Miscellaneous Income Forms |
| Federal Form 1096 | Transmittal for Form 1099 |
| Federal Form 1120 | Corporate Income Tax Return |
| Federal Form 1120S | S Corporation Income Tax Return |
| Federal Form 1040 | Individual Income Tax Return |
| | State Sales Tax |
| | State Employee Forms |
| | State License Fees |

Forms and taxes must be submitted throughout the year, so put away reserves and be ready to submit the forms when due.

## Accounting Methods Affect Taxes

Your tax liability changes according to the method by which you recognize your revenues and expenses. If you use the cash method, you recognize your revenue when you receive the check, and the expense when you send your payment. If you use the accrual method, you recognize revenue when you ship your product (assuming F.O.B. Shipping point), and recognize expense when you receive your purchase or commit to the payment (depending on type of transaction). From a tax standpoint, profits may shift from one period to another based on the method you use. For instance, let's suppose you buy $5000 worth of office supplies in December and pay for them in January. With accrual accounting, you would have a December expense that would decrease profits in year one by $5000, resulting in a tax savings of $1700 (assuming a 34% tax rate). On the other hand, if you use cash accounting, your expense would not go on your books until January, so you would have to wait a year to get the $1700 tax savings. With the cash method, however, you have the flexibility to accelerate your tax savings by paying the bill in December. With the accrual method, you must arrange shipment for the period in which you want the expense.

In most cases, cash accounting is simpler. Public corporations use accrual accounting. Small companies can use either. Ask your tax advisor which method is best for you.

## *More Than Just Contracts and Taxes*

You'd be surprised by how often your attorney and accountant can help you. For instance, I have turned to my attorney to collect money from a delinquent account. I have also used feedback from both my attorney and accountant to help me select business insurance. In the final analysis, your attorney and accountant are actually good all-around business advisors. By consulting your attorney, you can get help related to formation of your business, contracts, employee relations, antitrust, product liability, and protection of your intellectual property. Your accountant can set up your financial control system, give you cash management advice, help you reduce costs, and plan for compensation strategies. By using both, you increase your business viability and reduce problems.

Don't neglect other sources that can provide information and advice about legal and tax matters. Here, in Connecticut, I use the Connecticut Business and Industry Association. Software Publishers Association provides information and advice regarding software piracy and miscellaneous other software-related issues. The IRS, Small Business Administration, and OSHA produce many informative publications and have answer lines, as do most state agencies.

# Odds and Ends

I've covered the most important aspects of getting your company on solid ground, and keeping it there. However, there are a few odds and ends, and we'll cover them in this chapter.

## *Protecting Your Software Asset*

In 1993, with its introduction of MS-DOS 6.0, Microsoft decided it was going to take a hard line with software pirates. It had discovered that it was losing millions of dollars to these people. With MS-DOS 6.0, the company stopped licensing OEM's to replicate the disks and manuals, and instead provided access to authorized replicators who would, in turn, provide all MS-DOS software and manuals.

For each user license that an OEM or VAR ordered, it would receive the product, plus a certificate of authenticity that would include several anti-counterfeiting devices similar to those on dollar bills.

Microsoft was not going after the OEM's and VAR's, who were often innocent. They were going after the bootleggers, some of whom were pretty crafty. Printers that were working for the large OEM's, for instance, would make more copies than their customers ordered, then sell the over-run on the black market, making a lot of money at Microsoft's expense.

Like Microsoft, your software will be subject to piracy, too. And while you may not like it, you may decide to take steps to prevent it. According to Jody Morrison, litigation coordinator at The Software Publishers Association, the first step in protecting your software is to register your copyright with the copyright office in the Library of Congress. She says it is a short procedure and only costs a few dollars. After the copyright, she says your most effective protection is education, and when necessary, litigation.

## ☞ *Deterring Software Piracy* ☜

- Only license your source code to people you trust.

- Deter individual theft by requiring users to type in a registration number printed on the original program diskette or tape at installation. If they don't have the information on the original diskette, they can't install the program.

- Ask users to enter their name and company when installing your software, then record it on the diskette. If users are thinking about loaning diskettes to friends, they may think twice because the software is immediately traceable to the original owner.

- Place routines in your code that call a hardware "key" that is included with your software and placed into a port. If it finds the key, the software performs normally. If it does not, it stops. These keys are available from several third-party vendors.

- Copy-protect your disk. The problem with copy protection is that it also interferes with end users' ability to back up the software. Therefore, the user community does not like it.

- If you sell through retailers, include something in the box that is difficult to reproduce: for example, a distinctive marking such as a hologram. With such markings, savvy buyers can know whether they are buying the real thing or an illegal copy.

- If you grant license to your source code, deal only with people that you trust. Set up your licensing agreement so that they are responsible for any harm caused if the source code that you give them is illegally duplicated.

- When you license source code, put together a list of requirements that the licensee must abide by to obtain the code (i.e., can only make two copies; cannot be removed from the site; what it can be used for; and who can access it within the company). Your lawyer can help you put together the requirements into an agreement.

- If you sell through the channel, include a license agreement in each box. Make the agreement self accepting. Once users perform a specific task, such as opening the envelope or loading the tape, they automatically accept the license agreement.

There are others working on your behalf, too. A federal law has been passed, partly through the efforts of the Software Publishers Association, that has turned commercial bootlegging into a felony. With this law on the books, anybody convicted of commercial software piracy could face fines of $250,000 and up to five years in jail.

The SPA has taken an aggressive stance in attempting to educate the business community about the dangers of piracy. It has developed a software management guide, a self-audit kit, and videotapes to educate software users. It supplements these items with public relations support. When necessary, SPA instigates litigation.

When it comes right down to it, though, if your software is valuable, somebody will probably try to steal it. It is incumbent on you to protect it to keep it from losing its value.

## *Choosing Ethics*

Your top salesperson has just walked into your office and placed a purchase order on your desk for $100,000. Ecstatically, you congratulate her for winning a deal against your toughest competition. "Thanks" she says. But then she gives you the bad news. To get the deal, she had to tell the customer that the next version of your software would have a feature that you don't plan to put in. Is there an ethical problem here?

When faced with difficult business decisions, individuals react differently. In this case, your salesperson may have felt that you would change your design to accommodate this customer . . . or she may have lied to get the business. The only way to know is to understand the way she normally works.

If ethical questions were straight forward, there would be few disagreements about what constitutes ethical behavior. But many ethical decisions are made based on the interest of the person making the judgment. Your salesperson has to decide what to tell the customer to get the business. Your lawyer has to decide how strong a stance he must take when negotiating. Your accountant must decide how to make full use of the tax laws without breaking them. That leaves you to manage the entire process, because the decisions of all those people reflect on you. Sometimes they even have serious repercussions, such as legal liabilities, fines, or lost business.

In the case of the purchase order just presented, you have several choices:

1.  Accept the purchase order, then honor the commitment made by the salesperson by including the feature in your next release.

2.  Reject the purchase order and keep your original design specification.

3.  Accept the purchase order and hope that your customer doesn't notice. If he puts up a fuss, blame the sales person for overcommitting.

4.  Go to the customer (or have your salesperson approach him) and tell him that you cannot get the feature into the next release, but come up with a schedule that is acceptable to both parties.

Only you can make the call. If the salesperson has acted in a way that you feel is inappropriate, make sure you let her know why it was inappropriate and how you expect to do business.

If ethics are important to you, make sure your staff and business partners are aware of your convictions. Put together a code of ethics, either formally or by a model of your own actions. When you come across questionable situations, stick to your guns.

The same thing goes when your dealing with outsiders, even more so. If an outside company will be working with you, make sure that it stays within your acceptable ethical codes—at least in your business dealings and those that affect you. You can't always affect how they behave in general, but you can set barriers that keep you insulated. Dan Heller, President of Z-Soft, told me that, when starting his company, he was surprised by how unethical people can be. His belief was spurred by an arrangement he had put together with a software publisher. He has since solved the problem: he no longer works with that publisher.

The best way that you can impact how ethically your business partners act is to choose them wisely. If you don't trust an individual or company, don't do business with them.

## *Play Technological Leapfrog*

Will Rogers once said, "Even if you're on the right track, you will get run over if you just sit there." This certainly applies to the software business. Once you introduce your product, you have to start thinking about your next product (or version) because the market will change. To keep your product viable, it must change too. You're playing a continuous game of technological leapfrog. In January, you have the best product; in April, your competitor does. It's up to you to get the lead back. Even when you do, it will be temporary.

Because you can't keep the technology lead consistently, you should make sure your product stands on other merit too, such as your support or your knowledge of the user base. This helps you sell while your competitor has taken the lead.

In the mid-eighties, Intergraph used an in-place upgrade path to its advantage. The standard platform for CAD/CAM systems at the time was the 16-bit minicomputer, such as the Digital PDP-11, HP 1000 or Sperry-Univac V77. When several competitors announced VAX 32-bit versions of their software, Intergraph did too. But while it took months for most of the competition to deliver a VAX version, Intergraph had one almost immediately. That's because they delivered their current 16-bit software on the VAX, not a new 32-bit software package. Intergraph's software ran in PDP-11 16-bit emulation mode, so the user could buy his VAX, run the 16-bit version, then upgrade without having to change out the hardware. Even though Intergraph's 32-bit product came out later than other vendors, it used the in-place upgrade path to eliminate its competitors' advantage.

## *Plan for Contingencies*

Don't be surprised if things don't go as planned. Unexpected events will affect your market, sometimes in a positive way. McAfee Associates, Mergent Corporation, and other security software companies made out well when the Michelangelo virus scare became big news in 1991.

Sometimes, though, you must be ready to react to a threat. In 1993, Stac Electronics had to do that. Microsoft introduced DOS 6.0, an upgrade to the DOS operating system that included DoubleSpace file compression. Stac, at that time the leader in file compression utilities, had attempted to get Microsoft to use its compression code, but Microsoft opted for a competitive product. Inclusion of DoubleSpace in DOS posed a serious threat to Stacker, Stac's product.

Stac became aggressive. It enhanced Stacker with additional features such as a graphical interface. Then it sued Microsoft for infringement.[*] It got a break when DOS 6.0 users started to complain about corruption of data when they used DOS 6.0 compression. Stac immediately offered a Stacker Special Edition, which users, who had already installed DoubleSpace, could retrofit their drives with Stacker for $49. DOS 6.0 still hurt Stac. Several months after its introduction, Stac laid off 40 employees, 20% of its work force.

---

[*] On February 23, 1994, Stac won its suit, and was awarded $120 million in damages.

# *Protect Your Investment and Your Team*

As a business owner, you face many unforeseeable risks— accidents, employee mistakes, health problems, and natural disasters; any of these may strike at any time, causing you operational problems or even wiping out your entire business. You cannot always avoid the problems, but you can mitigate the financial consequences by obtaining insurance coverage. In its basic form, insurance is a pooling of risk. You make periodic payments to your insurance carrier instead of risking much higher one-time payments when something goes wrong. Even though you're betting against yourself, it's a good bet because one really large loss paid out of your own pocket (whether medical, liability or other) could put you out of business.

## Why You Need Insurance

It may seem like common sense to protect yourself against catastrophic risk; however, when choosing between paying for insurance to decrease risk and doing without insurance to conserve cash, some short-sighted entrepreneurs do without insurance. The only time it makes sense to do without insurance is when both risk (probability of loss) and the amount that you can lose are small. For instance, when I first started Marketing Masters, I did not insure my equipment because it was only worth $2000, and the insurance would have cost several hundred dollars per quarter. But I did get other kinds of coverage, and as soon as I bought more equipment, I promptly insured it. Your risks are probably larger. Consider the following situations in which insurance carries you over the hump:

- A fire in your building wipes out your computer equipment and keeps you from entering your offices for three weeks. Insurance reimburses you for fire-related expenses including new computers, staffing to reload the software, and temporary office space.

- A visitor to your office falls and suffers injuries that keep him from working for three months. He sues you. Your insurance carrier pays the bulk of the loss, as well as the legal costs.

- A computer vendor lends you a $50,000 workstation. You return it by external carrier, but it does not arrive at its destination or arrives in unusable condition. Proper insurance pays the bulk of the loss.

- An error in your software is blamed for the actions of a customer that result in the customer going out of business. The customer sues you. Proper insurance coverage pays your defense cost.

- You (or another critical employee) are injured while on vacation. Your disability coverage provides cash flow to help your business stay afloat while you recuperate.

The potential cost of being without insurance is much greater than the ongoing cost of coverage. Insurance is particularly important to small businesses, because unexpected losses or expenses can place severe financial burdens on the business or principals. Insurance helps you deal with extraordinary situations that can otherwise destroy your livelihood: loss of key employees, liability claims against your company, and other disasters. Whether you have a large staff or work by yourself, it is in your best interest to insure both your company and individuals.

You should have several types of coverage: coverage to protect you, your business, and your employees. In reality, they all protect you, even if only indirectly. Here are some of the most common types of coverage:

### TABLE 22-1: IMPORTANT TYPES OF INSURANCE COVERAGE

| Insurance to protect you: | |
| --- | --- |
| Medical | Pays your personal medical expenses |
| Life | Pays your beneficiary a prespecified amount if you die |
| Disability | Provides you with income, should you be unable to work |
| Overhead expense | Pays your business expenses while you are disabled (a type of disability insurance) |
| Life insurance to fund buy-sell | If one partner dies, provides funding for the survivors to buy out the deceased partner's share of the business. |
| **Insurance to protect your business:** | |
| Key Person | Protects you if a crucial member of your team dies |
| Liability | Protects you when someone is injured on your property or when business property is stolen |
| Inland Marine | Protects you when business property is lost or stolen while being transported |
| Errors and Omissions | Protects you if you harm a customer by way of error or omission in your product or service (for example, a bug in your software destroys a customer's data) |

| | |
|---|---|
| Credit | Insures against bad debt risk |
| Valuable Paper and Data | Protects you if valuable data or paperwork is destroyed, stolen, or lost |
| Business Income | Compensates you for lost income or provides cash to keep you going in case a mishap keeps you from operating |

**Insurance to protect your employees:**

| | |
|---|---|
| Workers Compensation | Compensates workers who are injured on the job |
| Unemployment Compensation | Compensates workers who lose their jobs |
| Life | Compensates the beneficiaries of workers who die |
| Medical | Pays the cost of medical care |
| Disability | Pays compensating "wages" in case the worker is disabled and unable to collect a paycheck. |

Federal law mandates that you have at least workers compensation and unemployment compensation insurance for your employees. Some states require other types of insurance. Check with your accountant, legal advisor, and insurance agent to determine what you need and where to get it in your state.

### NOTE

As this book goes to print, President Clinton is waging a political battle to reform health insurance in the United States. If he is successful, you will have to provide certain types and levels of health insurance for your employees. Your method of buying it will also change. Although we would love to provide more information here about your requirements as they will shake out, we can't. There's still a long way to go before the plans are solidified. At this time, there's not even a guarantee that major changes will happen.

If the changes occur before you read this, modify your actions to conform to the new plan. Otherwise, you are welcome to use this section as a guide. It's likely that the changes will take several years to implement.

Fine print on insurance documents can be confusing; you may mistakingly believe that you are covered when you're not. Therefore, seek the advice of a professional to make sure you're getting the coverage you really need.

## ☙ *The Peril of Self-Insurance* ☙

During recent years, an alarming number of companies have turned to self-insurance to reduce the cost of health care coverage. Under a self-insurance plan, the company pays the claims out of its own pocket instead of turning to an insurance company. Usually, the company hires an administrator. The administrator is not an insurance company. It simply processes the claims and tells the company how much is due. The company then puts the money into an account controlled by the administrator, who then disburses the funds. Some self-insured companies obtain an umbrella policy that reimburses them when total company claims exceed a prespecified amount (i.e., all employee health claims collectively total more than $10,000 for the month).

Well-intentioned companies obtain these umbrella policies to decrease their risk. However, the umbrella coverage normally has such a high deductible that the company often becomes burdened simply by paying the deductible amounts. Self-insurance—even through a reputable administrator—is no insurance! Your company cash flow becomes dependent on the health of your employees. Your company must find free cash to pay most employee medical bills. This compounds the burden that the company already faces if employees cannot work. Don't be misled by large companies that self-insure. Large companies can average their own risks. They can also put together large sums of cash much more easily than small companies. The risk of self-insurance is simply too great to be of value to small companies.

Self-insurance doesn't really protect your employees, either. Your company probably isn't in a position to handle the large and on-going claims that could result from an employee with a major illness, like AIDS, cancer, or Lyme Disease. And, should your company go out of business, your employees won't be protected adequately by federal law. If a company with standard health insurance coverage goes out of business, federal law mandates continued coverage by the insurance company for all displaced employees who want it. If a self-insured company goes out of business, employees may be stuck without any insurance because the government does not require insurance companies to pick up policies that they did not write. Self-insurance is high risk for both the company and employee and should be avoided.

## A Small Price for Big Protection

Insurance coverage should be obtained to cover any circumstances in which a potential loss might damage your business. You would be surprised at how quickly unforeseen costs can add up. Routine surgery can cost over $10,000. A fire can cost you tens of thousands of dollars in repair costs and lost revenue. A liability suit can cost you hundreds of thousands of dollars and wipe you out completely. And losses can come from unexpected events. In its first year of operation, for instance, Marketing Masters lost an $8000 peripheral in shipment, but was covered by an inland-marine policy which shielded us from most of the loss.

Statistically, you will probably end up laying out a bit more money by buying insurance than if you pay all your claims directly. But the majority of your payments will be on a predetermined schedule, allowing you to better manage your cash. You also benefit from the added protection against catastrophic losses—a protection that is well worth the price of your policy. Table 22-4 shows what kinds of agencies sell many important kinds of insurance:

*TABLE 22-2:* WHERE TO OBTAIN INSURANCE COVERAGE

| Type of Coverage | Sources |
|---|---|
| General Business Coverage | Independent Agent<br>Company Agent |
| Life Insurance | Independent Agent<br>Company Agent |
| Disability Insurance | Independent Agent<br>Company Agent |
| Health Care | Independent Agent<br>Company Agent<br>Group Plan |
| Unemployment Compensation | Independent Agent<br>Group Agent<br>Group Plan<br>Government Entity |
| Worker's Compensation | Government Entity<br>Independent Insurance Company |

# *Choosing the Proper Ownership Structure*

You can structure your company in two basic ways: as a proprietorship (sole proprietor or partnership), or as a corporation. Your choice affects the amount of risk to which you are exposed, how you are taxed, and your capacity to obtain funding.

If you choose proprietorship, you own and operate a company that is, for all intents and purposes, part of you. That is, in the eyes of the Internal Revenue Service, the business is the owner (and vice versa). Business income automatically becomes your personal income; its assets and liabilities are yours.

If, on the other hand, you incorporate, you (the owner) and the business (a.k.a. the corporation) become two distinct legal entities. This allows you to maintain an arm's length relationship with the company, including separating your assets, liabilities, and income from those of the corporation itself. This legal distinction is important, as you will see later.

There is a special type of corporation called an "S corporation" (a name derived from the title of the subchapter of the IRS code in which the definition exists). Just like "C corporations" (the name we will use to distinguish regular corporations from S corporations), S corporations are legally separate from the owners. However, the income and loss from the corporation flows directly to the personal income of the owners. Instead of being taxed as a corporation, the S corporation owners are taxed on their pro rata share of earnings.

## Ease of Administration

Starting a proprietorship is relatively easy. In many states you simply have to obtain state tax permits. And if you intend to have employees, you need an employer identification number (EIN) from the IRS. You're in business as "Joanne Q. Operator dba (doing business as) Nuevo Software." At the end of the year, you report your earnings to the IRS on your personal tax returns.

Starting a corporation is a more complex process. If you want to incorporate, you need to file incorporation papers. It's best to involve your attorney. He'll guide you through your incorporation decisions and file the papers for you. You must still obtain your EIN and state tax permits. At the end of the year, you must file separate business returns with the IRS and your state (because the business is now a legal entity). Additionally, you must follow corporate procedures, such as holding annual shareholder's meetings, keeping corporate minutes, and putting together a board of directors. Your lawyer can give you more information on how to do each of these.

Incorporating an S corporation is similar to that of a C corporation. You simply need to "elect" S corporation status on a form.

## Risk

One of the problems with proprietorships is that the individuals who own the company share all liabilities with the company. If the company owes money for any reason and does not have the cash to pay the suit, the individuals are responsible. So, if your company owes $100,000 to a creditor and you have not paid him, he can come directly after you and your personal assets. Your car, your house, and your personal savings accounts are all fair game.

This sharing of liability extends to lawsuits. If somebody injures herself on your property, if an employee thinks he lost a promotion because of illegal bias, or if somebody injures himself due to your software, your company may be sued. Your personal possessions are on the line.

Incorporation eliminates much of the risk because you are not automatically personably liable. In most cases, the risk is restricted to the corporate entity. That makes it difficult for creditors to latch onto your personal possessions. Of course, that doesn't mean that somebody won't sue you when he sues your corporation. It simply means that you are not *automatically* at personal risk. You are at personal risk if you have individually co-signed for a loan, but that type of decision can be made on a case by case basis, protecting you from the danger of unlimited risk. Figure 22-1 shows how corporate status separates your personal funds from the business.

## Taxes, Taxes, Taxes

The corporate structure you choose also has tax implications. C corporations, for instance, subject you to potential double taxation because corporate earnings are taxed as corporate income at the corporate tax rate; then, when you receive the money as dividends, you're taxed again on the same money, this time at individual rates.

If your corporation earns $100,000 (revenue minus expenses) after you have already taken your salary, it must pay about $23,000 in corporate income tax. If you receive the remaining $77,000 for your personal use (let's say as dividends) you will also pay personal income tax on the $77,000—possibly around $30,000. The dividends have been taxed twice: once as corporate income, once as your personal income.

If your business is a proprietorship or if you have elected S corporation status, you will only be taxed once on the earnings. However, your business earnings will affect your ability to take advantage of other tax benefits. Let's say you pay yourself a $100,000 salary, and your business has earnings of $500,000. Since

*FIGURE 22-1: CORPORATE ASSETS ARE LEGALLY SEPARATE FROM YOUR PERSONAL ASSETS*

your business is growing, you plan to use the $500,000 as working capital, so you keep the money in your business account, unavailable for personal use. The IRS doesn't care that you haven't put the money in your personal account. As far as your tax return is concerned, you have made $600,000 (the business earnings plus the $100,000 you paid yourself). That's an effective change of 600%! It may make you ineligible for exemptions and throw you into a higher tax bracket.

## Are You an Owner or an Employee?

One of the subtle differences between proprietorships and corporations depends on your own status as employee. In both cases, you are filling dual roles. You are an owner, directing the company, and an employee doing the everyday tasks. Where does one begin and the other end? This question is particularly important when determining your pay.

In the case of proprietors, there is no real distinction. During the course of the year, you can withdraw money at any time you want. According to the IRS, you are self-employed and subject to self-employment taxes. Your paycheck is considered to be a draw against retained earnings of the company. You will have been taxed the same amount whether you define it as wages or profit.

On the other hand, when you incorporate, every check you receive must be categorized appropriately. If you receive an employee's paycheck, your distribution is treated as if you worked for somebody else. All standard employment taxes and insurance must be paid. If instead you receive dividends as a stockholder, your money is not subject to employment taxes, but is subject to dividend taxes. (The considerations only apply to the owners. Other employees are treated identically under any ownership structure.)

Choosing an ownership structure is complex and varies depending on your needs and personal situation. The best advice is to consult your lawyer and accountant who can tell you which type of company is best for you.

*TABLE 22-3: COMPARISON OF SEVERAL OWNERSHIP STRUCTURES*

| Corporate Structure | Tax Rate | Separation of Assets | Owners | Owner Liability |
|---|---|---|---|---|
| **Sole Proprietor** | Individual | No | 1 | Yes |
| **Partnership** | Individual | No | 2 or more | Yes |
| **Private Corporation** | Corporate | Yes | Unlimited | No |
| **S Corporation** | Individual | Yes | Limited to 35 | No |

## Corporations Need Directors

If you incorporate, you are required by law to have a board of directors. Your board helps set company policy and ensures that you administer the policy. Although you can choose your board from virtually anybody you know, including family and friends, you are better served by selecting members who will significantly contribute to your corporation: investors, influential business leaders, retired executives, computer industry entrepreneurs, or executives from your end user markets. They will advise you on important decisions, help bring in new customers, and influence other business people. Corporations typically pay board members nominal fees for attending board meetings.

Even if you don't incorporate, it's not a bad idea to recruit a quality board of directors. Experienced executives on your board will keep you from wasting your money on imprudent activities, and make your job easier by using their experience to help you run your company effectively.

# *Thinking About Going Public?*

Many high tech entrepreneurs have made their fortune by going public. But it's not for the faint of heart. It's a complicated process that eats up your time, takes a lot of money, and requires more expertise than most entrepreneurial companies have.

When you go public, you will need to find an underwriter, file with the Securities and Exchange Commission, and put your company under a great deal of scrutiny as investors and regulators examine your company. On an ongoing basis, you will have to answer to a new set of stock holders and issue financial statements that conform with SEC guidelines. If your company is listed on a stock exchange, you will also have to obey the rules and regulations of that exchange. What's more, much of the information that you previously considered confidential will be available to the public—including to your competition.

So why go public at all?

The main reasons that companies go public are:

- The venture capitalists or owners are looking for a way to "cash out" and get a lump sum of money by selling stock.

- The company wants access to additional capital. Companies that are publicly traded can issue new shares fairly easily, thereby increasing the amount of cash available for business.

- The owner wants to become wealthy on paper. The value of Bill Gates' stock in Microsoft, for instance, is now over 7 billion dollars. (You can still be wealthy on paper if you don't go public. But by being publicly traded, you can readily sell your shares whenever you desire.)

If you have read this book from cover to cover, you already know it's not aimed at the entrepreneur who wants to make money by cashing out. Don't let that stop you. If you want to explore what it takes to go public, by all means do so. But you probably won't be in a position to go public until several years after your company is profitable; while there's no strict requirement that you have to be profitable to go public, several years of solid earnings and growth go a long way towards making your initial public offering payoff. You will also need to get plenty of advice. I suggest you obtain a book or two about the subject, then talk with your lawyer, accountant, and even an investment broker to help you understand what it's all about. Have them guide you through the steps you must take to issue your stock.

# *Is it Time To Collect Your Check?*

You have put together a terrific company. The members of your team are remarkable. The product you're developing will revolutionize the world. You have even set the world ablaze by marketing it superbly. Don't you deserve to be compensated for it? Sure you do. The real question is, "When?"

When you work for somebody else, you can be sure of a paycheck. But this is your own company. You must decide when you can afford to bring home a check. There are plenty of reasons to bring one home now. Your family has developed a nasty habit of requiring food every day and a roof over their heads. If you're single, your hobbies or love interests demand material objects. Yet, there are always ways for you to spend your money on the business, making it grow. It's a tough decision.

There are two trains of thought. The first is that you must put the business first so it can survive and thrive. "Throw every spare dollar into the business." This thinking truly belongs to the self-funded entrepreneur.

The alternative is to take out your personal money first, in a reasonable amount of course. Then use the remaining amount to fund the business. This is the way venture-funded companies pay their managers. The companies pay reasonable salaries so they can attract the best people. The investors hope for a rapid return, but realize that management cost is a standard cost of doing business.

In my opinion, there is a middle ground—but only if you have planned properly. During the initial stages of your company (assuming you have not been venture funded), you should be able to bring home a reasonable paycheck; perhaps not the same one that you became accustomed to when you worked for somebody else, but one that lets you pay your personal bills without pulling money out of your savings. You should not have to suffer economically to start your business or to continue operations.

The key is to plan for your salary when you plan your cash flows. If you cannot bring home enough money to live, why operate your own business? It seems a bit silly. If you include your own salary in your cash flow projections, and you are reasonably accurate, you will have no problem paying your personal bills and using the excess cash flow to fund your business. If you can't, you're probably undercapitalized. Raise the red flag. Your company is operating under a severe disadvantage. You need to rework your plans, and may need to raise additional money.

# *Now Get Out There!*

At this point you're probably ready to build your business into the next great software dynasty. Go out and do it. Keep this book within easy reach so you can use it when you need advice. Use the appendix to find resources to help you reach your goals. If you would like to get in touch with me or be put on my mailing list, you can contact me at the following address:

David Radin
Marketing Masters
Suite 765
60 Skiff Street
Hamden, CT 06517-1017

E-mail via Internet: radin@ora.com
E-mail via CompuServe Mail: 73234,3712

As you run your business, remember the words of Winston Churchill:

"Success is never final."

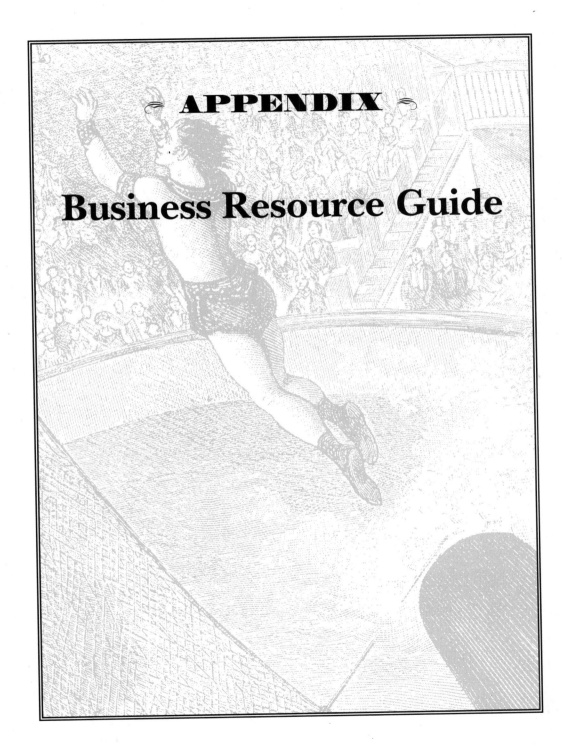

# APPENDIX

# Business Resource Guide

# Business Resource Guide

This resource guide has two types of listings. The first includes the types of people that you probably want to do business with: resellers, integrators, distributors, and hardware vendors. As partners, these companies will help you increase the effectiveness of your sales and marketing efforts. The second type shows where you can get information or other types of help: magazines, books, trade organizations, databases, and consultants.

Undoubtedly, some of the information will have changed, even as we go to print; one of the integrators has changed owners or name three times while I was writing this book. Even so, you will usually be able to track down the resource by calling the old number for a referral.

If you find any resources that should be included in our next printing, please send me an e-mail message. I'm always on the lookout for good sources.

## *Distribution Channels and Corporate Partners*

This section lists corporations that you will be working with, ranging from large resellers and distributors to vendors who have third-party programs.

### Large National Resellers

CompUSA Inc.
15160 Marsh Lane
Dallas, TX 75234
Attn: Merchandising
214-484-8500

Computerland
P.O. Box 9012
Pleasanton, CA 94566-9012
Attn: Vendor Relations
510-734-4019

Egghead Software, Inc.
22011 SE 51st Street
Issaquah, WA 98027
Attn: Merchandising/Advertising Dept.
206-391-0800

Electronics Boutique/Waldensoftware
Goshen Corporate Park
1345 Enterprise Drive
Westchester, PA 19380
215-430-8100

Entex Information Services
(formerly JWP/BusinessLand)
6 International Drive
Rye Brook, NY 10573
Attn: Product Management Department

Microage Computer Centers, Inc.
2308 S. 55th Street
Tempe, AZ 85282-1824
602-968-3168

Radio Shack
(Division of Tandy Corporation)
1500 One Tandy Center
Fort Worth, TX 76102
Attn: Product Marketing

Software Spectrum
2140 Merritt Drive
Garland, TX 75041
800-624-0503

UNIX Central
474 Potrero Avenue
Sunnyvale, CA 94086-9406
408-733-9400

## Top Systems Integrators

Andersen Consulting
69 W. Washington Street
Chicago, IL 60602
312-580-0069

Boeing Computer Services
P.O. Box 24346
Seattle, WA 98124
206-655-1131

Computer Sciences Corporation
2100 E. Grand Avenue
El Segundo, CA 90245
310-615-0311

Computerland Corp.
5964 W. Las Positas Blvd.
Pleasanton, CA 94566
510-734-4000

Digital Equipment Corp.
Professional Services
146 Main Street
Maynard, MA 01754
508-493-5111

Electronic Data Systems Corp.
5400 Legacy Drive
Plano, TX 75024
214-604-6000

GTE Corp
15000 Conference Center Drive
Chantilly, VA 22021
703-818-4000

IBM Integrated Systems Solutions Corp.
560 White Plains Road
Tarrytown, NY 10591
914-288-2267

Martin Marietta Information Systems
P.O. Box 590385
Orlando, FL 32859
407-826-1714

NCR Corporation
1700 South Patterson Blvd.
Dayton, OH 45479
513-445-5000

Science Applications International Corp.
10260 Campus Point Drive
San Diego, CA 92121
619-458-2660

Unisys Corp.
P.O. Box 500
Blue Bell, PA 19424
215-986-3848

TRW
One Federal Systems Park Drive
Fairfax, VA 22033
703-992-6201

# Large National and Regional Distributors

Arrow Electronics, Inc.
25 Hub Drive
Melville, NY 11747
1-800-323-4373

D&H Distributing
2525 North 7th Street
Harrisburg, PA 17110-0967
1-800-877-1200

Gates/FA Distributing
121 Interstate Blvd
Greenville, SC 29615
1-800-428-3732
1-800-332-2222

Ingram Micro
1600 East Saint Andrew Place
Santa Ana, CA 92705
714-566-1000
800-456-8000

Kenfil Distribution
16745 Saticoy Street
Van Nuys CA 91406
1-800-74 Kenfil
818-785-1181
FAX: 818-780-5472

Merisel
200 Continental Blvd
El Segundo, CA 90245
1-800-Merisel
310-615-3080

Micro Central, Inc.
55 Reid Street
South River, NJ 08882
908-257-7890
1-800-83-MICRO

Micro United
2200 East Golf Road
Des Plains, IL 60016
708-699-5000
1-800-755-8800

Microware Distributors
9400 Southwest Gemini Drive
Beaverton, OR 97005
1-800-888-6311
1-800-444-7300

Mini-Micro
2050 Corporate Court
San Jose, CA 95131
408-456-9500

Robec Distributors
425 Privet Road
Horsham, PA 19044-0965
1-800-223-7081

Tech Data Corporation
5350 Tech Data Drive
Clearwater, FL 34620
1-800-237-8931

# Vendors With Third-Party Programs

This is a partial listing of companies with formal third-party software programs that are meant to maintain relationships with independent software vendors like you. Even if a vendor doesn't have a formal program, it may be willing to cultivate a working relationship with you.

Borland International, Inc.
Developer Partners Program
100 Borland Way
Scotts Valley, CA 95066
408-431-5172

Hewlett Packard
Value Added Channel Support
3404 E. Harmony Road, MS-339
Fort Collins, CO 80525
303-229-3800

Convex Computer Corporation
Third Party Software
3000 Waterview Parkway
P.O. Box 833851
Richardson, TX 75083-3851
214-497-4000

IBM
1133 Westchester Avenue
White Plains, NY 10604
(Contact local office for applicable program)

Cray Research
1440 Northland Drive
Mendota Heights, MN 55120
612-452-6650

Intel Scientific Computers
15201 N. W. Greenbrier Parkway
Beaverton, OR 97006
503-629-7600

Data General Corporation
Software Business Unit
4400 Computer Drive
Westborough, MA 01580
508-366-8911

Kendall Square Research
170 Tracer Lane
Waltham, MA 02154-1379
617-895-9400

Digital Equipment Corporation
Independent Software Vendor Program
4 Results Way MR04-1/H18
Marlboro, MA 01752
800-DEC-ISVN

Lotus Development Corporation
Professional Developers Program
1 Rogers Street (Rogers 6 North)
Cambridge, MA 01242
800-DEV-RELS

MASPAR Computer
749 North Mary Avenue
Sunnyvale, CA 94086
408-736-3300

Microsoft Corporation
One Microsoft Way
Redmond, WA 98052-9953
206-882-8080

Pick Systems
1691 Browning
Irvine, CA 92714
714-261-7425

Santa Cruz Operations
Developer Relations
400 Encinal Street
P.O. Box 1900
Santa Cruz, CA 95061-1900
1-800-SCO-UNIX

Silicon Graphics, Inc.
IRIS Partners Program
2011 North Shoreline Blvd
P.O. Box 7311
Mountain View, CA 94039-7311
415-961-1980

Sun Microsystems
Catalyst Program
2550 Garcia Avenue, MS PAL1-317
Mountain View, CA 94043-1100
415-960-1300

UNIX Systems Laboratories, Inc.
190 River Road
Summit, NJ 07901
908-522-6555

WordPerfect Corporation
Developer Relations
1555 N. Technology Way
Orem, UT 84057-2399
801-225-5000

# *Trade Associations*

ABCD, The Microcomputer Industry
    Association
1515 E. Woodfield Road
Schaumburg, IL 60173-5437
708-240-1818
FAX: 708-240-1384
MCI 716-4951
AppleLink ABCD.IL

Apple Programmers and Developers
    Association
20525 Mariani Avenue MS 33G
Cupertino, CA 95014
800-282-2732
FAX: 408-562-3971

Association for Information Management
2026-C Opitz Blvd
Woodbridge, VA 22191
703-490-4246
FAX: 703-490-8615

Independent Computer Consultants
    Association
933 Gardenview Office Park
St Louis, MO 63141
800-438-4222
FAX: 314-567-5133

Information Technology Association of
America
(formerly ADAPSO: Computer Software and
Services Industry Association)
1616 North Fort Myer Drive, Suite 1300
Arlington, VA 22209
703-522-5055
FAX: 703-525-2279

Interactive Multimedia Association
3 Church Circle, Suite 800
Annapolis, MD 21401-1933
410-626-1380
FAX: 410-263-0590

National Computer Graphics Association
2722 Merrilee Drive, Suite 200
Fairfax, VA 22031
703-698-9600
FAX: 703-560-2752

Object Management Group
492 Old Connecticut Path
Framingham, MA 01701
508-820-4300
FAX: 508-820-4303

Open Software Foundation
11 Cambridge Center
Cambridge, MA 02142
617-621-8700
FAX: 617-621-0631

Software Entrepreneurs' Forum
P.O. Box 61031
Palo Alto, CA 94306
415-854-7219
FAX: 415-854-8298

Software Publishers Association
1730 M Street Northwest
Suite 700
Washington, DC 20036-4510
202-452-1600
FAX: 202-223-8756

Sparc International
535 Middlefield, Suite 210
Menlo Park, CA 94025
415-321-8692
FAX: 415-321-8015
e-mail: info@sparc.com

USENIX
2450 Ninth Street
Berkeley, CA

UniForum Association
2901 Tasman Drive, Suite 201
Santa Clara, CA 95054
408-986-8840
FAX: 408-986-1645

X/Open Company Ltd.
1750 Montgomery Street
San Francisco, CA 94111
415-773-5383
FAX: 415-421-4278

# *Publications*

As your business experience grows, you will undoubtedly build a library of books, industry periodicals, and other information resources. Your library is an essential resource: books can provide basic (or in-depth) advice on managing your business, while magazines and newsletters can be valuable sources of information on your competition and your market.

# Books

Here are some books that may help you in your endeavors. This list is divided by subject.

## Sales

*The Five Great Rules of Selling*
Percy Whiting
Dale Carnegie & Associates, 1974,1978
McGraw-Hill Book Co. 1947, 1957

*How To Master The Art of Selling*
Tom Hopkins
Warner Books

*How To Win Friends and Influence People*
Dale Carnegie
Simon and Schuster

*Major Account Sales Strategy*
Neil Rackham
McGraw-Hill, Inc.

*Strategic Selling*
Robert B. Miller and Stephen E. Heiman
William Morrow and Company

## Marketing

*The IBM Way*
Buck Rodgers
Harper and Row

*Marketing High Tech*
William Davidow
The Free Press, 1986

*MaxiMarketing*
Stan Rapp and Tom Collins
McGraw-Hill, Inc.

*Positioning: The Battle for Your Mind*
Al Reis and Jack Trout
McGraw-Hill

*Presentations Plus*
David A. Peoples
John Wiley and Sons

*Strategic Market Planning*
Derek R. Abell and John S. Hammond
Prentice-Hall

*Ogilvy On Advertising*
David Ogilvy
Vintage Books, 1985

*Winning Them Over*
James W. Robinson
Prima Publishing and Communications

## Finance and Business

*Economics Of the Firm*
Arthur A. Thompson, Jr.
Prentice-Hall

*Guerrilla Financing*
Bruce Blechman & Jay Conrad Levinson
Houghton Mifflin

*How To Raise Venture Capital*
Stanley Pratt
Charles Scribner's Sons

*Management of Working Capital*
Keith V. Smith
West Publishing

*The One Minute Manager*
Kenneth Blanchard, Ph.D. & Spencer
    Johnson, M.D.
William Morrow and Company

*402 Things You Must Know Before Starting*
    *a Business*
Philip J. Fox & Joseph R. Mancuso
Prentice Hall, Inc.

## Specialized Books and Publications

*Bacon's Publicity Checker*
Bacon's
332 S. Michigan Avenue
Chicago, IL 60604
800-621-0561

*The Software Support Handbook*
Tom Evans
Business Knowledge
101 First Street, Suite 130
Los Altos, CA 94022
415-961-7498

*Pocket Pal: A Graphic Arts Production Handbook*
Michael Bruno, Editor
International Paper Company

*Software Success Reference Book*
David H. Bowen
Software Success
P.O. Box 9006
San Jose, CA 95157-0006
408-446-2504

*The Print Production Handbook*
David Bann
North Light

*How To Write a Business Plan*
Corporation for Innovative Development
New York State Science and Technology
    Foundation
99 Washington Street, Suite 1730
Albany, NY 12210
518-473-9741

Booklets from Arthur Andersen & Company:

• *An Entrepreneur's Guide To Starting a Business*

• *The Life Cycle of a High Technology Company*

# Industry Periodicals

The following publications are excellent resources for keeping in touch with specific segments of the computer industry. In addition to the value of the information within each publication, most rent their subscriber lists and allow advertising, thereby increasing their value as marketing resources. Most are "controlled subscription magazines," meaning the publisher will grant you a free subscription if you meet qualification criteria. In addition to the publications on this list, there are many other leading computer publications (including *PC Magazine, Byte, MacWorld,* etc.) available at your local newsstand or by paid subscription.

Advanced Imaging
PTN Publishing Company
445 Broad Hollow Road
Melville, NY 11747
516-845-2700

Communications Week
CMP Publications Inc.
600 Community Drive
Manhasset, NY 11030
516-562-5000

Computer Graphics World
Pennwell Publishing Company
One Technology Park Drive
P.O. Box 987
Westford, MA 01886
508-692-0700

Computer Pictures
Montage Publishing
701 Westchester Avenue
White Plains, NY 10604
914-328-9157

Computer Reseller News
CMP Publications Inc.
600 Community Drive
Manhasset, NY 11030
516-562-5000

Computer Sources
Asian Sources Media Group
1038 Leigh Avenue
San Jose, CA 95126-4155
408-295-4500

Datamation
275 Washington Street
Newton, MA 02158
617-558-4281

DEC Professional
Cardinal Business Media, Inc.
101 Witmer Road
Horsham, PA 19044
215-957-4269

Digital News & Review
275 Washington Street
Newton, MA 02158
617-558-4281

Document Management & Windows Imaging
Pinnacle Peak Publishing, Ltd.
8711 E. Pinnacle Peak Road, #249
Scottsdale, AZ 85255
602-585-7417

HP Professional
Cardinal Business Media, Inc.
101 Witmer Road
Horsham, PA 19044
215-957-4269

International Spectrum
10675 Treena Street, Suite 103
San Diego, CA 92131
619-578-3152

LAN Times
McGraw-Hill, Inc.
1900 O'Farrell Street, Suite 200
San Mateo, CA 94403
415-513-6800

Midrange Systems
Cardinal Business Media, Inc.
101 Witmer Road
Horsham, PA 19044
215-957-4269

MicroStation Manager
ConnectPress, Ltd.
1580 Center Drive
Santa Fe, NM 87505-9746
505-438-3030

NASA Tech Briefs
Associated Business Publications Co., Ltd.
41 E. 42nd Street, Suite 921
New York, NY 10017-5391
212-490-3999

Network World, Inc.
161 Worcester Road
Framingham, MA 01701-9172
508-875-6400

New Media
901 Mariner's Island Blvd, Suite 365
San Mateo, CA 94404
415-573-5170

OEM Magazine
CMP Publications Inc.
600 Community Drive
Manhasset, NY 11030
516-562-5000

Open Systems Today
CMP Publications Inc.
600 Community Drive
Manhasset, NY 11030
516-562-5000

Pick World
Pick Systems
1691 Browning
Irvine, CA 92714
714-261-7425

Reseller Management
Elsevier Communications
301 Gibraltar Drive
Morris Plains, NJ 07950-0650
201-292-5100

RS/Magazine
Computer Publishing Group, Inc.
1330 Beacon Street
Brookline, MA 02146
617-739-7001

Scientific Computing & Automation
Elsevier Communications
301 Gibraltar Drive, Box 650
Morris Plains, NJ 07950-0650
201-292-5100

SCO Magazine
CMP Publications Inc.
600 Community Drive
Manhasset, NY 11030
516-562 5000

Software Magazine
1900 West Park Drive
Westborough Office Park
Westborough, MA 01581
508-366-2031

SunExpert
Computer Publishing Group, Inc.
1330 Beacon Street
Brookline, MA 02146
617-739-7001

Sunworld
Integrated Media, Inc.
501 Second Street
San Francisco, CA 94107
415-243-4188

Systems Integration Business
Cahners Publishing Associates, L.P.
275 Washington Street
Newton, MA 02158
617-964-3030

UNIX Review
411 Borel Avenue
San Mateo, CA 94402
415-358-9500

UNIX World
1900 O'Farrell St
San Mateo, CA 94403
415-513-6800

VAR Herald
Product News Publishing
1003A Mansell Road
Roswell, GA 30076
404-594-8833

VAR Business
CMP Publications Inc.
600 Community Drive
Manhasset, NY 11030
516-562-5000

Workstation (HP/Apollo)
Publications & Communications Inc.
12416 Hymeadow Drive
Austin, TX 78750-1896
512-250-9023

# Newsletters

ComputerLetter
Technologic Partners
419 Park Avenue South, Suite 500
New York, NY 10016

ComputerLetter analyzes trends, developments, and strategies in technology and finance.

Engineering Automation Report
P.O. Box 3593
Englewood, CO 80155-3593

Engineering Automation Report covers engineering workstations, personal computers, CAE/CAD/CAM software, document management software, data communications software, and other products of interest to the engineering market.

Marketing Masters
Suite 765
60 Skiff Street
Hamden, CT 06517-1017

Marketing Masters does not currently publish a traditional newsletter. Use this address to get on Marketing Masters' mailing list to receive periodic information of interest to software companies.

Release 1.0
EDventure Holdings, Inc.
104 Fifth Avenue, 20th Floor
New York, NY 10011-6987

Release 1.0 covers PC's, software, CASE, groupware, text management, connectivity, artificial intelligence, intellectual property law.

Soft-letter
17 Main Street
Watertown, MA 02272-9154

Soft-letter includes analysis of technical trends, new marketing strategies, industry statistics, and other topics of interest to software developers and publishers.

# Databases and Reference Volumes

## Hiring and Staffing

*The Directory of Executive Recruiters (annual)*
Kennedy Publications
Templeton Road
Fitzwilliam, NH 03447
603-585-6544
FAX: 603-585-9555

*The Prentice-Hall Directory of Executive
Search Firms*
William Lewis & Carol Milano
Prentice-Hall, Inc.

Reference guides from the United States Department of Labor:

- *Employment Cost Indexes and Levels*

- *Employment and Wages Annual Averages*

- *Occupational Outlook Handbook*

Available from Bureau of Labor Statistics (call 703-487-4600 for current ordering information)

Magazines that publish computer industry salary surveys:

- *Datamation*

- *EE Times*

- *Electronic Buyers News*

- *Information Week*

## Your Markets

*Computer Intelligence*
3344 North Torrey Pines Court
La Jolla, CA 92037
619-450-1667

*Data Sources*
Ziff Communications Company
One Park Avenue
New York, NY 10016
800-289-9929

*The Corporate Technology Directory* (CorpTech)
Corporate Technology Information
Services, Inc.
12 Alfred Street, Suite 200
Woburn, MA 01801-9998
617-932-3939

*Million Dollar Directory*
Dun & Bradstreet Information Services
3 Sylvan Way
Parsippany, NJ 07054-3896
800-526-0651
201-605-6000

*ParaTechnology Directory of Systems and Network
    Integrators*
ParaTechnology, Inc.
4038 - 128th Avenue SE, Suite 266
Bellevue, WA 98006
206-641-5483

*Standard Industrial Classification Manual*
Executive Office of the President
Office of Management and Budget

Available from:
National Technical Information Service
5285 Port Royal Road
Springfield, VA 22161
Order number PB 87-100012

Gives definitions of Government SIC codes.

## Finding Funding

*National Business Incubation Association*
One President Street
Athens, OH 45701

*Annual Directory of Business Incubators*
International Venture Capital Institute
P.O. Box 1333
Stamford, CT 06904

*Thomas Register*
Thomas Publishing Company
One Penn Plaza
New York, NY 10001
212-290-7277
FAX: 212-290-7365

*Directory of American Savings and Loan
    Associations*
T.K. Sanderson
1115 Thirtieth Street
Baltimore, MD 21218

# Other Resources

American Management Association
135 W. 50th Street
New York, NY 10020
212-903-8160
FAX: 212-903-8168

Resource for business and management issues

Bacon's Clipping Services
332 S. Michigan Avenue
Chicago, IL 60604
800-621-0561
312-922-2400

Service that finds the articles that appear about your product or company.

Bruno Blenheim, Inc.
P.O. Box 1422
Englewood Cliffs, NJ 07632
800-829-3976

## Organizers of trade shows, including UNIX Expo, Networks Expo, PC Expo.

Technology Research Center
CMP Publications Inc.
600 Community Drive
Manhasset, NY 11030
516-562-5000

## Market research organization

Datapro Information Services Group
600 Delran Parkway
Delran, NJ 08075
800-328-2776
609-764-0100

## Produces reports about various segments of the computer industry

Dataquest Incorporated
1290 Ridder Park Drive
San Jose, CA 95131-2398
408-971-9000

## Information/consulting services

Dialog Information Services
3460 Hillview Avenue
Palo Alto, CA 94304
800-334-2564
415-858-3785
FAX: 415-858-7069

## Online information service

Engineering Automation Report
P.O. Box 3593
Englewood, CO 80155
303-770-1728
FAX: 303-770-3660

## Information about trends in engineering automation

InfoCorp
2880 Lakeside Drive, Suite 300
Santa Clara, CA 95054
408-980-4300

## Industry analysis and market research; hardware and software

The Interface Group
300 First Avenue
Needham, MA 02194-2722
617-449-6600

## Organizes COMDEX

International Data Group
Five Speen Street
Framingham, MA 01701
508-872-2700
FAX: 508-879-0184

## Publisher and provider of industry information

Interop Company
480 San Antonio Road
Mountain View, CA 94040
1-800-468-3767

## Produces Interop Conference and Exhibition

Marketing Masters
301 Field Point Drive
Branford, CT 06405
203-483-5440
FAX: 203-481-5314

## Helps companies introduce new products via consulting, planning, and execution of marketing programs

New Science Associates
One Glendinning Place
Westport, CT 06880-1242
203-221-8900

## Information and consulting on the computer industry

O'Reilly & Associates, Inc.
103 Morris Street, Suite A
Sebastopol, CA 95472
707-829-0515
FAX: 707-829-0104

## Publishes books for the computer industry

Professional And Technical Consultants Association (PATCA)
3381 Mount Diablo Boulevard, Suite A
Lafayette, CA 94549
510-284-8703
FAX: 510-283-6258

# ⸙ Index ⸙

# About the Author

David Radin, President of Marketing Masters since 1990, designs and executes strategic and tactical marketing programs for companies in the computer industry. He's worked with such clients as Apple, WordPerfect, Hewlett Packard, Logitech, Corel, SCO, Dell, Xyvision, and Silicon Graphics as well as a number of smaller companies. Prior to founding Marketing Masters, David was Director of Industry Planning for Multiflow Computer Corporation, and Regional Manager for Ana Tech Corporation. He began his work in the computer industry at Auto-trol Technology Corporation as Assistant to the Director of Marketing and Customer Services, where he had also been a top-performing salesperson and branch manager. As a permanent group leader for Dale Carnegie courses, David has had articles published by *Mass High Tech*, *VAR Digest*, American Management Association's *Small Business Reports*, *New Science*, and *DEC Professional*. He holds an MBA from Duke University (Fuqua) and a B.S. from Yale University.

When he's not working, you can usually find him playing basketball, strumming a guitar with friends, or participating in family activities with his wife and children.

# Colophon

Edie Freedman designed the cover of this book, using a 19th-century engraving from the Dover Pictorial Archive. The cover layout was produced with QuarkXPress 3.2 using Adobe New Baskerville and Madrone fonts.

The inside layout was designed by Jennifer Niederst. The interior fonts are New Baskerville, Madrone, and Woodtype Ornaments, all from Adobe. Lenny Muellner implemented the design in The Free Software Foundation's GNU *gtroff*, using macros developed by Steve Talbott. The figures were created in Aldus Freehand 3.1 by Chris Reilley.

# Programming

## UNIX, C and MULTI-PLATFORM

*Books from O'Reilly & Associates, Inc.*

Fall/Winter 1994-95

## Fortran/Scientific Computing

### Migrating to Fortran 90

*By James F. Kerrigan*
*1st Edition November 1993*
*389 pages, ISBN 1-56592-049-X*

Many Fortran programmers do not know where to start with Fortran 90. What is new about the language? How can it help them? How does a programmer with old habits learn new strategies?

This book is a practical guide to Fortran 90 for the current Fortran programmer. It provides a complete overview of the new features that Fortran 90 has brought to the Fortran standard, with examples and suggestions for use. The book discusses older ways of solving problems—both in FORTRAN 77 and in common tricks or extensions—and contrasts them with the new ways provided by Fortran 90.

The book has a practical focus, with the goal of getting the current Fortran programmer up to speed quickly. Two dozen examples of full programs are interspersed within the text, which includes over 4,000 lines of working code.

Topics include array sections, modules, file handling, allocatable arrays and pointers, and numeric precision. Two dozen examples of full programs are interspersed within the text, which includes over 4,000 lines of working code.

"This is a book that all Fortran programmers eager to take advantage of the excellent feature of Fortran 90 will want to have on their desk." —*FORTRAN Journal*

### High Performance Computing

*By Kevin Dowd*
*1st Edition June 1993*
*398 pages, ISBN 1-56592-032-5*

*High Performance Computing* makes sense of the newest generation of workstations for application programmers and purchasing managers. It covers everything, from the basics of modern workstation architecture, to structuring benchmarks, to squeezing more performance out of critical applications. It also explains what a good compiler can do—and what you have to do yourself. The book closes with a look at the high-performance future: parallel computers and the more "garden variety" shared memory processors that are appearing on people's desktops.

### UNIX for FORTRAN Programmers

*By Mike Loukides*
*1st Edition August 1990*
*264 pages, ISBN 0-937175-51-X*

This handbook lowers the UNIX entry barrier by providing the serious scientific programmer with an introduction to the UNIX operating system and its tools. It familiarizes readers with the most important tools so they can be productive as quickly as possible. Assumes some knowledge of FORTRAN, none of UNIX or C.

## C Programming Libraries

### POSIX.4

By Bill Gallmeister
1st Edition Winter 1994-95 (est.)
400 pages (est.), ISBN 1-56592-074-0

A general introduction to real-time programming and real-time issues, this book covers the POSIX.4 standard and how to use it to solve "real-world" problems. If you're at all interested in real-time applications—which include just about everything from telemetry to transaction processing—this book is for you. An essential reference.

### POSIX Programmer's Guide

By Donald Lewine
1st Edition April 1991
640 pages, ISBN 0-937175-73-0

Most UNIX systems today are POSIX compliant because the Federal government requires it for its purchases. Given the manufacturer's documentation, however, it can be difficult to distinguish system-specific features from those features defined by POSIX. The *POSIX Programmer's Guide*, intended as an explanation of the POSIX standard and as a reference for the POSIX.1 programming library, helps you write more portable programs.

"If you are an intermediate to advanced C programmer and are interested in having your programs compile first time on anything from a Sun to a VMS system to an MSDOS system, then this book must be thoroughly recommended."
—*Sun UK User*

### Understanding and Using COFF

By Gintaras R. Gircys
1st Edition November 1988
196 pages, ISBN 0-937175-31-5

COFF—Common Object File Format—is the formal definition for the structure of machine code files in the UNIX System V environment. All machine code files are COFF files. This handbook explains COFF data structure and its manipulation.

### Using C on the UNIX System

By Dave Curry
1st Edition January 1989
250 pages, ISBN 0-937175-23-4

This is the book for intermediate to experienced C programmers who want to become UNIX system programmers. It explains system calls and special library routines available on the UNIX system. It is impossible to write UNIX utilities of any sophistication without understanding the material in this book.

"A gem of a book.... The author's aim is to provide a guide to system programming, and he succeeds admirably. His balance is steady between System V and BSD-based systems, so readers come away knowing both." —*SUN Expert*

### Practical C Programming

By Steve Oualline
2nd Edition January 1993
396 pages, ISBN 1-56592-035-X

C programming is more than just getting the syntax right. Style and debugging also play a tremendous part in creating programs that run well. *Practical C Programming* teaches you not only the mechanics of programming, but also how to create programs that are easy to read, maintain, and debug. There are lots of introductory C books, but this is the Nutshell Handbook®! In this edition, programs conform to ANSI C.

"This book is exactly what it states—a practical book in C programming. It is also an excellent addition to any C programmer's library." —Betty Zinkarun, *Books & Bytes*

### Programming with curses

By John Strang
1st Edition 1986
76 pages, ISBN 0-937175-02-1

Curses is a UNIX library of functions for controlling a terminal's display screen from a C program. This handbook helps you make use of the curses library. Describes the original Berkeley version of curses.

# C Programming Tools

## Software Portability with imake

*By Paul DuBois*
*1st Edition July 1993*
*390 pages, ISBN 1-56592-055-4*

*imake* is a utility that works with *make* to enable code to be compiled and installed on different UNIX machines. *imake* makes possible the wide portability of the X Window System code and is widely considered an X tool, but it's also useful for any software project that needs to be ported to many UNIX systems.

This Nutshell Handbook®—the only book available on *imake*—is ideal for X and UNIX programmers who want their software to be portable. The book is divided into two sections. The first section is a general explanation of *imake*, X configuration files, and how to write and debug an *Imakefile*. The second section describes how to write configuration files and presents a configuration file architecture that allows development of coexisting sets of configuration files. Several sample sets of configuration files are described and are available free over the Net.

## Managing Projects with make

*By Andrew Oram & Steve Talbott*
*2nd Edition October 1991*
*152 pages, ISBN 0-937175-90-0*

*make* is one of UNIX's greatest contributions to software development, and this book is the clearest description of *make* ever written. It describes all the basic features of *make* and provides guidelines on meeting the needs of large, modern projects. Also contains a description of free products that contain major enhancements to *make*.

"I use *make* very frequently in my day to day work and thought I knew everything that I needed to know about it. After reading this book I realized that I was wrong!"
—Rob Henley, Siemens-Nixdorf

"If you can't pick up your system's *yp Makefile*, read every line, and make sense of it, you need this book."
—*Root Journal*

## Checking C Programs with lint

*By Ian F. Darwin*
*1st Edition October 1988*
*84 pages, ISBN 0-937175-30-7*

The *lint* program checker has proven time and again to be one of the best tools for finding portability problems and certain types of coding errors in C programs. *lint* verifies a program or program segments against standard libraries, checks the code for common portability errors, and tests the programming against some tried and true guidelines. *Linting* your code is a necessary (though not sufficient) step in writing clean, portable, effective programs. This book introduces you to *lint*, guides you through running it on your programs, and helps you interpret *lint's* output.

"I can say without reservation that this book is a must for the system programmer or anyone else programming in C."
—*Root Journal*

## lex & yacc

*By John Levine, Tony Mason & Doug Brown*
*2nd Edition October 1992*
*366 pages, ISBN 1-56592-000-7*

Shows programmers how to use two UNIX utilities, *lex* and *yacc*, in program development. The second edition contains completely revised tutorial sections for novice users and reference sections for advanced users. This edition is twice the size of the first, has an expanded index, and now covers Bison and Flex.

## Power Programming with RPC

*By John Bloomer*
*1st Edition February 1992*
*522 pages, ISBN 0-937175-77-3*

RPC, or remote procedure calling, is the ability to distribute the execution of functions on remote computers. Written from a programmer's perspective, this book shows what you can do with RPCs, like Sun RPC, the de facto standard on UNIX systems. It covers related programming topics for Sun and other UNIX systems and teaches through examples.

## Multi-Platform Programming

### Guide to Writing DCE Applications

*By John Shirley, Wei Hu & David Magid*
*2nd Edition May 1994*
*462 pages, ISBN 1-56592-045-7*

A hands-on programming guide to OSF's Distributed Computing Environment (DCE) for first-time DCE application programmers. This book is designed to help new DCE users make the transition from conventional, nondistributed applications programming to distributed DCE programming. In addition to basic RPC (remote procedure calls), this edition covers object UUIDs and basic security (authentication and authorization). Also includes practical programming examples.

"This book will be useful as a ready reference by the side of the novice DCE programmer." —*;login*

### Distributing Applications Across DCE and Windows NT

*By Ward Rosenberry & Jim Teague*
*1st Edition November 1993*
*302 pages, ISBN 1-56592-047-3*

This book links together two exciting technologies in distributed computing by showing how to develop an application that simultaneously runs on DCE and Microsoft systems through remote procedure calls (RPC). Covers the writing of portable applications and the complete differences between RPC support in the two environments.

### Understanding DCE

*By Ward Rosenberry, David Kenney & Gerry Fisher*
*1st Edition October 1992*
*266 pages, ISBN 1-56592-005-8*

A technical and conceptual overview of OSF's Distributed Computing Environment (DCE) for programmers, technical managers, and marketing and sales people. Unlike many O'Reilly & Associates books, *Understanding DCE* has no hands-on programming elements. Instead, the book focuses on how DCE can be used to accomplish typical programming tasks and provides explanations to help the reader understand all the parts of DCE.

### Encyclopedia of Graphics File Formats

*By James D. Murray & William vanRyper*
*1st Edition July 1994*
*928 pages (CD-ROM included), ISBN 1-56592-058-9*

The computer graphics world is a veritable alphabet soup of acronyms; BMP, DXF, EPS, GIF, MPEG, PCX, PIC, RTF, TGA, RIFF, and TIFF are only a few of the many different formats in which graphics images can be stored. The *Encyclopedia of Graphics File Formats* is the definitive work on file formats— the book that will become a classic for graphics programmers and everyone else who deals with the low-level technical details of graphics files. It includes technical information on nearly 100 file formats, as well as chapters on graphics and file format basics, bitmap and vector files, metafiles, scene description, animation and multimedia formats, and file compression methods.

Best of all, this book comes with a CD-ROM that collects many hard-to-find resources. We've assembled original vendor file format specification documents, along with test images and code examples, and a variety of software packages for MS-DOS, Windows, OS/2, UNIX, and the Macintosh that will let you convert, view, and manipulate graphics files and images.

### Multi-Platform Code Management

*By Kevin Jameson*
*1st Edition August 1994*
*354 pages (two diskettes included), ISBN 1-56592-059-7*

For any programmer or team struggling with builds and maintenance, this book—and its accompanying software (available for fifteen platforms, including MS-DOS and various UNIX systems)—can save dozens of errors and hours of effort. A "one-stop-shopping" solution for code management problems, it shows you how to structure a large project and keep your files and builds under control over many releases and platforms. The building blocks are simple: common-sense strategies, public-domain tools that you can obtain on a variety of systems, and special utilities developed by the author. The book also includes two diskettes that provide a complete system for managing source files and builds.

## Understanding Japanese Information Processing

*By Ken Lunde*
*1st Edition September 1993*
*470 pages, ISBN 1-56592-043-0*

*Understanding Japanese Information Processing* provides detailed information on all aspects of handling Japanese text on computer systems. It brings all of the relevant information together in a single book and covers everything from the origins of modern-day Japanese to the latest information on specific emerging computer encoding standards. Appendices provide additional reference material, such as a code conversion table, character set tables, mapping tables, an extensive list of software sources, a glossary, and more.

"A programmer interested in writing a computer program which will handle the Japanese language will find the book indispensable." —*Multilingual Computing*

"Ken Lunde's book is an essential reference for everyone developing or adapting software for handling Japanese text. It is a goldmine of useful and relevant information on fonts, encoding systems and standards."
—Professor Jim Breen, Monash University, Australia

## Business

## Building a Successful Software Business

*By Dave Radin*
*1st Edition April 1994*
*394 pages, ISBN 1-56592-064-3*

This handbook is for the new software entrepreneur and the old hand alike. If you're thinking of starting a company around a program you've written—and there's no better time than the present— this book will guide you toward success. If you're an old hand in the software industry, it will help you sharpen your skills or will provide a refresher course. It covers the basics of product planning, marketing, customer support, finance, and operations.

"A marvelous guide through the complexities of marketing high-tech products. Its range of topics, and Radin's insights, make the book valuable to the novice marketeer as well as the seasoned veteran. It is the Swiss Army Knife of high-tech marketing." —Jerry Keane, Universal Analytics Inc.

## ORACLE Performance Tuning

*By Peter Corrigan & Mark Gurry*
*1st Edition September 1993*
*642 pages, ISBN 1-56592-048-1*

The ORACLE relational database management system is the most popular database system in use today. Organizations, ranging from government agencies to small businesses, from large financial institutions to universities, use ORACLE on computers as diverse as mainframes, minicomputers, workstations, PCs, and Macintoshes.

ORACLE offers tremendous power and flexibility, but at some cost. Demands for fast response, particularly in online transaction processing systems, make performance a major issue. With more organizations downsizing and adopting client-server and distributed database approaches, performance tuning has become all the more vital.

Whether you're a manager, a designer, a programmer, or an administrator, there's a lot you can do on your own to dramatically increase the performance of your existing ORACLE system. Whether you are running RDBMS Version 6 or Version 7, you may find that this book can save you the cost of a new machine; at the very least, it will save you a lot of headaches.

"This book is one of the best books on ORACLE that I have ever read.... [It] discloses many Oracle Tips that DBA's and Developers have locked in their brains and in their planners.... I recommend this book for any person who works with ORACLE, from managers to developers. In fact, I have to keep [it] under lock and key, because of the popularity of it."
—Mike Gangler

# O'Reilly & Associates—
# GLOBAL NETWORK NAVIGATOR™

The Global Network Navigator (GNN)™ is a unique kind of information service that makes the Internet easy and enjoyable to use. We organize access to the vast information resources of the Internet so that you can find what you want. We also help you understand the Internet and the many ways you can explore it.

*In GNN you'll find:*

## Navigating the Net with GNN

 The *Whole Internet Catalog* contains a descriptive listing of the most useful Net resources and services with live links to those resources.

 The *GNN Business Pages* are where you'll learn about companies who have established a presence on the Internet and use its worldwide reach to help educate consumers.

The *Internet Help Desk* helps folks who are new to the Net orient themselves and gets them started on the road to Internet exploration.

## News

 *NetNews* is a weekly publication that reports on the news of the Internet, with weekly feature articles that focus on Internet trends and special events. The Sports, Weather, and Comix Pages round out the news.

## Special Interest Publications

 Whether you're planning a trip or are just interested in reading about the journeys of others, you'll find that the *Travelers' Center* contains a rich collection of feature articles and ongoing columns about travel. In the *Travelers' Center*, you can link to many helpful and informative travel-related Internet resources.

 The *Personal Finance Center* is the place to go for information about money management and investment on the Internet. Whether you're an old pro at playing the market or are thinking about investing for the first time, you'll read articles and discover Internet resources that will help you to think of the Internet as a personal finance information tool.

*All in all, GNN helps you get more value for the time you spend on the Internet.*

 **The Best of the Web**

*GNN* received "Honorable Mention" for **"Best Overall Site," "Best Entertainment Service,"** and **"Most Important Service Concept."**

The *GNN NetNews* received "Honorable Mention" for **"Best Document Design."**

## Subscribe Today

GNN is available over the Internet as a subscription service. To get complete information about subscribing to GNN, send email to **info@gnn.com**. If you have access to a World Wide Web browser such as Mosaic or Lynx, you can use the following URL to register online: `http://gnn.com/`

If you use a browser that does not support online forms, you can retrieve an email version of the registration form automatically by sending email to **form@gnn.com**. Fill this form out and send it back to us by email, and we will confirm your registration.

*O'Reilly on the Net—*
# ONLINE PROGRAM GUIDE

O'Reilly & Associates offers extensive information through our online resources. If you've got Internet access, we invite you to come and explore our little neck-of-the-woods.

## Online Resource Center

Most comprehensive among our online offerings is the O'Reilly Resource Center. Here, you'll find detailed information and descriptions on all O'Reilly products: titles, prices, tables of contents, indexes, author bios, software contents, reviews... you can even view images of the products themselves. We also supply helpful ordering information: how to contact us, how to order online, distributors and bookstores world wide, discounts, upgrades, etc. In addition, we provide informative literature in the field: articles, interviews, and bibliographies that help you stay informed and abreast.

 **The Best of the Web**

The *O'Reilly Resource Center* was voted "**Best Commercial Site**" by users participating in "Best of the Web '94."

### *To access ORA's Online Resource Center:*

Point your Web browser (e.g., `mosaic` or `lynx`) to:

`http://gnn.com/ora/`

For the plaintext version, `telnet` or `gopher` to:

`gopher.ora.com`

(telnet login: `gopher`)

## FTP

The example files and programs in many of our books are available electronically via FTP.

### *To obtain example files and programs from O'Reilly texts:*

`ftp` to:

`ftp.ora.com`

or

`ftp.uu.net`

`cd published/oreilly`

## Ora-news

An easy way to stay informed of the latest projects and products from O'Reilly & Associates is to subscribe to "ora-news," our electronic news service. Subscribers receive email as soon as the information breaks.

### *To subscribe to "ora-news":*

Send email to:
**listproc@online.ora.com**

and put the following information on the first line of your message (not in "Subject"):
**subscribe ora-news** "your name" **of** "your company"

For example:
**subscribe ora-news Jim Dandy of Mighty Fine Enterprises**

## Email

Many customer services are provided via email. Here's a few of the most popular and useful.

**nuts@ora.com**
For general questions and information.

**bookquestions@ora.com**
For technical questions, or corrections, concerning book contents.

**order@ora.com**
To order books online and for ordering questions.

**catalog@ora.com**
To receive a free copy of our magazine/catalog, "ora.com" (please include a postal address).

## Snailmail and phones

**O'Reilly & Associates, Inc.**
**103A Morris Street, Sebastopol, CA 95472**
Inquiries: **707-829-0515, 800-998-9938**
Credit card orders: **800-889-8969** (Weekdays 6a.m.- 6p.m. PST)
FAX: **707-829-0104**

# O'Reilly & Associates—
# LISTING OF TITLES

## INTERNET

!%@:: A Directory of Electronic Mail
Addressing & Networks
Connecting to the Internet: An O'Reilly Buyer's Guide
Internet In A Box
The Mosaic Handbook for Microsoft Windows
The Mosaic Handbook for the Macintosh
The Mosaic Handbook for the X Window System
Smileys
The Whole Internet User's Guide & Catalog

## SYSTEM ADMINISTRATION

Computer Security Basics
DNS and BIND
Essential System Administration
Linux Network Administrator's Guide (Winter '94/95 est.)
Managing Internet Information Services
Managing NFS and NIS
Managing UUCP and Usenet
sendmail
Practical UNIX Security
PGP: Pretty Good Privacy (Winter '94/95 est.)
System Performance Tuning
TCP/IP Network Administration
termcap & terminfo
X Window System Administrator's Guide: Volume 8
The X Companion CD for R6 (Winter '94/95 est.)

## USING UNIX AND X

### BASICS

Learning GNU Emacs
Learning the Korn Shell
Learning the UNIX Operating System
Learning the vi Editor
MH & xmh: Email for Users & Programmers
SCO UNIX in a Nutshell
The USENET Handbook (Winter '94/95 est.)
Using UUCP and Usenet
UNIX in a Nutshell: System V Edition
The X Window System in a Nutshell
X Window System User's Guide: Volume 3
X Window System User's Guide, Motif Ed.: Vol. 3M
X User Tools (with CD-ROM)

### ADVANCED

Exploring Expect (Winter 94/95 est.)
The Frame Handbook
Learning Perl
Making TeX Work
Programming perl
sed & awk
UNIX Power Tools (with CD-ROM)

## PROGRAMMING UNIX, C, AND MULTI-PLATFORM

### FORTRAN/SCIENTIFIC COMPUTING

High Performance Computing
Migrating to Fortran 90
UNIX for FORTRAN Programmers

### C PROGRAMMING LIBRARIES

Practical C Programming
POSIX Programmer's Guide
POSIX.4: Programming for the Real World
(Winter '94/95 est.)
Programming with curses
Understanding and Using COFF
Using C on the UNIX System

### C PROGRAMMING TOOLS

Checking C Programs with lint
lex & yacc
Managing Projects with make
Power Programming with RPC
Software Portability with imake

### MULTI-PLATFORM PROGRAMMING

Encyclopedia of Graphics File Formats
Distributing Applications Across DCE and
Windows NT
Guide to Writing DCE Applications
Multi-Platform Code Management
ORACLE Performance Tuning
Understanding DCE
Understanding Japanese Information Processing

## BERKELEY 4.4 SOFTWARE DISTRIBUTION

4.4BSD System Manager's Manual
4.4BSD User's Reference Manual
4.4BSD User's Supplementary Documents
4.4BSD Programmer's Reference Manual
4.4BSD Programmer's Supplementary Documents
4.4BSD-Lite CD Companion
4.4BSD-Lite CD Companion: International Version

## X PROGRAMMING

Motif Programming Manual: Volume 6A
Motif Reference Manual: Volume 6B
Motif Tools
PEXlib Programming Manual
PEXlib Reference Manual
PHIGS Programming Manual (soft or hard cover)
PHIGS Reference Manual
Programmer's Supplement for Release 6 (Winter '94/95 est.)
Xlib Programming Manual: Volume 1
Xlib Reference Manual: Volume 2
X Protocol Reference Manual, R5: Volume 0
X Protocol Reference Manual, R6: Volume 0
(Winter '94/95 est.)
X Toolkit Intrinsics Programming Manual: Vol. 4
X Toolkit Intrinsics Programming Manual,
Motif Edition: Volume 4M
X Toolkit Intrinsics Reference Manual: Volume 5
XView Programming Manual: Volume 7A
XView Reference Manual: Volume 7B

## THE X RESOURCE

### A QUARTERLY WORKING JOURNAL FOR X PROGRAMMERS

The X Resource: Issues 0 through 13
(Issue 13 available 1/95)

## BUSINESS/CAREER

Building a Successful Software Business
Love Your Job!

## TRAVEL

Travelers' Tales Thailand
Travelers' Tales Mexico
Travelers' Tales India (Winter '94/95 est.)

## AUDIOTAPES

### INTERNET TALK RADIO'S "GEEK OF THE WEEK" INTERVIEWS

The Future of the Internet Protocol, 4 hours
Global Network Operations, 2 hours
Mobile IP Networking, 1 hour
Networked Information and
Online Libraries, 1 hour
Security and Networks, 1 hour
European Networking, 1 hour

### NOTABLE SPEECHES OF THE INFORMATION AGE

John Perry Barlow, 1.5 hours

# O'Reilly & Associates—
# INTERNATIONAL DISTRIBUTORS

Customers outside North America can now order O'Reilly & Associates books through the following distributors. They offer our international customers faster order processing, more bookstores, increased representation at tradeshows worldwide, and the high-quality, responsive service our customers have come to expect.

## EUROPE, MIDDLE EAST, AND AFRICA
*(except Germany, Switzerland, and Austria)*

**INQUIRIES**

International Thomson Publishing Europe
Berkshire House
168-173 High Holborn
London WC1V 7AA
United Kingdom
Telephone: 44-71-497-1422
Fax: 44-71-497-1426
Email: ora.orders@itpuk.co.uk

**ORDERS**

International Thomson Publishing Services, Ltd.
Cheriton House, North Way
Andover, Hampshire SP10 5BE
United Kingdom
Telephone: 44-264-342-832 (UK orders)
Telephone: 44-264-342-806 (outside UK)
Fax: 44-264-364418 (UK orders)
Fax: 44-264-342761 (outside UK)

## GERMANY, SWITZERLAND, AND AUSTRIA

International Thomson Publishing GmbH
O'Reilly-International Thomson Verlag
Attn: Mr. G. Miske
Königswinterer Strasse 418
53227 Bonn
Germany
Telephone: 49-228-970240
Fax: 49-228-441342
Email: anfragen@orade.ora.com

## THE AMERICAS, JAPAN, AND OCEANIA

O'Reilly & Associates, Inc.
103A Morris Street
Sebastopol, CA 95472 U.S.A.
Telephone: 707-829-0515
Telephone: 800-998-9938 (U.S. & Canada)
Fax: 707-829-0104
Email: order@ora.com

## ASIA
*(except Japan)*

**INQUIRIES**

International Thomson Publishing Asia
221 Henderson Road
#05 10 Henderson Building
Singapore 0315
Telephone: 65-272-6496
Fax: 65-272-6498

**ORDERS**

Telephone: 65-268-7867
Fax: 65-268-6727

## AUSTRALIA

WoodsLane Pty. Ltd.
Unit 8, 101 Darley Street (P.O. Box 935)
Mona Vale NSW 2103
Australia
Telephone: 61-2-979-5944
Fax: 61-2-997-3348
Email: woods@tmx.mhs.oz.au

## NEW ZEALAND

WoodsLane New Zealand Ltd.
21 Cooks Street (P.O. Box 575)
Wanganui, New Zealand
Telephone: 64-6-347-6543
Fax: 64-6-345-4840
Email: woods@tmx.mhs.oz.au